The Regency of Tunis, 1535–1666

The Regency of Tunis, 1535–1666

GENESIS OF AN OTTOMAN PROVINCE IN THE MAGHREB

LEÏLA BLILI

Translated by Margaux Fitoussi and Anna Boots

The American University in Cairo Press
Cairo New York

First published in 2021 by
The American University in Cairo Press
113 Sharia Kasr el Aini, Cairo, Egypt
One Rockefeller Plaza, 10th Floor, New York, NY 10020
www.aucpress.com

First published in French in 2012 by Editions SCRIPT as *Sous le toit de l'Empire: La Régence de Tunis, 1535–1666: Genèse d'une province ottomane au Maghreb, tome 1*

Dar el Kutub No. 26214/19
ISBN 978 977 416 989 2

Dar el Kutub Cataloging-in-Publication Data

Blili, Leïla Temime
The Regency of Tunis, 1535–1666: Genesis of an Ottoman Province in the Maghreb / Leïla Temime Blili.—Cairo: The American University in Cairo Press, 2021.
p. cm.
ISBN 978 977 416 989 2
1. Tunisia—History—1535-1666
2. Tunisia—Civilization—Foreign influences
961.1

1 2 3 4 5 25 24 23 22 21

Designed by Westchester Publishing Services
Printed in the United States of America

I thank Mr. Hazem Ben-Gacem and the team for the translation of this book.

Contents

Figures

Introduction

This book is a study of the emergence of modern Tunis starting in the sixteenth century, conducted through a reexamination of the Ottoman occupation of the ancient Hafsid Ifriqiya. I trace the long process of the establishment of the Regency of Tunis, both its territory, through the gradual solidification of what had been loosely defined borders, and its society. The territorial and social identities of this new province were marked by many distinctive characteristics in terms of its relationship with Istanbul: the new borders of the regency were drawn as an imperial province, and individuals originating from throughout the vast territory of the Ottoman Empire settled in Tunis and succeeded in creating a new elite. These people could be categorized into two groups: Muslim Turks coming from the vast Anatolian plateaus, and those who had been captured by pirates—Christians by birth who had converted to Islam and thus were also considered Turks. Belonging to this latter group was Mourad Coursou, founder of the Mouradite house and a product of the underworld of captivity.

Under the Ottoman Empire, Tunis became a meeting place for these people with unique pasts, who, in spite of their varied geographic and religious backgrounds, were able to form kinship ties through intermarriage and to improve their standing through alliances with powerful local families. These new arrivals secured wealth and seized political power; thus, poor soldiers from the Anatolian plateaus as well as Mediterranean renegades were able, in a very short time, to form the new nobility of the Regency of Tunis. It is this complex process—the interaction of the social with the political and the religious—which we try to follow here.

The precise contours of the Regency of Tunis were produced by a rapidly changing situation, one marked by a series of fits and starts, that must be reconstructed, even if this requires going back in time and rethinking traditional periodizations in order to better understand the sixteenth century, with its crises and its upheavals, as a fundamental moment of transition. For a sixty-year period, from 1530 to 1595, it is difficult to delineate the exact borders of the Hafsid territory of Ifriqiya. The period of July and August of 1574 seems to have represented a major shift, with the capture of Tunis and La Goulette, the departure of the Spanish and the last Hafsid rulers, and the installation of the Ottoman Turks. This important military victory did not mean that the Ottomans controlled the territory completely; rather, it initiated a difficult period during which the new authority strove to establish itself.

Historians have traditionally divided Ottoman history into three chronological phases beginning with 1574: the period of the pashas (1574–91); the period of the deys (1591–1631); and the period of the Mouradite beys (1631–1702). This chronology highlights the weakening authority of the pashas and the Turkish deys, in favor of the Mouradite beys. Such a convulsive succession of rulers suggests an effort to establish indigenous identity in opposition to the foreign Turks. This work proposes an alternative chronology, one that begins in 1535 and ends with the death of Hamouda Pasha Bey in 1666. It returns to the founding of Algiers by Barbarossa and its consolidation by Khayriddine as part of the project to create a Maghrebi state under Ottoman control, in which the Andalusian population would form the linchpin. The military victory of 1574 would in this context have been one step toward the ultimate aim of the great corsairs, which their successors continued to pursue until 1587. But this plan failed. Instead, three *oujak*s, or provinces, were established in the Maghreb: Algiers, Tripoli, and Tunis. They were autonomous from one another but shared a common fate, and people circulated among them with incredible frequency. After being caught in the pincers of both the Turks and the Spanish, the territory of Hafsid Ifriqiya shrank considerably. Tunis fell sometimes under the rule of Algiers and sometimes of Tripoli. When the sultan caliph decided to bring an end to the unity of the three *oujak*s of the Maghreb, each of the three embarked on its own political and social path. Borders that had been fluid and ambiguous began to solidify. The ruling powers that established themselves in the three cities were distinct from one another, and their destinies depended, in part, on the men who governed them. The features of each province began to take form, accentuated by geographical conditions that promoted increasing centralization in the Regency of Tunis.

A Difficult Reconstruction of Historical Events

Reconstructing events, establishing a chronology, and identifying individual men and women are necessary steps toward renewing and refining readings of macrohistory. This is an essential but difficult process, because the sources do not always answer the questions being posed. There is also the problem of local sources from this long, blurry era, during which the end of Hafsid rule, Spanish occupations, tribal insubordination, the rise of Marabout powers, and Ottoman interventions all coincided. Tunisian chronicles, which were often written much later than the events they describe and which build off one another, constitute the bulk of local sources in the absence of official documents dating back to this period. Nevertheless, it is possible to gain "new" insights from these sources if we rethink the way that we use them. There is also a formidable collection of narratives from European travelers, diplomats, and former captives, which historians have used with eagerness, given the gaping void in local sources. And yet, despite the detailed work done by these authors, their stories impose a version of the facts heavily shaped by their authors' biases. I am not suggesting that these sources lack objectivity, but merely underlining that, in common with all writers, the authors of these narratives describe local political institutions and their mode of operation through an individual lens. I will bring a different reading to official Spanish, Italian, and French sources that have previously been published in historical reviews, and I will make use of important Turkish documents that have been translated into Arabic. This deliberately descriptive approach will allow for a precise reconstruction of historical events, in order to better recreate several episodes, with a focus on the long demise of the Hafsids (1535–74) and the so-called period of the pashas (1574–91). We discover that the three ruling powers—the pashas, the deys, and the beys—were overlapping, not successive dynasties, and that the beys and the deys were linked by strong family ties. If these family relationships have escaped attention until now, it is because scholarship wasn't concerned with the roles of women. The reconstruction of marriages and matrimonial alliances will allow us to identify the houses—the *dar*s and the *bayt*s—which were formed by both symbolic and material inheritances, and which enabled parvenus to access nobility. This notion of a "house," which relies on an analysis of kinship, strategies of inheritance, and the transfer of power, will enable us to understand the political and institutional landscape and begin to make sense of the social cohesion of this formative period.

The Ottoman-Turkish occupation was accompanied by significant new diversity in the population. How were the newcomers identified? What ties united them? What sorts of relationships did they have with the authorities? Should our textbooks continue to list each new group on top of the many others that have populated Tunis? Should we not instead attempt to capture the dynamics of these various groups, the processes by which they construct their identity, and the manner in which they define themselves and their relationship to power? The affiliation of the Regency of Tunis with the Ottoman world established a new configuration that gave each group of new arrivals a political position, both within and outside the corridors of power, in lasting or temporary alliances. These fluid and cyclical dynamics must be identified in order to understand the connections between society and power. We will not look at them in their macrohistorical form, however, but by focusing on marriages, matrimonial alliances, and women's roles in political networks. In opting for a social analysis of power, we aim to reconsider the place of family ties in establishing inheritance, access to spheres of power, and even the acquisition of "titles of nobility." Contrary to what took place in nobiliary societies in which social belonging was linked to birth and marriages subject to strict social and religious control, the Muslim southern Mediterranean was distinguished by a different set of practices that this work attempts to disassemble: in this world, any adventurer could attain a position of authority if circumstances placed him in the proximity of power. Once such an individual had reached the top of the social hierarchy, the discourse surrounding his legitimacy would be constructed a posteriori.

The historian is a product of his or her time. At a moment in which history thinks less in terms of national identity, this study departs from the path that locates the formation of the state and the modern nation in the opposition between the Turks and the indigenous populations. If a Turkish identity existed, as we shall see, it was as a political identity and a generic term for all those who fell under the Ottoman banner. Moreover, local populations cannot be defined only by their indigeneity, as this designation did not correspond to their own self-perception: they identified first and foremost with their familial or tribal affiliations, and then with their cities or their lands (the *watan*); and for nomads, with their eponymous ancestors and with their rangelands. The respective imaginations of local populations did not extend beyond these familiar territories and the kinship ties that linked them to their groups, whether these ties were real, as in the case of the extended family, or imagined, as in the case of the tribe. The territory of these communities was not that of the state, and the difference would persist for a long time. The former corresponded to ancestral lands and carried an emotional charge so strong that its inhabitants would give their lives to protect it, while the latter was a political construction of a central authority, made by taking hold of territory that was not necessarily continuous and controlling it through coercive means, with the help of a mobile army that travelled throughout it, collecting taxes and demanding signs of submission. This connection of politics to territory explains its great elasticity and how insurrections and uprisings challenged its limits. It requires the historian to begin not with a defined territory constantly being brought into question, but with the visions carried by those who contested the land.

Over the course of the contentious sixteenth century, many protagonists coveted this territory and produced different visions for it. The vision of the Spanish—who sought to isolate the coast and establish a string of fortresses, the presidios, to supply and protect their Mediterranean fleet—would have transformed Ifriqiya, cut off from its coast, into a region with its back to the sea, facing the Sahara. The great corsairs, 'Arrouj and Khayriddine, for their part, hoping to establish themselves on both shores of the Mediterranean, sought to unify the coasts from west to east and to found a republic of the sea populated by Andalusian settlements, under the control of Algiers and the protection of the Ottoman Empire. Faced with these two colonizing projects, the impoverished local powers chose to submit more to the Spanish than the Turks, while the tribal leaders granted their allegiance to one or the other according to the interests of the moment. In this unstable situation, the Maghreb remained unmapped (apart from coastal charts drawn by the Spanish); it would be unfounded to speak of defined territorial powers. From Fes to Tripoli, regions both large and small escaped the control of the central powers and developed autonomously, making space for new configurations of power.

To better grasp the drama of this century, I have chosen to situate this study more widely, in the context of the Mediterranean world, if not of the world as a whole—an ancient world as well as a new one that had just been discovered, and was ushering in so many revolutions, even in small nations. At this moment in history, the Mediterranean world was highly complex and its political situation had global ramifications. The historian Fernand Braudel masterfully described the globalized world of the sixteenth century, and proved that local histories could only be understood in the context of significant innovations in technology, economics, and ideas throughout the century.

I. AT THE MARGINS OF THE EMPIRE

1
The Mediterranean Scene

At the beginning of the sixteenth century, nothing seemed to foreshadow the imminent perishing of the old Hafsid dynasty, after decades of agony, at the hands of a great Ottoman expedition. Situated in the heart of the Mediterranean, the Hafsid territory was completely integrated into the world surrounding it. The acceleration of events would throw this centuries-old power into turmoil.

A Tormented Mediterranean

The Mediterranean world is a vast space encompassing the Iberian Peninsula, the Balkans, Southern Europe, Asia Minor, and North Africa, into the Sahara Desert.[1] This expanse was divided by fragmented geography but endowed nonetheless with a single people, linked since antiquity by a shared destiny. If the region was dominated by numerous powers throughout its long history, it was also home to many forms of resistance (as much to Christianity as to Islam), which flourished in the protection of the region's mountains. Since time immemorial, the Mediterranean, an inland sea, has allowed the inhabitants of its coasts to form both combative and friendly relationships: of war and peace, of prohibitions and transgressions, of religious struggles and commercial exchanges. The area around the Mediterranean seems to have been a world of contrasts between plains and mountains, nomadic populations and shepherds, and both transhumant and sedentary populations. There were also stark contrasts between wealth and poverty, abundance and need. A space of mobility and circulation, the Mediterranean displayed these dimensions in the sixteenth century when two giants, the Spanish and Ottoman empires, each developing on their own fronts, collided. From this violent encounter, a different Mediterranean was born, one marked as much by war and violence as by the mixing of people and cultures.

States in Reconstruction

In the Middle Ages, the northern periphery of the Mediterranean was organized into city-states: Granada, Istanbul, and the most vibrant of them all, Venice. Beginning in the fifteenth century, these city-states fell into crisis, unable to meet their political or financial obligations. One by one, they fell under the control of their rivals, the territorial states that were gradually taking shape in Europe and Turkey. These new powers were not yet modern nation states, but rather lands and peoples united under the person of the ruler.

As the Christian Mediterranean was beginning to unify, the Islamic Mediterranean was disintegrating. The Maghreb was by this time divided into four kingdoms named after their capitals: Marrakech, Fez, Tlemcen, and Tunis. In the sixteenth century, the Hafsid Kingdom still asserted authority over the regions of Bjaïa, Constantine, Tripoli, and Zab. But these territories were gradually slipping out from under the rule of Tunis and forming small independent kingdoms led by tribal leaders who were constantly falling out and fighting one another, making them easy prey for the expanding Spanish Empire.

The Spanish Expansion

The marriage of Ferdinand of Aragon and Isabella of Castile in 1469 and the resulting union of their Crowns spurred the unification of Iberia and the emergence of the Kingdom of Spain. This new kingdom grew steadily through acquisitions, integrating Granada in 1492 and then Spanish Navarre in 1512. The profoundly Catholic Spanish rulers were occupied with the crusade and the religious struggles amplified by the fall of Granada. A true "imperial mystique" motivated the Spanish expansion toward Italy. The additions of Sardinia and Sicily further enlarged the Kingdom of Aragon's possessions. In 1503, Ferdinand seized Naples, an opulent kingdom in a strategic position. His successor, Charles V, was crowned Emperor in Aix-la-Chapelle in September 1520. He made it his mission to unify Christianity behind a single leader and establish a universal monarchy.

Further south, from 1492 until the death of Ferdinand the Catholic in 1516, the African wars began to be assimilated into the new crusades, as much due to the religious fanaticism that motivated them as by the desire of the Catholic Church to push back the frontiers of Islam. The papacy inserted itself into this war, especially under Alexander VI, who from 1493 onward gave his blessing to the African Crusade. The Catholic kings, backed by the Church, were eager to continue their battle against the infidels on African territory: in 1497, the Spanish fleet occupied Melilla; in 1505, Mers el-Kebir; and in 1508 Peñón de Vélez. Oran was occupied in 1509 by an army commanded by Pedro Navarro, assisted by Father Ximénes. The following year, Bjaïa was taken. To avoid destruction, Algiers surrendered without a fight and declared itself to be under Spanish rule. A fortress, the "Peñón," was immediately erected on the island facing the city. On July 24, 1510, Tripoli fell. The seemingly unstoppable Christians caused terror, but also inspired several acts of resistance: one of these, in 1511, led to the defeat of the Spanish fleet in its attempt to conquer Djerba.

The Spanish established presidios, small fortresses occupied by soldiers, at various locations along the African coast that they occupied. Local leaders in the African hinterlands rarely attacked these enclaves, as they were preoccupied with waging wars against one another and so incapable of uniting against their common enemy. The role of the presidios was to give Spanish galleys en route to their Italian possessions refueling points and shelter from the scourge of the Mediterranean: piracy. This ancient activity had been revived in the sixteenth century as a result of an exceptional situation and a significant new phenomenon: the Moriscos fleeing religious persecution in Spain for more hospitable Muslim lands.

The Persecuted Moriscos

The Christian reconquest of Muslim Spain has a long history. It began in 1118, stopped in 1248 with the capture of Seville, and did not resume until the end of the fifteenth century, with the fall of the Muslim Kingdom of Granada in 1492. On the surrender of this last Islamic capital, the Spanish authorities recognized the religious liberty of the subject populations. However, they did not keep this promise, and in 1499 the Muslim Granadans were forced to convert under orders from the government. Book burnings were carried out and religious authorities set fire to manuscripts and Qur'ans. These measures provoked outrage in the Muslim communities, which soon reached a boiling point. An uprising broke out in the neighboring mountains in 1502 that proved difficult to suppress. When calm returned, the Moriscos faced a choice between conversion and exile. Many chose to adopt Christianity rather than leave their homeland. The wave of conversions, entrusted to the "old Christians" among whom the Muslims (the Mudejares) lived, were carried out in haste and often accompanied by cruelty and violence. According to a diplomatic testimony reported by Braudel, one Morisco village brought a complaint against its pastor for treating them with such hatred, even though their children were born with eyes as blue as their own.[2]

The new converts were treated as second-class Christians because the religious authorities were aware that many had converted merely for show. But despite the oppression that it suffered, Granadan Morisco society remained cohesive. Elites—nobles of refined taste that wore silk clothing and led discreet lives while ruling over a population of agriculturalists and being experts in raising silkworms and doing intensive fieldwork—remained in power in their villages. However, certain markers of Islamic identity irritated the Spanish authorities. At the end of 1566, the advisers of Philip II suggested several measures to better integrate the Moriscos. They forbade men and women from wearing traditional clothing and from speaking Arabic. Moorish baths were closed. The equilibrium that had existed until then, maintained by the protection that Christian landowners offered to the Muslims in their service, was breaking down, foreshadowing the disappearance of Muslim civilization from Spain.

A large uprising began in the mountains surrounding Granada, where outlaws were prevalent. On Christmas Eve 1568, they descended from their mountain hideout and led the Granadans in a rebellion. A groundswell of revolt broke out, bringing widespread pillage and slaughter. The unrest lasted for almost two years. When the uprising was finally crushed, the order was given to expel Granadan Muslims from the region. Several thousand Granadans were exiled to Castile in chains. There, their fate could have been much worse: they were at least able to work and earn money, profiting from favorable economic circumstances, as the region was being flooded with precious metals from the Americas.

But the Moriscos did not always assimilate. Under the cover of conversion, their culture remained intact. In 1580, a conspiracy was discovered in Seville. In 1588, trouble between the "Old Christians" (those who had been born Christian) and new converts was brewing in the Kingdom of Aragon. The disturbances were usually short-lived but were enough to generate some nervousness and much suspicion on the part of certain distrustful men of the Church. For how long, they wondered, would they need to endure these false Christians who never confessed, didn't go to mass, didn't baptize their children, and only recited the last rites when the dying person was no longer in a state to receive them? This was the debate among most Christian authorities, which suggested a radical solution: the definitive expulsion of the Moriscos. The implementation of this measure would be deferred until 1609, as the king was occupied with foreign wars. But the plight of thousands of Morisco refugees, their journey out of Spain, and their settling in host countries would become central to the history of the Mediterranean.

The Maghrebi narrative of these events has been oversimplified, seeing the Muslim populations as persecuted, expelled from their homeland, and welcomed by their coreligionists. In reality, their history is much more complex. Certainly, thousands of Moriscos left Spain, voluntarily or involuntarily. The Spanish government itself organized many of these departures to avoid the refugees landing in Muslim countries, where their expertise could be used to benefit the enemies of Christianity. However, many Moriscos arranged their own voyages so that they could choose their destinations. The conditions of departure varied according to region. Castilians, for example, were authorized to sell their goods and to bring a part of their revenues with them, a freedom that was not accorded elsewhere. Some Moriscos left on merchant boats destined for the shores of the Maghreb. Others went to France, Italy, and Turkey. Sources retain the traces of the suffering that raiders inflicted on many men, women, and children. They also preserve the memory of the poor treatment of these refugees by the Muslims of the Maghreb themselves, which was bad enough to cause some to return to their villages of origin.

The ties between Andalusia and the Maghreb were not new; they date back to the beginning of the Hafsid period. The princes of this dynasty collaborated closely with the Andalusians and encouraged them to immigrate to the Maghreb, particularly to Tunis, due to the close ties between the ruler Abu Zakariya (1236–49) and the Muslim kingdoms of Spain. In the thirteenth century, several cities in Ifriqiya had received Muslims from Valencia and Seville who settled down and built a variety of trades. The first wave of immigrants, made up of scholars, poets, traders, and craftsmen, lent a spark to the Hafsid court and encouraged a flurry of economic and cultural activity. It created an enlightened elite in the service of a state that had been founded originally by austere Berber preachers. We consider Khayriddine Barbarossa, as having embarked on a similar project in the sixteenth century, which would rely heavily on the Muslims of the West, a project that the Ottoman sultan caliphs supported.

The question of the settlement of Moriscos in the Maghreb is being revisited. The integration of these refugees was not as simple as has been represented. There are many indications that the Barbarossa brothers, Khayriddine in particular, intended to build a state in the Maghreb in which the Andalusians would have been colonizers, populating and bringing their expertise to regions that lacked a workforce. He organized expeditions on the Spanish shores and the surrounding islands to bring back Morisco families. His successors in Algiers, especially 'Ilj 'Ali, would continue these policies.

The Ottoman Empire in Full Power

The Ottoman Empire is Asian, in terms of both its geography and its origins. But its military expansion and the conditions of the sixteenth century pushed it farther and farther toward the western Mediterranean. The founders of the empire were originally from the frontiers of Asia Minor, a vast region that was Orthodox and Greek before it became Muslim and Turkish through the evangelization of the mystic Muslim orders, the Babais and the Mevlevis. At the beginning, the Ottoman expansion was directed toward Europe. It progressed slowly, despite encountering little resistance, as European peasants saw no interest in defending feudal regimes and the great oppression of their lords. The Ottoman soldiers advanced into the Balkan region, taking the routes that followed the many rivers flowing into the Danube. They also advanced in the plains of the East, successively occupying Bulgaria and Thessaly. Over the course of the second half of the fifteenth century, Greece was occupied. Athens fell in 1456, the Morea in 1460, Bosnia in 1466, and Herzegovina in 1481. Only some mountainous regions resisted this tidal wave.

The vast, newly conquered territory would gradually be tamed. At the beginning of the Ottoman occupation, agrarian policy was relatively flexible. In Serbia, the fleeing of the lords left open territory, which was transformed partly into *waqf*, land permanently belonging to religious institutions. As for the rest, it was granted to sipahis, soldier-peasants, in the form of concessions or *timar*. These new concessionaires, unlike the ancient feudal lords, asked only for royalties and renounced the practice of the *corvée*—unpaid labor—which was ill-tolerated by the peasants and often considered abusive. For this reason, and for the fact that it required no forced conversions, the Turkish occupation met little resistance. In Bosnia, for example, voluntary conversions became commonplace, especially in the area around Sarajevo, where a longstanding, powerful heresy, Bogomilism, introduced Islam to its followers. In Albania, faced with the Turkish onslaught, many lords fled toward the Venetian enclaves and from there to Italy, where their families settled permanently. Others remained on their land, sometimes at the cost of forced repudiation of their faith. The Turkish conquest in Christian countries mixed violence with integration: while thousands of Kossovan Serbs were sold as slaves, others were enlisted in armies as mercenaries. In other regions, the institution of the Devshirme plundered the region of its young children, whom the central authority enrolled in the elite Janissary corps. Later, the Turks accorded the conquered populations new cadres in which they could evolve: the establishment of the millet system permitted nations founded on confessional communities to exercise certain religious and legal rights.

Once the Balkan world had been pacified, the Ottomans turned toward the lands of the Mamluks. The occupations of Syria in 1516 and Egypt in 1517 by Sultan Selim were major events in the history of the empire. These two regions were conquered without great difficulty because the Turks possessed artillery and the Mamluks did not. The new provinces of Egypt and Syria would give the Ottoman Empire access to African gold and spices from India, essential products for commerce with Christendom. At a symbolic level, the Ottoman sultan received the Sharif of Mecca as a refugee in Egypt, the gatekeeper of the Ka'ba, the symbolic center of Islam. Sultan Selim thus became the 'Commander of the Faithful' beginning in 1517, a title that would legitimize many of his future conquests in Islamic lands.

Selim died in 1520. His son Suleiman took the throne and expanded the conquests. Belgrade fell into his hands in 1521 and the island of Rhodes in December 1522. By breaking this final bolt—Rhodes had been controlled until then by the Knights of Saint Jean—Suleiman opened the western Mediterranean. As the Ottoman sultan turned his focus toward wars with the Persian Empire, he found in the Barbarossa brothers the best executors of his Mediterranean policies.

The stage of the Mediterranean in the sixteenth century was set: two giants fought over sea and coastline against the backdrop of political rivalries, religious hatred, human displacement through captivity and expulsions, suffering and repudiations, and integration and exclusion. The sixteenth century was a time of globalization, during which regions were drawing closer to one another due to revolutions in navigational techniques. Men and women, merchandise, and ideas all circulated with new intensity across seas, oceans, and through Saharan circuits, creating enormous intermixing and giving rise to an exceptional melting pot of people and culture.

At the political level, the Spanish and Ottoman empires both granted themselves the right of interference in the local affairs of the Maghrebi kingdoms, where conflicts between factions and rival families were settled partly in Madrid and partly in Istanbul. The great autonomy that the Maghreb had enjoyed throughout the Middle Ages was beginning to disappear—its destiny becoming, for the moment, Mediterranean.

2
Back to a Medieval Era

Let us leave this turbulent sixteenth century for a moment and go further back to ascertain the dynamics that gave the Maghreb its most fundamental traits, and on which the rupture of modern times would act. Maghrebi history saw two contradictory pushes, a century apart. The first, in 1050, was the arrival of Arab tribes from the south of Egypt, who swept aside existing rulers and broke up their territories into infinite numbers of principalities. The second, in 1152, was a push for unification coming out of the western Maghreb led by the iron will of the Berber tribe of Masmouda, the founders of the great Almohad dynasty. These two powers marked the medieval Maghreb, which churned with territorial deconstructions and reconstructions that ignited conflicts between sedentary populations and nomads, city and countryside, and orthodoxy and heresy.

The Disintegrating Maghreb

When the Governor of Ifriqiya, al-Mu'izz ibn Badis, proclaimed his allegiance to the Caliphate of Baghdad in 1048, his master, the Fatimid al-Mustansir in Cairo, decided to crack down. He gave the Arab nomads, the Banu Hilal and Banu Sulaym, who were encamped in the south of Egypt and forbidden from crossing the Nile, permission to make their way to the Maghreb and pillage the territories. The Zirid Prince al-Mu'izz did not anticipate the magnitude of the invasion. When the Arab invaders arrived in Ifriqiya, al-Mu'izz tried to approach them and enlist them in his army. He tried to find common ground, going so far as to marry his daughter to a prince of the Ryahs (one of the main branches of the Hilali). But the tribes refused to submit and behaved as invaders in conquered land. In 1052, they devastated the Zirid army at Haydaran, near Gabes. Not long after, Kairouan was invaded and pillaged. By whom? The Arab Bedouins? Or Ibn

Badis himself, who would have destroyed his own capital for fear of his subjects defecting? That's what Jacques Berque asserts based upon a close reading of Ibn Khaldun, going so far as to suggest that the Zirid ruler would have invited the Arabs into Ifriqiya to punish his own population.[1] But al-Mu'izz had miscalculated and he found himself isolated, abandoned by the Arab contingents in his service, without the support he had expected from his Berber kin. Nevertheless, he continued to strengthen his alliances with the Arabs by giving them three more of his daughters in marriage. But the invaders continued to pillage, and al-Mu'izz, exhausted by all this turmoil, ultimately abandoned Kairouan and retired to Mahdia, which he thought was more resistant to attack due to its geography. However, in 1057, this new capital met the same fate as Kairouan. Now, without the protection of the Zirid ruler, other cities—Gabes, Gafsa, Béja, Tunis, Tozeur—also fell to the Arab kinglets.

The Hilali invasion and its consequences have been interpreted in different ways. Did the invaders set back agriculture in favor of nomadism, thereby destroying villages and all forms of urbanism? Were they the agents of a profound crisis that shook the Maghreb? Were historians' views on the Hilali turbulence influenced by the perspective of the great medieval historian Ibn Khaldun, which was shaped by his position as an urban scholar and an authority figure with a harsh opinion of the Bedouin? Were Ibn Khaldun's writings interpreted unequivocally? In rereading *Kitab al-'ibar* Jacques Berque detected ambivalence in Ibn Khaldun's attitude toward the Arabs.[2] While treating them like a "swarm of locusts," he also glorifies their warrior spirit, their esprit de corps, and their harmony with nature (far from the "urban softness"), traits that helped them found dynasties. A new reading of Hilali history would likely add nuance to certain judgements and show that pre-Hilali Ifriqiya was not as prosperous as some studies would have liked to show.

Colonial studies such as Gauthier's *Les Siècles Obscurs du Maghreb*, for their part, considered the Hilalis the destroyers of Roman heritage—a heritage that French colonization then sought to restore by highlighting its archaeological remains.[3] History has attributed the worst traits to the Hilalis, depicting them as destroyers, bandits, predators, and thieves. Hilali tales, on the other hand, paint a much richer portrait of the culture, recounted through oral legends of heroes such as the unstoppable Jazia, enveloped in her long hair, or Dhiab, the repentant lover.

The Banu Hilal and Banu Sulaym, who came after, are estimated to have consisted of around two hundred thousand people. In one century, they spread throughout the Maghreb spontaneously, first in search of rangelands and later when they were exiled by the Almohad prince, who deported entire tribes to the West. This event provides the setting for the epic poem *Taghribat Bani Hilal*.[4] The Arabs thus became a sociological reality that would definitively mark the Maghreb. The political breakdown that followed benefitted the smaller kingdoms, formed primarily by tribal sheikhs who had taken advantage of the reigning insecurity to establish themselves as local potentates. The impact of the Hilali invasions collapsed the existing structures of the Maghreb. But the collapse was fortunately counterbalanced by an event concomitant to the arrival of the Hilalis: a movement of sainthood, part of the mythical *saguia al hamra*, extending to the east. Saints, who became quite famous, such as Abu al-Hassan al-Chadouli, Abu Midyan, and others, expanded across the entire Maghreb, spreading their doctrines, gathering followers, and forming powerful fraternal solidarities. The spread of sainthood, which characterizes Maghrebi Islam, was a powerful source of social cohesion that can be observed throughout the entire medieval period, during which the number of santons and sanctuaries multiplied and participated actively in a mass Islamization of the population. The *zawiyas* played several roles, such as feeding and caring for the poor and teaching and spreading knowledge.

The Arab Bedouins were late to join these fraternal movements. Throughout the Middle Ages, they were known for their brutality, their ignorance of Qur'anic precepts, and their lawless lifestyles. Legal sources categorized them as *mustaghriqi al-dhimma*, lacking honor or good reputation, and went so far as to forbid commercial transactions with some of them. In the legal opinions, there are several clear allusions to regions inhabited by the Bedouins, where Shari'a did not apply and bandits raped and pillaged.[5] This lack of adherence to religious and social codes was perceived to be the principal trait of Bedouin society.

It was not until the fifteenth century that these populations began to believe in the power of the intercession of saints. A movement of repentance and tranquility, called *tawbat al-'Arab*, gradually began to appear in rural areas. Rich men who had accrued fortunes illicitly now offered their belongings to *zawiyas* as a sign of repentance. Men and women became curious about religious practice and sought to devote themselves to it. For some Bedouins, this movement of consecrated repentance marked the beginning of their integration into the wider society.

Sustained over some time, this turmoil shaped the fate of Ifriqiya. The new authority that emerged in the thirteenth century, the Hafsids, who originated among the Berbers of Masmouda, oscillated between autonomy from Marrakech, the capital of the Almohad empire, and dependence on it. The new dynasty sought local support by negotiating with the rebellious Arab tribes, over whom they alternately exercised brutal repression or an irresistible call.

The Hafsids Leading Ifriqiya

A century after the arrival of the Hilalis and the subsequent territorial and political fragmentation, another event occurred on the periphery of the Maghreb that gave the region a new source of unity: the appearance of the Almohads. Originating in southern Morocco, this modest movement formed around a rigorist sect founded by the preacher Ibn Tumart, who drew support from the Berber population of the High Atlas. The preaching of the *mahdi*, simple and accessible to the Berbers, was strengthened by an effective propaganda machine that helped transform disciplcs into formidable warriors. From their mountain stronghold, the Almohads set off on an assault against Morocco and Spain before turning toward the East. This great Berber offensive would give the Maghreb another nexus of power, which would be constructed against the Arab Bedouins. The conquest happened in three stages: first, they captured Moroccan and Andalusian villages, then those of the central Maghreb and Bjaïa, and finally, they won an overwhelming victory against the Hilali princes in the Battle of Sétif in 1153. This victory opened Ifriqiya to the Almohads—the final stage in the unification of the Maghreb.

Ifriqiya at the time was extremely divided. The last Zirids were entrenched in small villages, the Hilali princes dominated the vast interior regions, and the Normans were based in Mahdia. Two campaigns conducted by Caliph ‘Abd al-Mu’min, in 1152 and 1159, eventually crushed the Arab Bedouins, the Christians, and the small kinglets in the main urban centers. Ifriqiya, now attached to the Almohad Empire, was then divided into two provinces with two capitals: Bjaïa, and the newly declared capital of Tunis.

Would this emerging province know peace under its new masters? A short period of tranquility followed the annexation of Ifriqiya, but the province was too far from Marrakech, the capital of the empire, to fall completely under its control. The former local leaders did not waste time before beginning to fight for autonomy or stir up dissent, while the central power, weakened by problems of succession, saw its control over the outlying territories weaken. A large part of Ifriqiya slipped from its authority under the government of Yahya ibn Ghalia, the Hilali chief who submitted to the vassalage of the Abbasids of Baghdad.

The Almohad Caliph al-Nasir reacted boldly, and, with one of his lieutenants, 'Abd al-Wahid bin abi Hafs al-Hintati, an important state dignitary and brother-in-law of the caliph, set off to retake the province. Back in Marrakech, al-Nasir decided to entrust the newly recaptured territories to his lieutenant, who accepted this responsibility on the condition that he have complete liberty to choose his deputies. This is how the first Hafsid ruler established himself in Tunis in May 1207, where he would die in the course of duty in February 1221. Following a difficult period, in 1226, the caliph named the son of 'Abd al-Wahid al-Hintati as the new governor, inaugurating three centuries of Hafsid rule. Prince Abu Zakariya (1228–49), the brother and successor of 'Abd al-Wahid al-Hintati, would expand the territory of his province toward Tripolitania, ensuring domestic order and achieving autonomy. Abu Zakariya's power grew so much that, once ensured of the decline of the Almohad Empire, he began to covet the Moroccan regions and part of Spain, where he came to the aid of local leaders fighting the Christians of the reconquest. This was how Valencia, Seville, Jeres, Tarifa, and Almería came to request Abu Zakariya's help and some cities declared themselves to be under his authority. In 1237, he received a second *bay'a* declaring him prince. Ifriqiya would have an extraordinary destiny under Abu Zakariya, becoming the capital of the Maghreb and of part of Spain. The territory was discontinuous and rebellions incessant, but recognition of Abu Zakariya's political authority made Tunis the capital of the Maghreb. When Abu Zakariya died, his son al-Muntasir, born of 'Atif, his legal concubine, succeeded him and took the title of Amir al-Mu'minin (Commander of the Faithful). His spiritual power was recognized as far away as Mecca, from where he received a *bay'a* in 1259.

Charged with governing a difficult province and faced with endless uprisings, the first Hafsids tried to achieve a balance between the different populations with their divergent interests. The Hafsids depended mainly on the Almohad sheikhs, Berbers who had arrived during the conquest and who considered themselves the sole bearers of legitimacy in the region.

Abu Zakariya also relied on the Andalusians and the freed Christian captives. Even though a division of responsibilities emerged within the circles of power, a strong rivalry formed between the Andalusians and the old Almohad families. If the latter invoked legitimacy based on their kinship with the founder of the dynasty, the Muslim refugees from Spain prided themselves on being urbanites and on their skills in various domains, in particular the art of governing. The Hafsids inherited the Almohads' political structures, including a rather rudimentary administration and imprecise guidelines for the chancellery. The ruler was surrounded by close advisers (*wazirs*); a chancellery made up of secretaries (*katibs*), Andalusians or Maghrebis trained in Andalusia; a chamberlain *(hajib)*; and a minister of finance *(sahib al-ashghal)*. The Andalusians made the courts sparkle with their poets, musicians, and architects, and caused the Hafsids to distance themselves, little by little, from the austere practices of their origins. Tunis was receiving many Muslim refugees expelled by the Reconquista, as well as Christians leaving their countries and settling permanently in Ifriqiya. The social landscape was thus changed. As for the local Arab and Berber populations, they alternated between allegiance and rebellions that the ruling powers tried to contain, sometimes by means of incentives such as offering fiefs to the sheikhs, and sometimes by repression.

On the military side, in the beginning the Hafsids relied on the Berber troops from Morocco. They encountered Arab tribes, whom they considered enemies, but over time, some of these Hilali branches were integrated into the Berber units, which helped to neutralize them by creating divisions among their men. This policy achieved its intended outcome, but it also created a dependency on the Bedouins that would be felt until the disappearance of the Hafsids in the sixteenth century. Yet these troops were just an auxiliary force, for the true military force was a Christian militia, which appears in the sources around 1254.[6] It was made up of mercenaries, vassals of the Crown of Aragon, and had many horsemen, often appointed by the kings of Aragon themselves.[7] Moreover, until the first quarter of the fourteenth century, the Christian militia was a body serving the king of Tunis but detached from its head, the Crown of Aragon. Later, this body lost its allegiance to the Christian state. The soldiers were then placed under the jurisdiction of their leader, who held the title of caid. The first sources mention a caid named Abu 'Abdallah, but shortly thereafter only speak of *'uluj*: the converted Christians, whose roles included governing the cities in which they were based. In Tunis, the neighborhood of Bab al-'Uluj was reserved for them. In the fifteenth century, the traveller Marmol described *al-rabatin*, the Christians from the peripheral neighborhoods who were descendants of these first militias. The sultan's chosen guards, they formed three groups commanded by the caids, who possessed parts of the region as fiefdoms.[8] Their customs were heavily Arabized. They dressed like Moors (except for the hoods), had their own places of worship, and their wives were invited to the palace. These working-class people had the privilege of ringing the bell of their church, dedicated to Saint Francis. The Spanish used them as translators throughout the occupation of La Goulette in 1535.[9]

Drawing from this Christian guard may seem unusual for a time when the crusades were pitting the West against the East (Saint Louis died at Carthage in 1270). In fact, these wars, amplified by the religious authorities, included the defense of shared political and economic interests. Abu Zakariya maintained excellent relations with many Christian kings, in particular Frederick II, the king of Sicily. Upon the death of Saint Louis and after the signing of a peace agreement, the two armies established a fruitful commercial relationship. In these circumstances, reliance on Christian soldiers should not be surprising, for professional mercenaries showed more loyalty than the indigenous populations, who changed sides or fled when faced with the enemy.

The Hafsids were sufficiently aware of the Bedouins' fickleness not to fully trust them with the security of the state. Moreover, when it came to techniques of warfare, the Arabs had only cavalry, while at the same time infantry was developing in the West.

The role of the Arab tribes in Hafsid history was decisive: through their attitudes, they alternately strengthened or weakened Hafsid power and influenced its economic policy.

To the extent that the Hafsid state was cultivating relations with Venice, it was with the goal of reorienting itself toward the sea and reducing the importance of the ancient caravan routes of the south. Mediterranean commerce was essential for the Hafsids. The rulers placed a strong emphasis on trade because the taxes collected from these transactions were their most stable source of revenues, given the weakness of agricultural revenue and the difficulty of collecting taxes from rural areas. Agricultural tax collection depended on tenant farming and was corrupted by the misappropriation of funds, which the authorities could not control, except by occasionally executing tax collectors and confiscating their goods. Under these circumstances, maritime taxes became regular royalties, and rulers had everything to gain from developing Mediterranean commerce and from the concessions given to European merchants. The Hafsids were the first to embark on this economic policy, which created stiff competition with local traders by expanding the state's monopoly over products for export such as copper, coral, wax, honey, and cereals. The ruler enriched himself at the expense of the local populations, deepening a rupture within the society.[10]

What must be remembered about the long Hafsid reign, from 1209 to 1574, was the difficulty they had holding on to Maghrebi territory, despite having an administration that was experienced in governing. The Hafsids struggled to contain the Arab Bedouins, despite their attempts using many forms of courtship and repression. Was this why they depended on the *'uluj*? This practice, of relying on political or military personnel of Christian origin, was not uniquely Hafsid: in the Ottoman Empire, the Janissary corps was only open to converted Christians, and the most meritorious rose to the highest levels. This was a dominant feature of the modern history of the entire Islamo-Mediterranean world.

The sixteenth century opened to a dramatic situation for the Hafsid rulers: they were effectively caught between the tribes and their frequent about-faces, the Spanish crusade and its expansion toward the Mediterranean coasts, and the hegemonic threat of Ottoman intervention. This uncomfortable situation began with the disappearance of Sultan Muhammad (1494–1526), so the period of his rule is rightly considered the last long reign of the Hafsid dynasty. A lover of pleasure, this prince ordered the construction of palaces such as the famous residence of al-'Ibdilliya in La Marsa, a symbol of this lavish era. However, he could not contain either the Spanish offensive or the Arab tribes that were gnawing at the borders. Little by little, Sultan Muhammad's territory was torn apart. He lost Bjaïa and Tripoli in 1510. A crisis of succession followed his death. Unable to find dependable support within the region, the contenders called on foreign powers: the Spanish and the Ottomans. After a series of clashes, this war of succession would culminate with the disappearance of the Hafsid dynasty against a backdrop of change in the Maghreb.

The Maghreb Reconstructed

When the Spanish Empire broke beyond its Iberian borders during these African wars, in a crusade against the Moors and Islam, it did not meet much resistance. Rulers surrendered readily, probably due to military incapacity. Opposition would come from elsewhere: the corsairs, specifically the Barbarossa brothers, were destined for greatness, having harnessed the exceptional circumstances in the Mediterranean for their benefit. The control of the seas, the defense of religions, maritime commerce and profit, and the practice of piracy were inextricably linked during the early modern period. For too long, scholarship has privileged the religious nature of these conflicts as the most obvious and acceptable explanation for the atrocities committed by both sides, the Christians and the Muslims. Certainly, everything about the Spanish offensive recalls religious wars, with its fanaticism and its desire to push the frontiers of Islam off Spanish territory, territory that included much of Italy at this time, thereby involving the pope and the Church authorities in the conflict. Inquisition documents reveal numerous proceedings against renegades tracked down in a ferocious witch-hunt.

Another institution, the Knights of Rhodes, which was originally founded by the Knights Hospitaller, and which became, in 1309, a maritime power engaged in piracy and combat on the seas, halted the Ottoman advance in the eastern Mediterranean. Not yet in possession of their own fleet, the Turks called on Greek corsairs to fight the Knights of Rhodes. The Knights occupied the island of Mételin, the homeland of the Barbarossa brothers, which had been captured by the Turks in 1457. The island became the refuge of the Islamicized Greek corsairs, who defended it fiercely when a coalition of Christian states tried to seize it in 1501. The Ottoman sultans, Selim and later his son Suleiman, realized that their empire would never know peace while the Knights controlled Rhodes. The provinces of the Levant, Egypt, Syria, Caramania, and the islands of Morea, Mételin, and Negroponte were constantly threatened. Sultan Suleiman pronounced the following in 1522 during the siege of the island:

> Only the city of Rhodes, located at the heart of my empire, at the doors of my best provinces, stands in the way of my grandeur. . . . [The Knights] intercept my messages, they steal my tributes, they rob our merchants, they intimidate my galleys, they receive Christian corsairs, criminals, the disowned, fugitives, and rebels against our faith and my justice . . . they haggle and negotiate with me as if we were equals, are these things not unbearable? Is it not a shame and a reproach to us Ottomans to further defer punishment and vengeance? To this end, I sent as many ships, cannons, soldiers, and good captains, as if it were a question of conquering an entire kingdom . . . [11]

This religious and military rivalry between the Knights of Rhodes and the Ottoman Empire intensified in the sixteenth century in the eastern Mediterranean. At the same time, in the western region, Spain was beginning a crusade against Islam. The religious hatred between Christians and Muslims did not exclude material considerations—the lure of riches and loot. It was not uncommon for the emperor's ships to spend more time engaging in piracy than in expeditions against Muslim cities. The decades-long Spanish offensive was able to succeed because the lands of the Maghreb did not resist, so great were the divisions and rivalries between leaders, clans, and tribes. The Maghreb had not stopped breaking apart, with the Hafsid states to the East and Merinid states to the West losing control of large swathes of their respective territories. While the local tribes rebelled, their sheikhs returned to power.

The remainder of the central territory of the Maghreb was subject to other powers. Constantine fell under a Hafsid prince fairly autonomous from Tunis, whose authority extended to the neighboring regions of Collo and Bône. The vast plateaus and plains of eastern Algeria submitted to the authority of a strong Arabized Berber tribe, the Houara, later known by the name Hnansha. On top of the territorial fragmentation of the Maghrebi states, they were also behind in acquiring modern weapons and learning the art of maritime war. Under these circumstances, defending the coasts became a difficult mission. It was at this moment that the Barbarossa brothers intervened in the Maghreb.

3

The Barbarossas in the Maghreb

The arrival of the Barbarossas in the Maghreb would have far-reaching consequences for the fate of the region, which found itself plunged into the global conflict between the Spanish and the Ottomans. The Hafsid dynasty, with its borders being encroached upon, was suspicious of these corsairs with great political ambitions.

'Arrouj and the Founding of a Barbary State

The founding of a Barbary state in Algiers was the work of one of these corsairs, legendary for his intrepidness: 'Arrouj Barbarossa. All of 'Arrouj's biographies say that he was born into a family of four brothers on the island of Lesbos, in Mytilene (or Mételin). He was the son of a poor potter, and like many Greeks sailed off on a Turkish galley at the age of twenty. While at sea, he earned a reputation as an invincible sailor. The Arab sources claim that he was born a Muslim: his father, an Albanian, allegedly took refuge on Mytilene as a fugitive, where he converted to Islam and became a *sipahi*, a soldier holding a fief. He married the widow of a Greek priest who bore him six children, four of them boys. Each specialized in a different trade: 'Arrouj became a sailor, while Khayriddine (called Khidr at birth) became a potter. 'Arrouj and his brother Ilyes ventured into piracy. During one expedition, Ilyes perished and 'Arrouj was taken prisoner by the Knights of Saint John, who imprisoned him on Rhodes. His captivity allowed him to closely observe the way this order was organized and operated, and he swore to use this knowledge to defeat the Christians.[1] Thanks to his ingenuity, he managed to escape.

Shortly after, Turkish merchants who wanted to commission a galiot for corsairing solicited 'Arrouj to be its commander. He agreed and recruited two of his brothers, Ishaq and Khayriddine. They decided to attack the Maghrebi coastline, parts of which had recently come under

Christian control. During this expedition, he trained another sailing crew. They arrived in La Goulette in 1504, where he obtained the Hafsid sultan's permission to enter the ports and resupply. His first seizures were two papal galiots, which he captured near Tuscany, earning him immense popularity and great wealth. The following year, bolstered by this recognition and the goodwill of the sultan of Tunis, 'Arrouj was able to arm the two captured galiots, as well as his own galley, and embark on a new expedition in the spring of 1505. He succeeded in capturing a ship sent by the king of Spain to the Kingdom of Naples, which earned him enormous revenue in both ransom and goods. Henceforth, 'Arrouj's fleet consisted of four well-armed vessels, two of which he gave to his brothers, Ishaq and Khayriddine. In 1510, 'Arrouj's reputation and fortune established, the sultan of Tunis granted him the island of Djerba. He became its caid, a governor responsible for administration and collecting taxes.

The Hafsid sultan, Muhammad, maintained good relations with 'Arrouj, whose fleet spent the winter in Djerba. The corsair even moved to Tunis himself with his brother Khayriddine, and the two men arranged several of their victorious expeditions at sea from La Goulette. In return, the sultan of Tunis received one-fifth of their earnings, as well as the magnificent gifts Barbarossa never failed to offer him. It was only once they began to feel their power threatened that the attitude of the Hafsid kings towards the Barbarossas began to change.

The two corsairs, 'Arrouj and Khayriddine, came to the rescue of Bjaïa, which had been captured by the Spanish. It was there that 'Arrouj injured his arm and eventually had to have it amputated. Once healed, he returned to sea with his brother and stormed the city of Djidjelli, which had been in Spanish hands since 1514. After this victory, the brothers established contact with Sultan Selim, sending him precious gifts and offering their allegiance. This recognition encouraged many Berbers to align with them and to participate in the attack on Bjaïa, which they besieged for twenty-four days. As the gunpowder was about to run out, Khayriddine requested more from the sultan of Tunis, who refused to supply it. The sixteenth-century Turkish chronicler Sinan Chaouch explains this refusal as stemming from the sultan's jealousy of the two corsairs. It likely had more to do with his anxiety about collusion between the corsairs and the Ottoman Turks, which made him fear for his throne.

However, the sultan's attitude did not put an end to collaboration with the corsairs. After having abandoned the siege of Bjaïa, 'Arrouj settled in

Djidjelli, and Khayriddine returned to La Goulette to prepare his fleet for a new campaign. It was there that an envoy of the sultan entrusted him with several of his ships armed for privateering.

His injury healed, 'Arrouj restored his fleet and returned to Bjaïa in August 1514. Thanks to the support of the former governor and the population, he succeeded in destroying one of the fortifications, but he had to give up the capture of the city after the Spanish sent strong reinforcements and the people withdrew to the mountains to sow their crops. 'Arrouj retreated to Djidjelli and returned to privateering, capturing several Sicilian ships full of wheat destined for Spain and distributing the goods to the populations suffering from famine. This earned him great popularity, and the people appointed him king. Emboldened by his new role, he fought and killed his neighbor, the king of Kouko in Kabyle, thereby enlarging his territorial possessions.

'Arrouj, King of Algiers

The events of 1516 would establish 'Arrouj as the new king of Algiers. During this year, the Catholic King Ferdinand died, which encouraged the people of Algiers, led by the Arab Sheikh al-Tumi, to ask 'Arrouj to free them from the yoke of the Spanish. He accepted their proposition, as he had secretly yearned for a long time to become king of the entire region. His expedition was carried out in two phases: he sent a fleet of sixteen galiots by sea and led an army of Arabs and Turkish mercenaries by land. Before heading to Algiers, 'Arrouj decided to conquer Cherchell, which had recently been governed by his former friend Gara Hassan, whom he now feared as a rival. 'Arrouj entered the city unexpectedly, killed Gara Hassan even though he had surrendered, and seized the city and its riches. He then travelled on to Algiers where he was well received by Sheikh al-Tumi. 'Arrouj attempted to dislodge the Christians from Peñón but failed due to his weak artillery. He settled in the city with his soldiers. The presence of 'Arrouj and his soldiers in Algiers concerned Sheikh al-Tumi, as much due to the corsair's arrogance as to the brutality of the Turks who accompanied him. 'Arrouj, who harbored pretensions to rule Algiers, decided to get rid of the sheikh, strangling him to death in the bath while he was performing his ablutions. The terrified inhabitants of Algiers did not resist, and the Turks proclaimed 'Arrouj as the new king of Algiers. The son of the assassinated king quickly fled to Oran, which was under Spanish control. He was welcomed there by the Marquis of Comares, the captain-general of the province. The people of Algiers began to stir, making contact with both the Spanish and the people of the Mitidja plain (the latter wished to avenge the dead king, who was one of their own). Together, the Christians and Arabs organized a plot against 'Arrouj, but he was informed of it in advance and massacred the conspirators in the Great Mosque.

In 1516, the Spanish decided to intervene at the request of Selim al-Tumi's son, who had settled in Spain in the interim. They equipped a fleet, not of three hundred boats (as recorded by Sinan), but of eighty warships, including galleys, vessels, and simple transport ships. On September 30, 1516, the fleet entered the Bay of Algiers. 'Arrouj, having gotten wind of the fleet's arrival, prepared his Turkish soldiers and the Arab troops that had come to the rescue. The Spanish troops were routed. Many Spanish historians have tried to conceal the defeat, following the lead of Cardinal Ximénés himself, who downplayed its seriousness in his report to Charles V. All the blame was placed on the leader of the expedition, Francesco de Véro. He managed to escape and return to Spain, leaving behind almost his entire army, either dead or imprisoned. He became an object of ridicule in his land. Children used to sing:

> Certainly Véro was neither the strongest nor the most clever, for despite having two arms, he let himself be defeated by a one-armed man.[2]

After the Spanish armada failed in its attack, the people of Algiers turned to the king of Ténès and asked him to help them regain their freedom. 'Arrouj, outpacing the attack, set out with his Arab and Morisco soldiers and routed the enemy. He pursued the fleeing army and entered Ténès, which submitted to him after the king fled into the Atlas Mountains. News of 'Arrouj's exploits spread, and some inhabitants of Tlemcen proposed that he come occupy their city to drive out their king, who supported the Spanish. Tlemcen was governed by Abu Zayan, who had recently overthrown his nephew, the rightful king Abu Hammou. The Turkish army, led by 'Arrouj, defeated Abu Zayan, and in September 1517 entered Tlemcen and reaped its vast wealth. The eldest of the Barbarossa brothers managed to secure the support of the king of Fes.

By that time, a large portion of the central Maghreb was in the hands of the Barbarossas: 'Arrouj was in Tlemcen, Khayriddine was occupying Algiers, and Ishaq controlled the *qal'a* of the Beni Rashid. The latter were massacred by Arab soldiers, supported by the Spanish, in 1518. During this same period, Charles V, responding to a request from the Governor of Oran, sent an army of ten thousand soldiers to fight 'Arrouj. He defended the city for close to six months but abandoned it when the Spanish breached the city gates and the people of Tlemcen betrayed him. He left the city in secret with his loyal companions and headed toward Algiers, closely pursued by the Spanish soldiers of the Marquis of Comares. With the Spanish hot on his heels, he strategically left part of his booty on the road to slow them down, but they caught him nonetheless. The Turks defended themselves bravely, but their forces were crushed. 'Arrouj Barbarossa was killed by Garcia de Tineo, who brought back his head as a trophy. And so, the first chapter in the adventure of the Barbarossas came to a close. Haedo, a Spanish priest who was in Turkish captivity, wrote:

> According to those who knew him, Arrouj was forty-four years old at the time of his death. He was not very large, but very strong and robust. He had a red beard; bright, fiery eyes; an aquiline nose; and a swarthy complexion. He was energetic, very courageous, fearless, magnanimous and extremely generous; he never showed himself to be cruel, except in war and when he was disobeyed. He was at once very loved, very feared, and very respected by his soldiers who wept bitterly at his death. He left behind no offspring. He spent fourteen years on the Barbary Coast where he did much harm to the Christians; he was King of Gigelli [sic] and the neighboring lands for four years, king of Algiers for two years, and a usurper of Tlemcen for one year.[3]

The death of 'Arrouj would allow his brother Khayriddine to move into the foreground.

4

Khayriddine Barbarossa and the Project of a Maghrebi State

In a few years, 'Arrouj had succeeded in carving out a territory around Algiers, but his early death prevented him from consolidating it. After the loss of his brother in 1518, Khayriddine was desperate to keep control of the city. Most of his troops had perished in the siege of Tlemcen, and he doubted the ability of his remaining forces to confront the Spanish army. The second of the Barbarossas learned from his brother's death that he could not stand up to the Spanish Empire alone. He had two options: abandon Algiers lest he be killed in an attack by the Governor of Oran, or put himself under the protection of the Sublime Porte.

Khayriddine at the Head of the *Oujak* of Algiers

Khayriddine considered abandoning Algiers, but several of his friends and relatives dissuaded him. To explain Khayriddine's decision, his historian, Sinan Chaouch, relies on a conventional method: the premonitory dream. Khayriddine had seen the Prophet Muhammad in his sleep, who commanded him to not abandon Algiers. In reality, when Khayriddine learned that the Marquis of Comares, the Spanish Governor of Oran, had demobilized and sent his troops back to Spain, he regained hope and was encouraged by those close to him to proclaim himself king of Algiers. He was strengthened by this new title but decided to still seek the protection of the Ottoman Sultan Selim. The sources contradict each other about this move: Did the request for protection come from Khayriddine himself, who said it came from the people of Algiers to give it more weight? When exactly did the delegation set off—1518 or 1519? Who led it?

There were in fact two delegations. For the first, Khayriddine commissioned Hajj Hussein to establish contact with Sultan Selim, who was in Egypt, and to offer his vassalage. The Sultan accepted the proposal and sent his insignia, which made Algiers a *sanjak*, a small province, and Khayriddine, a *beylerbey*.[1] A second delegation, led by Ahmad ibn al-Qadi, was sent to Istanbul in 1519, carrying a letter from the people of Algiers requesting the protection of the Empire.[2] The sultan-caliph accepted their submission, appointed Khayriddine Governor-Pasha of Algiers, and, to confirm their vassalage, dispatched a corps of two thousand Janissaries. He also encouraged Turkish peasants to go to Algiers by according them privileges normally reserved for the Janissaries of Istanbul and paying for their travel costs. The *oujak* of Algiers was born.

The sources have little good to say about this first group of soldiers, describing them as the dregs of the population. This point, mostly made by European historians, was used to justify the hatred that was developing in Europe, France in particular, toward the Turkish soldiers of Algiers. Plantet summarized this hatred best:

> In addition to the two thousand janissaries sent by the Great Lord to the Barbarossas to conserve their power, a company of four thousand volunteers soon came to join them, drawn by the lure of easy as well as illicit gains. These six thousand Turks formed the body of the militia and became this proud *oujak* [sic] that could exploit without mercy, up to the last day, the Arabs, the Jews, the Moors exiled from Spain who were living in Algiers. . . . We found among them only the outcasts and renegades, pirates of every nation and criminals escaped from every jail, beggars from the cities and vagabonds from the countryside, the dregs of the population and the scum of all Turkish ports. These were arrogant, crass people, with no country and no home, debt-ridden bandits who had lost their reputation, and who formed in only a few short years this society of ten thousand janissaries that no one could defy.[3]

The year 1518–19 constituted a turning point in the history of Algiers, which was now under the protection of the Ottoman Empire and therefore causing the Spanish great concern. When the delegation returned, Khayriddine became Governor of Algiers, assuming the title of pasha. He built his house in a style befitting a high official. He married a woman from Algiers described in several sources as Moorish and in others as descending from a family of *shurafa*.[4] This marriage produced a son named Hassan, who would one day succeed his father. Hassan spoke Spanish like a native of Spain, according to the Spanish priest Haedo, which leads us to believe that his mother was an Andalusian whose family claimed Sharifian descent.

Khayriddine's choice of spouse was not accidental. It was an expression of his broader ambitions to make Algiers the capital of a great Maghrebi province, protected by the Ottoman Empire, in which the Andalusians would occupy an essential place. The city's new status as vassal of the empire and protector of the Moriscos alarmed the Spanish, and they chose to act swiftly.

The First Expedition against Algiers

In May 1518, Charles V decided to expel the Turks from Algiers. He ordered the preparation of an expedition of 4,500 well-trained soldiers, thirty ships, eight galleys, and brigantines for transport, all overseen by Hugo of Moncada, his viceroy of Sicily. He added a chief of artillery charged specifically with attacking the city. With such strong a force, the fall of Algiers seemed inevitable. The fleet headed first toward Bjaïa to recruit soldiers, then to Oran, whose commander was sowing panic by repeatedly attacking the surrounding territories. He signed an agreement with the king of Tlemcen to lead a ground offensive. On August 17, 1518, the fleet anchored in the Bay of Algiers, and the soldiers seized the highest point of the city. The people of Algiers prepared themselves for a ground offensive that was a long time coming: the Spanish chief of artillery was awaiting the arrival of reinforcements from among the Arab soldiers of Tlemcen. The war council was still debating the best strategy for attacking Algiers when a violent storm hit, battering Spanish forts and causing considerable losses, both human and material. By the time the Tlemcenians arrived, the Spanish army had been devastated and a large portion of their ships destroyed. The soldiers who had managed not to drown raised the sails to depart, and then a second storm hit. It flung the ships onto the coast, where some of the soldiers were massacred and others were taken as slaves.

This is how the events are described by Spanish sources, which only hint at the full magnitude of the catastrophe. Sinan Chaouch's version differs, insofar as it describes Khayriddine's soldiers as courageously attacking the Christians as soon as they came ashore, forcing any who escaped to return immediately to their ships. It was then that the storm hit and completed the rout of the Spanish army.

The Spanish version of this history is more plausible as these two armies were not evenly matched, and the Christians' position on land should have been an advantage. However, the Turkish and Spanish sources concur that Algiers was a divinely protected city. Chaouch's text is riddled with divinatory references. The Christian historians, for their part, take into account a Moorish woman's prophecy that the Christians would suffer three defeats, one led by a great prince, a reference to the campaign that would be led by Charles V in 1541.[5]

This monumental Spanish defeat contributed to Khayriddine's notoriety and the legend of the Turks of Algiers' invincibility. Shortly after, the galleys that had been repaired using the debris of the Spanish fleet departed to ravage the coast of Valencia, bringing back riches and Andalusian refugees. Questions must be asked about Khayriddine's policy, which we see throughout the history of Algiers, of bringing back Morisco refugees. We might accept the routine explanation that he wanted to save the souls of men from religious persecution and forced conversion. But we should also consider that Khayriddine wanted to use these populations to establish a settler colony. He hoped that the Moriscos would become the social core of Algiers, which, in his view, lacked sophistication due to its uncivilized and little policed Arab population as well as its military character, created by the sizeable presence of Turkish soldiers. All of the testimonials describe Algiers in the sixteenth century as an Andalusian city, populated by men and women brought over, in large part, on Barbarossa's galleys.[6] This wish to resettle Algiers also explains Khayriddine's policy toward Spanish prisoners from the defeat of 1518: he kept the notables in captivity, likely hoping that they would convert. But his plans were thwarted when the captives rebelled against him and attempted to reach the small island facing the city, which was still under Spanish control. The resulting repression was bloody. Four hundred of the five hundred men were massacred. Khayriddine even refused a hefty ransom for the officers, whom he beheaded instead.

The Spanish defeat, Barbarossa's power, and the Ottomans support for him eventually worried the Hafsid sultan.

The Anxieties of the Hafsid Sultan

The Hafsid sultan became afraid of Khayriddine's growing notoriety and rising power. Seeking allies, he sent a letter to the king of Tlemcen revealing his fear of Khayriddine, an enterprising figure who had built a kingdom using only his sailors. What would he be able to accomplish with the support of the Sublime Porte? Possibly he would usurp the thrones they had inherited from their fathers! The Hafsid sultan proposed a plan to poach

Khayriddine's two lieutenants charged with protecting the border territories, Muhammad bin 'Ali and Ahmad ibn al-Qadi.[7]

The plan was not entirely successful: Ahmad ibn al-Qadi proved unwilling to betray Khayriddine, as he had enjoyed comfort and security since the corsair's arrival. The king of Tlemcen, Moulay 'Abdallah, however, did agree, remembering the resentment that Khayriddine felt toward him because he had helped the Spanish during their campaign against Algiers in 1518. He incited the Arab populations of the regions surrounding Algiers to rise up against the Turks. In return, Khayriddine provoked sedition within the Kingdom of Tlemcen by encouraging the king's brother, Massoud, who was living in exile in Fes, to dethrone the king, who was forced to put himself under the protection of the Spanish in Oran. Yet once in power, Massoud made a deal with the Spanish to expel Khayriddine and the Turks from Algiers. It was at this moment that Moulay 'Abdallah sent a sheikh to Khayriddine to repent for his past betrayal and request his help. It was decided that Khayriddine would attack Mostaganem and, with the help of Moulay 'Abdallah, take back Tlemcen.

Thanks to their massive fleet and large army, the plan succeeded. The Turks seized the city of Tlemcen. Sultan Moulay 'Abdallah, back in power, agreed to give the *khutba* (Friday sermon) in the name of Sultan Selim and to print currency with his image. Moulay 'Abdallah was granted a Turkish garrison of 150 men. The dissident king Massoud went to the borders of the Sahara to mobilize the sheikhs of Arab and Berber tribes to join him in laying siege to Tlemcen again. But the Turks defended Moulay 'Abdallah, forcing his brother to flee. Not long after, Massoud was betrayed by a friend with whom he had sought refuge. He spent the rest of his days in a cramped prison in Tlemcen. Again, Tlemecen became a vassal to the Turks. With the conflict resolved, Khayriddine's fleet headed back toward the coast of Andalusia to collect Muslim refugees to settle in Algiers.

The kingdom that Khayriddine built in the central Maghreb and the submission of Tlemcen worried the Hafsid prince, who renewed his efforts to recruit Ahmad ibn al-Qadi to his aid. Ahmad ibn al-Qadi ultimately declared his dissidence. A Turkish army sent to the Eastern provinces was obliterated thanks to the joint efforts of the kings of Tunis and the prince of Kouko. Khayriddine was forced to turn back to Algiers, pursued by Ibn al-Qadi, who laid siege to the city. Famine followed soon after. A peace was signed between the Turks and the Kabyles, but it fell apart quickly, forcing the Turks to fight Sheikh ibn al-Qadi, who retreated to his territories.

Khayriddine sent a unit under the command of Cara Hassan of Satalie to fight Ibn al-Qadi. But Ibn al-Qadi had bribed Cara Hassan, promising him part of his provinces.

Ibn al-Qadi continued plotting to destroy the Turks of Algiers. He conspired with the *baldis*, the old families of Algiers, whose support he had gained. The Turks discovered the conspiracy. Khayriddine convened the *ulama* and asked them to deliver a message of peace to the *baldis*, but they refused it, choosing instead to attack the government palace to which the Turks had withdrawn. The townspeople, inexperienced with weapons, were massacred. Only a few survived. Against the advice of his soldiers, Khayriddine showed relative clemency toward the survivors, sentencing only the main conspirators to death.

Khayriddine remained in Algiers for two years following the sedition of the *baldis*. Life there was difficult, and many of his Turkish soldiers chose to return to Istanbul. Those who remained married and had children, losing their skills as warriors.

Surrounded by Arab populations whose allegiance was never certain, and boxed in by the Spanish in Oran, in Bjaïa, and on the small island facing Algiers, Khayriddine struggled to see a way out. In 1526, with his authority reduced to a small territory that he was unable to expand, Khayriddine decided to leave Algiers. According to his biographer, the inhabitants of Algiers did not try to stop him. He settled in Djidjelli, where he left his family and resumed his life as a corsair. He armed several vessels and captured ships at sea, which saved his territory from food shortages. To avenge himself against the Hafsid sultan, he attacked several Tunisian vessels. His maritime expeditions were fruitful: he multiplied his seizures from the Christians and brought more and more Andalusians to Djidjelli.

Khayriddine's Return to Algiers

At this point in Khayriddine's story, his biographer writes, the hero had a premonitory dream in which the Prophet encouraged him to return to his fair city of Algiers. The recourse to dreams is a common rhetorical exercise in such chronicles, used to emphasize the profundity of political actions and to lend them legitimacy. In my view, Khayriddine's decision to return to Algiers was a response to favorable economic conditions. At this point, the corsair had at his disposal an Andalusian colony large enough to repopulate Algiers, with whom he would find stronger ties than with the native population of Algiers, and who would be his best allies in founding a state.

Since Khayriddine's departure, Algiers had been governed by Ahmad ibn al-Qadi. Khayriddine found a pretext for attacking the city. Ibn al-Qadi was showing increased hostility toward the corsair, going so far as to fire on one of Khayriddine's ships, which had stopped in Algiers for supplies of food and water during a privateering mission. According to Chaouch's version of events, it was the rais and his crew, outraged by al-Qadi's attitude, who pushed Khayriddine to retake the city he had long protected. He fought al-Qadi's troops, and once defeated, al-Qadi himself was killed by one of his own men. Some time later Khayriddine decided to depose his former lieutenant, Cara Hassan, who had settled in Cherchell. Several years before, Hassan had betrayed Khayriddine by volunteering to help the Spanish capture Algiers, which had been without leadership since the death of Ibn al-Qadi. Khayriddine, determined, entered the city and had Cara Hassan and his bodyguards beheaded.

In the midst of this unrest, the king of Tlemcen reclaimed his independence and renounced all signs of allegiance to the Ottoman Empire. The Turkish army forced the king into submission by the sword. Between 1528 and 1530, Khayriddine devoted himself to fighting the brother of Ahmad ibn al-Qadi, who had retaken al-Qadi's former territories, stretching from Bône to La Calle. Khayriddine led an army on a long and difficult expedition through the mountainous region, leaving it slashed and burned. The Turks even captured the wives and children of the sheikh, who begged for mercy and agreed to pay an annual tribute in return for being able to keep their lands.

After these campaigns, Khayriddine consolidated his control over a large swathe of territory around Algiers and imposed vassalage on the territories to the east and west of the city. However, a thorn remained in his side: the small island that faced the city and which had been under Spanish control for fifteen years.

The Destruction of Pènon of Algiers: May 1530

Khayriddine could not fully claim Algiers while the fort—which the Spanish had built on one of the small islands facing the city, just two hundred meters from shore—continued to hinder the departure of his ships. An opportunity came to remove this thorn—this enemy fortress—when a

Spanish soldier swam ashore in secret to warn Khayriddine that the people in the fort were starving because their appeals to the Spanish still had not been answered. Khayriddine proposed an honorable surrender to the Spanish Governor, Martin de Vargas, but he flatly refused.

Khayriddine sent two spies to the fort under the pretext of wanting to convert to Christianity. They were well received, until their true motives were discovered and they were hanged. Khayriddine tried again to negotiate a surrender, but still the governor refused. And so, beginning on May 6, he launched a relentless assault on the island. On May 16, a large portion of the fortress was demolished. Many of the besieged surrendered, and the others fell prey to starvation. The Turks took the fort, dismantled it, and used the debris to build a jetty connecting the small island to the land.

The commander of the old fort, Martin de Vargas, was treated with great respect due to his position and his sense of honor. Khayriddine pressed him to surrender. Faced with his resistance, he sentenced him to death. When nine Spanish vessels finally arrived to assist the fort, they found only ruins. The 2,700 captured Spanish soldiers were made to rebuild the damaged areas of the city.[8]

The taking of Peñón of Algiers disrupted the Spaniards' freedom of movement in the Mediterranean and was a devastating loss to their navy. It left two great men, Khayriddine and André Doria, face to face with one another. This conquest is considered one of Khayriddine's most remarkable achievements. It enabled him to definitively control the port of Algiers and to open it up to corsairs of all nationalities. Some historians trace the founding of the Regency of Algiers to this moment.

From this point on, Khayriddine began to expand his territory. He conquered Collo, a fishing port that exported wool, leather, and wax. He annexed the cities of Constantine and Bône. His privateering brought him great riches. In 1529, he established an alliance with the Kabyle leaders, the kings of Kouko, and the *qal'a* of the Beni 'Abbas. He also increased his support for the Moriscos of Valencia who wished to come to Muslim territory.

In 1531, Khayriddine began to develop the port of Cherchell. For the Spanish, this initiative threatened the Balearic Islands, leading André Doria to attack the city to free the many captives employed in constructing the port. In July 1531, Doria left Genoa with twenty galleys. He arrived soon after, not far from the port of Cherchell, and dispersed his soldiers, who took the inhabitants of the city by surprise. They were able to free the captives, who hurried back to the galleys.

The Spanish soldiers, invigorated by their easy victory, began to loot. This left time for the Turks and the Moriscos to regroup and capture them. Fearing for his ships, Doria sailed off, leaving behind six hundred men. The victory strengthened Khayriddine's reputation and his sense of invincibility. He sent an emissary to Istanbul to bring word of all he had accomplished in the last several years and of the importance of the territory he had incorporated into the Empire: he had taken his first steps on the path to a promising career.

5

Khayriddine, Grand Admiral of the Ottoman Navy

We owe the most comprehensive account of Khayriddine's rise to the rank of captain pasha, or Grand Admiral of the Ottoman Navy, to Prudencio de Sandoval, the sixteenth century monk and historian of the reign of Charles V.[1] Examining the conditions in which Khayriddine was promoted to this important rank can help us make sense of the action that he later took against Tunis. The new possibilities created for Khayriddine through his control of the port of Algiers, his capture of the Spanish boats sent to fight him, and his raids on the Spanish coasts outraged Charles V. André Doria reassured Charles V that he could defeat "this Turk" if the emperor gave him twenty well-rigged and well-armed vessels. An alliance with the King of France, even though he was an enemy of the Spanish crown, was necessary if Charles V were to defeat the corsair. And so Charles V wrote to the king of France and requested twenty armed vessels to reinforce Doria's fleet. With these, Doria succeeded in capturing the Greek town of Koroni from the Turks.

Khayriddine, aware of this new alliance between the French and Spanish kings, called for reinforcements from the Jewish corsair Sinan Rais, based in Djerba, who had formerly served under him. André Doria raided the city of Cherchell while Khayriddine was in Algiers, but the attack failed and he was forced to retreat to the sea. As soon as the news reached Khayriddine, he attempted to track down Doria. He went toward Marseille and anchored in Hyères, where he captured a galley and faced off with several Christian vessels. Despite his efforts, Khayriddine failed to find Doria and was forced to return to Algiers to recuperate. It was during this period that Khayriddine's ships brought back seventy thousand people from Andalusia to the coasts of the Maghreb over the course of seven voyages.[2]

In retaliation, Charles V sent a fleet to wreck the land of Albania, the population of which complained to Sultan Suleiman. The sultan hastened to warn Khayriddine. At the same time, in 1533, the king of Hungary, anticipating an attack by the Ottoman army, requested help from the Spanish. On the advice of his close advisors, Charles V plotted to provoke a rebellion in Algiers: he pressed Prince 'Abdallah, the king of Tlemcen, to revolt against Khayriddine so as to keep him occupied and far from the eastern Mediterranean. The king of Tlemcen led an army against Algiers, but it was crushed by Khayriddine, who, once again, pardoned the Tlemcenian king for his betrayal. The rout of the King of Tlemcen temporarily derailed Charles V's plan and he went himself to the rescue of the Hungarians. But before the emperor arrived in Hungary, Suleiman, the sultan-caliph, had taken the citadel of Ankerous, and he had to turn back. It was in the context of this long war against Hungary that Suleiman decided to entrust the imperial fleet to Khayriddine, the only one strong enough to stand up to André Doria.

Sinan Chaouch offers a different take on these events. He affirms that once Suleiman had decided to attack Spain he needed Khayriddine, who knew the Spanish coasts well and whose support would guarantee an easy victory.[3] According to Chaouch, using subterfuge to spread false information in the enemy camp was a common practice at the time. It is therefore likely that the Ottomans spread rumors of an Ottoman attack against Spain to lure Charles V away from the Hungarian battlefield.

In this context of Ottoman expansion in the heart of Europe, Khayriddine was granted the position of Admiral of the Sea. It was bestowed on him following his personal victories in the Mediterranean and the failures of the Ottoman fleet against André Doria.

Khayriddine in Istanbul

Khayriddine's first move was to bring stability to Algiers by making peace with the King of Kouko and signing a truce with the King of France. Then he prepared gifts to present to the sultan-caliph: slaves, eunuchs, and wild animals. He handed over the city of Algiers to his twenty-year-old son, Hassan, who would be supervised by Shalabi Ramadan, one of Khayriddine's relatives, and to Captain Hassan Agha. Among the men who accompanied Khayriddine on this voyage was Moulay Rachid—the brother of Hassan, the King of Tunis, to whom Khayriddine had promised the throne of the land, with the help of the sultan-caliph.

Khayriddine left Algiers in the middle of August 1533 for a long journey. He captured several galleys along the way, eventually arriving in

Istanbul with forty sails in good order. He was well received by Suleiman and his officials, who inquired about the corsair's well-known maritime exploits in Spain, Italy, and the Maghrebi states. However, with Ibrahim Pasha, the first minister and adviser to the sultan, absent from Istanbul, many courtiers tried to dissuade the sultan from entrusting the entire Ottoman fleet to Khayriddine, a corsair.

In December 1533, the sultan informed Khayriddine that there would be no expedition without the consent of Ibrahim Pasha, and ordered the corsair to go meet him in Syria. Khayriddine disarmed his ships and headed to Syria by land. When Khayriddine arrived, Ibrahim Pasha received him with great respect and assessed his plan for waging war against Charles V in Spain, Italy, or Tunis. Ibrahim then wrote to the sultan affirming his support for Khayriddine's mission.

Fortified by Ibrahim Pasha's support, Khayriddine returned to Istanbul. He was warmly welcomed by the sultan and his pashas, who invited him to outline his strategy of attack: he would take control of the coasts of Tripoli up to the Strait of Gibraltar, and from there, plan the attack on Spain. As for the islands of the Mediterranean—Sicily, Sardinia, Corsica, and Mallorca—he knew them well enough to know that they would not be able to resist his powerful fleet. Furthermore, the occupation of Sicily would starve Genoa and the coasts of Italy. Finally, Khayriddine proposed attacking Tunis first, in order to replace Moulay Hassan—the enemy of the Turks and little loved by his own subjects—with his brother, Moulay Rachid.

Despite the sultan's reservations about Khayriddine's advanced age, he gave him the title of Grand Admiral, delivering the insignia of the office: a *yatagan* (an Ottoman knife), an imperial sign decorated with a crescent, and a scepter that symbolized his absolute power in the ports and the islands under his control. Khayriddine was also decorated with a diamond egret, the *chélik*, which the sultan himself attached to Khayriddine's turban.

Khayriddine spent the winter in the armory of Istanbul building boats for the imperial fleet. When summer arrived, he was able to cast off toward the Mediterranean with eighty boats, carrying eight hundred Janissaries and eight thousand soldiers and volunteer rowers. He also had eight hundred thousand ducats set aside for unforeseen needs. He was ordered to attack Italy first—Genoa, to be exact—and then Tunis.

The Short-lived Occupation of Tunis by Khayriddine

Khayriddine's occupation of Tunis has been diversely interpreted. According to Haedo, the Tunisians themselves appealed to Khayriddine because they were angry at the cruelty of their king, Moulay Hassan, who had violently disposed of several of his brothers and many notables. Khayriddine did not follow the sultan's plan to the letter: rather than follow his orders to attack Genoa first, he settled for razing several coastal towns. Then he set off directly toward Bizerte. We do not know the reasons for this trajectory. Chaouch claims that the winds pushed Khayriddine north. But there is another possible reason for Khayriddine's delays: he may have been in the midst of secret negotiations with Charles V, and therefore hoping to avoid a frontal attack.

Accompanied by an army of 1,800 Janissaries, 6,500 Greek, Albanian, and Turkish soldiers, and six hundred renegades, the majority of which were Spanish, Khayriddine landed in Bizerte on August 15, 1534. He was welcomed enthusiastically. The pretext for his arrival was to put Rachid on the throne in place of his brother Hassan. Hassan had come to power as a result of the scheming of his mother, al-Jaziya bint Awlad Yahya, daughter of the celebrated tribe of the Riah. Al-Jaziya forced her spouse to kill many of his other sons so that they would not stand in the way of her son, Hassan, taking the throne. Rachid, who was away serving as the Governor of Constantine at the time, was the only one of Hassan's brothers to escape this grisly fate.

We do not know the details of the dealings between Rachid and Khayriddine, but it seems likely that the two men had agreed that Khayriddine would help put Rachid on the throne in exchange for Rachid's submission to Istanbul. It was likely with this plan in mind that Rachid accompanied Khayriddine to the imperial capital. But in a surprising twist, Rachid was taken prisoner in Istanbul and prevented from returning to Tunis. A plan had been hatched in the imperial capital—or perhaps even before, in Algiers—to gain the support of the people of Tunis by dangling before them the prospect of their prince's return. As soon as the fleet had docked in Bizerte, Khayriddine's emissaries spread the rumor that Rachid was in the galley, indisposed by the heat. They asked that an accommodation and a meal be prepared for him and even allowed his wife and children to come aboard, where they were temporarily taken prisoner. Thanks to this subterfuge, Bizerte was occupied without resistance.

Khayriddine's Capture of Tunis

From there, Khayriddine made for La Goulette, all the while making it seem as though Rachid was aboard the ship. He occupied La Goulette without force and built a Turkish garrison there. In Tunis, Hassan—finding no one to lead a resistance—left the city, believing that he had left the throne to his brother. Khayriddine quickly entered Tunis, and on August 22, 1534, took over the Kasbah, thanks to his five thousand Turkish soldiers and his renegades. Not seeing Rachid with Khayriddine, the people of Tunis understood that they had been deceived. They rebelled against the Turks and called for the return of their king. Chased from the city streets, the Turks retreated into the Kasbah. However, a strategy concocted by a Spanish renegade allowed Khayriddine's soldiers to exit through two separate breaches in the walls, trap the Tunisian insurgents in a crossfire and defeat them, killing three thousand Tunisians and losing only four hundred of their own. Following this defeat, Hassan was forced to leave the area and headed toward Constantine. The Tunisians were given a three-day cease-fire to bury their dead. Khayriddine took advantage of this period of calm to convince the notables to submit to the Sultan-Caliph Suleiman. A few days later, Khayriddine was proclaimed Governor of Tunis on behalf of the sultan-caliph.

Khayriddine reestablished order in the city and proceeded to make improvements to the port of La Goulette in order to shelter his fleet there. He divided his army into two contingents. One, under the authority of Hassan Agha, was charged with subjugating the rest of the land. The other was commanded by 'Ali, the Janissary officer to whom he entrusted the city guard. He sent them a contingent of soldiers from Turkey, whom he had already paid, and began to fortify La Goulette. It wasn't long before Khayriddine began to encounter difficulties, as he was unable to pay the salaries of the Janissaries in his service. The soldiers revolted for the first time in October 1534, and for the second time in November of the same year, obliging Khayriddine to brutally suppress the revolts with the help of his renegades.

This reconstruction of events leading to Khayriddine's entry into Tunis is based on the Spanish archives.[4] It differs in several respects from the version offered by Sinan Chaouch, which is more favorable to Khayriddine. Chaouch claims that Khayriddine's arrival in Bizerte was accidental: he had intended to go to Algiers but was diverted by the winds. The people of Bizerte were surprised and somewhat concerned by the sight of the great fleet, but nevertheless did not hesitate to welcome Khayriddine with joy and declare their loyalty to Sultan Suleiman. As for the commander of the fortress, he fled by night to Tunis and informed the king, who decided to leave the capital with his family for Djerid (an error by Sinan Chaouch—the sultan of Tunis did not go that far).

As soon as the people of Tunis learned of the king's departure, they wrote a letter to Khayriddine. He arrived at La Goulette with his fleet and was received by many men—close to ten thousand—led by the *ulama* and the sheikhs, who installed him on the throne. However, the residents who favored the Hafsids resisted and pitilessly massacred many Turks. The enraged Turks began attacking the Tunisians who had taken refuge in the city's mosques and *zawiyas*. Eighty Turks and three hundred Tunisians were killed.

As soon as he heard of this ordeal, Khayriddine mounted his horse and rode to Tunis, hoping to put an end to the clashes. He ordered his troops to retreat. However, the supporters of the Hafsids, whose numbers were growing, called on their sultan to return to Tunis. In a single night, al-Hassan al-Hafsi succeeded—using a mix of persuasion and threats—in convincing a great number of men to attack the Kasbah by surprise. But the plan was thwarted and the Tunisians were chased down and massacred, leaving the city streets littered with their corpses. Without waiting for the fighting to end, the Hafsid king returned to his Arab allies. Many Tunisians who had been marginalized until then welcomed this submission to Khayriddine and the empire, seeing it as potentially beneficial to their commercial interests. After having ensured his hold over Tunis, Khayriddine wrote to the Drid and Nmamcha sheikhs, promising 30,000 ducats to whoever could bring him the Hafsid sultan. They responded that if he could grant them the same amount of money and commodities the Hafsids had promised, they would put themselves in his service.[5]

Once he had been assured the support of the Arab sheikhs, Khayriddine demanded that his lieutenant in Algiers send him three hundred soldiers and four hundred cavaliers to reinforce the garrisons. Meanwhile, Moulay al-Hassan incited the Arabs, who rose up against Khayriddine once again.

Ibn abi Dinar offers yet another version. When the Tunisians realized Khayriddine's deception, they demanded that al-Hassan, who had fled with his mother to the Bedouins, return. Fighting broke out on January 18, 1535, between Khayriddine, positioned at Bab al-Jazira, and al-Hassan, at

Bab Souika. But al-Hassan failed to defend the city and fled once again, and the Turks attacked the Tunisians, their allies. Khayriddine tried to win the support of the Arab tribes by distributing burnous (brown woolen robes) and money.[6]

Together, the three versions of this history show the weakening of Hafsid power. They concur on the violence of the Tunisians' reaction to the arrival of the Turks, and the equally violent response by Khayriddine's soldiers.

Tunis Caught Between Khayriddine, al-Hassan, and the Spanish: August 1534 to July 1535

The character of Hassan al-Hafsi, who ruled between 1526 and 1543, is central to the history of the last Hafsids. As one among many of Sultan Muhammad's sons, he was not necessarily destined for the throne—that is, until the harem plot hatched by his mother, al-Jaziya, eliminated his rivals. A Spanish survey of the sheikhs and the Arabs of the Kingdom of Tunis states that the Ouled Yahya of Riah had 1500 cavaliers, among them two sheikhs who were brothers and uncles of the King of Tunis. One was named 'Ali and the other Talem (sic), probably Salem. Their vast territory stretched west for a hundred miles, from Kairouan to Teboursouk.[7] Al-Hassan was therefore connected to the Bedouins through his mother and would not have hesitated to call on them when threatened.

The sources contradict each other as to whether there really was a conspiracy allowing Hassan al-Hafsi to eliminate his brothers. The version told by Moulay Hamida, Hassan's son, to Charles V, whom he met in Brussels in 1555, reported that al-Jaziya drove her spouse to kill twenty-eight of his sons so that they would not dispute Hassan's claim to the throne. The number of al-Jaziya's victims varies according to the sources, ranging from twenty-two, to thirty-four, or even forty-five, according to Hammer.[8] Only Rachid, then Governor of Constantine, escaped the ordeal. Hassan thus appears unsure of himself from the start, having risen to power by questionable means. After eight years in power, his downfall began when he was driven from Tunis by Khayriddine in August 1534.

There are no direct sources concerning the eleven months that Khayriddine spent in Tunis. Charles V sent a spy disguised as a merchant, Don Lays de Présendes, to inform him of the situation in Tunis and to sow discord between the Turks and the Arabs. But the spy was denounced by his Morisco companion and promptly executed by Khayriddine.[9]

The ousted king of Tunis found himself in a grim spot and pleaded with the Spanish to intervene.[10] Before making a decision, Charles V interrogated Don Bernadino de Mendoza about the situation, who responded "that it was better to seize the kingdom directly than to try to keep a prince there who was so incapable and also so universally detested." The prince nevertheless obtained the help of two thousand soldiers while he waited for the emperor's decision. The emperor ultimately chose to intervene, motivated by the fear that had taken hold among the Christians of the Mediterranean. The Knights of Malta, in particular, were frightened by the proximity of the Turks. Their leader, the Grand Master, succumbed to this fear. His successor insisted that Charles V intervene.

Meanwhile, hiding somewhere with the Bedouins, the ousted ruler of Tunis strengthened his appeals to both the Knights of Malta and Emperor Charles V for a rapid intervention. Throughout this period, the role of spies and intermediaries was decisive: it was through them that the king of Tunis could contact the Christian powers and send messages, in which he described the fear that had gripped him since the arrival of the Turks, "who were but five hundred, but are joined by all who wish me ill." The King of Tunis later wrote that if the emperor did not send help, he could not hold on much longer, and that he was counting on his friend to win back the land of the Christians. In an undated letter, the Hafsid Sultan al-Hassan asked that:

> His majesty sent him an army to drive the Turks from the kingdom and help him bring back the rebellious Moors. He offers to hand over to the officers of his majesty the fortresses of his choosing, and his majesty can preserve them or dismantle them, as he sees fit. As this army cannot come soon enough, the king asks for two thousand soldiers to begin the war immediately. If his majesty cannot supply them, he begs his majesty to send him ships, so that he can keep his majesty's lands secure. It is impossible for him to hold on much longer in Tunis. He also asks to be allowed to purchase arms and munitions.[11]

At the insistence of the Order of Malta, the pope agreed to intervene. Charles V, having planned the intervention in secret, began to make arrangements.

The Capture of Tunis by Charles V

The Emperor of Spain prepared a powerful army and set off from Barcelona on July 20, 1535. Khayriddine understood that the balance of power was not in his favor and decided to cede his place. He sent his vessels toward Bône by sea but went himself by land, accompanied by his soldiers and corsairs. Arriving at the Port of Bône, he set off on a series of maritime expeditions, heading first toward Minorca, taking care to disguise his sailors as Christians and to fly the Spanish flag. He took the island by force, ransacking and burning it. Six thousand men were taken prisoner. Having taken his revenge for the defeat of Tunis, Khayriddine returned to Algiers. At the same time, Charles V entered La Goulette, established his headquarters, and signed a treaty with Hassan after returning him to the throne.

The Treaty Between Hassan and Charles V

The treaty signed in La Goulette on August 6, 1535 began by describing how the King of Tunis had been expelled from his kingdom by Khayriddine Barbarossa, who had occupied the city using cruelty and violence toward its subjects, and that the king had put himself under the protection of the emperor who had liberated the harbor and city of La Goulette.[12] As a result:

> The king of Tunis pledges to liberate all the enslaved Christians without ransom and foster their return to Christendom. He pledges, both now and in the future, not to capture any subject of the countries that are part of the Kingdom of Spain, and the emperor also commits to not taking any Tunisian captives.[13]
>
> It will also be permitted for Christians to live throughout the Kingdom of Thunès, to maintain their places of worship, and to establish new ones. Moreover, the king of Tunis commits to not accepting the Moriscos in his kingdom, those of Valencia and Granada, nor of any other areas under the protection of the Spanish Empire. He will pursue them as enemies and deny them refuge or commerce, with the exception of those who carry a letter from his imperial majesty or his representatives.
>
> The king of Tunis authorizes the emperor to guard all the strongholds conquered thus far and in the future against the Turks, those of Bizerte, Bone, Africa (Mahdia), and others, and renounces all of his rights to these maritime places at present and in the future.

La Goulette, occupied at great cost and with much risk, belongs now to his imperial majesty, along with the two miles of territory surrounding it, including the water tower (called the *burj al-'uyun*). The Spanish will not prevent the inhabitants of the region from reaching Carthage to obtain water from the wells there. The Spanish are authorized to navigate on the canal as far as Tunis, and to trade with the city by paying ordinary taxes. Any abuse will be punished by the captain and the caid of the fort of La Goulette according to law and justice.

The king of Tunis will pay 2,000 ducats of gold annually, in two payments, one on Saint-Jacques day, the 25th of July, and the other in January of each year. In cases of failure to pay on time, the captain of La Goulette will force the administrator of finances to pay.

The mining, sale, and trade of coral will be exclusively reserved to his majesty and his representatives. A consul and a judge will be designated to look after the interests of his majesty's subjects without the king of Tunis intervening.

In recognition of the great benefit that the king of Tunis receives from his majesty's protection of his states, the king of Tunis, along with his successors, pledges to provide on the day of Saint-Jacques six good Morisco horses and a dozen falcons, under the penalty of a fine of 50,000 ducats in the case of a failure to provide them, and double that if the mistake is made again. After the third time, the Spanish authority herself will undertake the collection.

The king of Tunis will not make any alliances with a Muslim or Christian state that holds prejudices against his imperial majesty. The two countries will be able to trade all legal merchandise peacefully by both sea and land routes, and the king of Tunis commits to not sending any aid to pirates or enemies of the Crown, who he will instead chase away.

Four copies of this treaty were prepared, two in Castilian and two in Arabic, and they were signed in front of witnesses in the tent that Charles V set up two miles from La Goulette, at the foot of the water tower. There were four Spanish witnesses, all advisors to his majesty. On the Tunisian side, Mahomet Tantem, Hamet Garamazan, and 'Abd al-Rahim witnessed the signing, all Moorish servants of the king.

An addendum stipulated that if the terms of the treaty were respected, his majesty would no longer seek to occupy any place within the Kingdom of Tunis, except if Africa (Mahdia) were returned to the King of Tunis, in which case his majesty the emperor could dispose of it at his whim and retain it for himself and his successors.

The treaty of August 6, 1535 made the Hafsid Kingdom a true protectorate. The conditions imposed on the King of Tunis made him a vassal of the Crown of Spain. Khayriddine was, for the moment, ousted from Tunis.

The story of a man as famous as Khayriddine is often clouded by the ways it is written over time, by his enemies as well as his friends. In the abundant literature devoted to him, even during his lifetime, it is often difficult to distinguish events that really happened from fabrications, contradictory interpretations, accusations, and praise.

The Ottoman sultans established the tradition of having an official history of the empire written. When Khayriddine reached a high enough status, Sinan Chaouch was charged with documenting his celebrated feats, which make up the laudatory Turkish biography. In the midst of war, Charles V was accompanied by writers and artists who recorded events and delivered information about enemies. All these authors recognized how impressive the intrepid corsair's achievements had been—whether it was the Turkish chroniclers who traced his life as a trajectory toward fame, with neither mistakes nor setbacks, or Sandoval, the official historian of Charles V, who acknowledged the virtues of this enemy of Spain and Christianity.

Many questions remain about this figure whom the local historiographies present as unblemished—a man motivated by the sole desire to defend Islam whose reward was a great imperial career. Khayriddine embraced his reputation as master of the Mediterranean. After having reorganized and reinforced the sultan's fleet, he participated in the war against Venice. Venice had been allied to the kingdom of the pope and to Charles V, who had formed a grand fleet and entrusted it to Doria. But Doria would not face Barbarossa, which only bolstered Khayriddine's reputation. When King François I declared war on Charles V in 1543, he appealed to the sultan-caliph for help. Khayriddine left with his fleet toward France, along the way pillaging several Calabrian cities under Spanish rule, such as Gaete. There, he met a beautiful young woman, the daughter of the governor, and took her as his wife. He attacked the city of Nice, an ally of the Spanish emperor, which submitted to him. Then he wintered in Toulon and charged one of his corsairs, Salah Rais, with attacking the Catalan coasts. Khayriddine left Toulon in 1544 on the basis of a peace treaty between the French and the Spanish. On the way back, he freed another important corsair, Dargouth, from the Genoese in exchange for a large ransom. He established himself in Istanbul, where he constructed several buildings, notably mausoleums and baths. If he never returned to Tunis again, Khayriddine Barbarossa had still sealed the fate of this city, which would be largely tied to that of Algiers. His failure in Tunis did not change his perspective. He clung to his plan to form a state in the Maghreb under his authority, especially since being designated Grand Admiral had given him enormous power over the maritime territory. He ensured that the governors appointed to Algiers belonged to his house and pushed to occupy Tripoli so as to be able to take hold of Hafsid territory.

This strategy, which Khayriddine's successors carried on after his death, continued for some forty years with some progress and some setbacks. Throughout this era, the Bedouins had the upper hand, and all the protagonists sought their allegiance. Khayriddine died in July 1546. He left a son, Hassan, who would become King of Algiers and nourish ambitions for Tunis.

6

The Dismantling of the Hafsid Territory by the Spanish, Turks, and Marabouts: 1535–57

The major event of these years was that the Marabouts appeared to challenge the established authorities. This was made possible by the weakening of the Hafsid king, who became incapable of playing the roles expected of the sultan: protecting his subjects, securing the roads, and ensuring the free practice of religion. It was in respecting this code that all power derived its legitimacy. By opening the city to the Spanish and allowing them to treat the local population however they pleased, Moulay Hassan violated his sovereign duties. As a result, the Shabbia brotherhood rose to power and dared to dispute the king's legitimacy.

The Birth and Spread of the Shabbia Brotherhood

In the medieval Maghreb, saints and brotherhood movements proliferated. At the origin of what has come to be known as "popular religion" were pious men who lived exemplary lives and dedicated their time to the worship of God. Little by little, they would gather disciples around them. This practice of recruitment led to the creation of subgroups, the establishment of large fraternal networks, and a dramatic increase in the number of followers. Religious rites and practices quickly organized around *zawiyas*, madrasas, and the tombs of the founders, giving birth to large social networks that, in times of political turmoil, acted as ready-made cadres able to mobilize the fervor of the population and organize protests.

The Shabbia brotherhood was born as part of this movement. Its founder was Ahmad ibn Makhlouf, a native of Shabba who had moved to Kairouan to teach after having studied religion in Tunis. Concerned with cementing his saintly image, his family traced several stages of Makhlouf's biography.[1] It records his marriage in 1470 to Amat al-'Aziz, a young woman born to a notable family in the town, and the story of his pilgrimage, during which he intuited that his wife, who had remained in Kairouan, had just given birth to a boy whom he decided to name 'Arafa after the sacred mountain 'Arafat. Back home, it did not take long for him to earn a reputation as a wise man. He surrounded himself with followers and began to teach his *tariqa*, inspired by the great founders of Maghrebi Sufism, Ibn 'Arabi and Abdul Hassan al-Shadhili. Among his young, dedicated students was a man belonging to the Hnansha, who would glorify his master's reputation and spread it across Tell, the region where his tribe lived, which extended over two hundred kilometers from Kairouan. The members of this tribe became his most loyal followers and paid him considerable sums of money, which gave the newborn order fame and power. This influx of funds guaranteed lodging and upkeep for the order's followers, whose numbers grew and grew. Ahmad ibn Makhlouf died in an aura of sainthood on November 11, 1482, leaving behind eight children, among them one girl, Umm al-'Aziz.

Leadership of the order fell to Makhlouf's eldest son, Muhhammad al-Kebir, who died two and a half years later. Makhlouf's youngest son, 'Arafa, replaced his brother, which prompted a challenge from Makhlouf's adopted son, a young Hnanshi named Gamash al-Mass'oudi. He belonged to the Ouled Mass'oud, a branch of the Hnansha in Souk Ahras that had united en masse behind Ahmad ibn Makhlouf and constituted one of his strongest sources of support. Gamash felt better qualified to lead the order because of his spiritual proximity to its founder, from whom he had learned the order's teachings. 'Arafa challenged him, claiming that blood ties made him the natural successor to his father.

This double claim to Makhlouf's legacy divided the Hnansha. They ultimately rallied around 'Arafa, who, according to sources close to these events, was the victim of an assassination attempt organized by his adversary. Whether or not this was true, it demonstrates the Hnansha's attempt to claim the legacy of the brotherhood and to use this power to subjugate the vast region across which they roamed. Having failed to establish themselves as the rightful inheritors of the order, they conceded to joining 'Arafa, giving the brotherhood influence over a section of Ifriqiyan territory. Beyond that, they helped grow the order's followers, riches, and notoriety. Many other tribes submitted to 'Arafa and served, when needed, as formidable warriors, for Sidi 'Arafa was simultaneously a religious leader and a political and military one, who claimed leadership of a land beset with political instability. Western sources, Spanish ones in particular, characterized him as a *faqih*, a king, a lord, and even a pope, emphasizing his dual spiritual and political roles.[2] 'Arafa knew how to speak to country folk. He used simple, widely accessible language to spread his spiritual message and teach his dogmas to his followers. This method aroused the wrath of his adversaries, who accused him of educating shepherds about the oneness of God.

'Arafa al-Shabbi made enemies of the great Ifriqiyan scholars of his time. They were jealous of his fame and saw it as a threat—as much to political stability as to their own religious power, which was based on pedantic teachings designed for elites. The brotherhood offered a very different kind of education. The majority of Shabbia's followers were rural people who were sometimes ignorant of the basic premises of Islam. When Sidi 'Arafa began preaching to the Hnansha, he understood that they were not familiar with Islamic religious practices, except perhaps for the fast during the month of Ramadan. The Trud didn't even recognize this obligation. He addressed himself to them in simple language: his *da'wa*, or preaching, was diffused in the "language of love" among the Trud, the Hammama, the Hnansha, the Ouled Said, the Ouled Mhalhal, the Ouled Bellil, and their allies. This simple language, as well as the desire of the Hnansha to be among the tribes who benefitted from proximity to power, made them into the principal ally of the Shabbia.

With the renown of the order secured, 'Arafa turned to its material consolidation. He imposed a common law tax—an *'ada*—on his followers in place of the traditional *zakat*. Because of this measure, revenue that would have otherwise gone to the Hafsids flowed to the order instead, and the Hafsids found themselves in competition with 'Arafa for the same land tax base. This customary tax signified the beginnings of a Shabbi state, based on the tribes of the Tell and bidding for Kairouan as its capital. After all, the ability to tax the population and raise an army are the foundations of all political projects, more so than fully developed state organizations or control over continuous territory. This particular political project would begin to materialize as a result of the unrest of the sixteenth century.

'Arafa and the Hafsid Sultans

Even before the conflict between the Shabbia and the Hafsids broke out in 1535, the Hafsids had been concerned about the order's growing influence, fame, and wealth. The council of the ulama was appalled by the reputation of this master of obscure origins who addressed his message to the peasantry, or what they called "vulgar cow keepers." Old Kairouan society watched with concern the dazzling rise of this leader who was dominating urban spaces. Because so many of his followers came to visit him, food prices shot up. After an uptick in consumption, meat would disappear completely from the markets. Moreover, the order's success had weakened other, older orders—notably the Ghariani, who issued threats against the interlopers. 'Arafa had also been harshly criticized for his principles by other Sufis, such as 'Amor al-Kammad of Constantine (d. 1522), the author of an epistle denouncing the Shabbia brotherhood.[3]

Thus warned, the Hafsid powers wasted no time cracking down on 'Arafa, subjecting him to a variety of ordeals and ultimately, during the reign of Muhammad al-Hafsi, throwing him in prison. As recounted in the saint's hagiography, even while he was in prison 'Arafa did inspiring things. The cause of his imprisonment was the jealousy of a powerful Tunisian scholar, Muhammad al-Tonoussi—called "Maghûche," *qadi 'askar* (judge of the army)—who persuaded the sultan that Sidi 'Arafa was conspiring against him. 'Arafa was arrested in Kairouan and brought to Tunis. But divine retribution was meted out to everyone who took part in his arrest and they were unable to put him in chains; 'Arafa put them on himself.

He remained in the dungeon for seven months. This whole time the sultan was ill and no doctor could cure him. Realizing that the sultan's illness was a punishment from God, Muhammad al-Hafsi eventually ordered 'Arafa's release. The edifying aspects of this version of the story aside (it was recounted by one of 'Arafa's followers), it reminds us that there were serious concerns about the brotherhood's political aims. These would come to light before long.

'Arafa's political project—to form a Maraboutic state in Ifriqiya—required that he be capable of leading a revolution against the Hafsid power. The Mediterranean at the beginning of the sixteenth century, with the great Spanish offensive that the religious authorities equated to a crusade, presented an ideal opportunity to oppose the Christian advance with religious resistance. The first occupations of Hafsid territory by the Spanish took place under the reign of Muhammad al-Hafsi (1493–1525), who lost Tripoli and Bjaîa. He did not seek to take back those cities so much as to fight the Bedouins, who took advantage of this period of turbulence to rebel against him. It is possible that the uprisings in the countryside surrounding Kairouan had been incited by Sidi 'Arafa, who deplored the negligence and treachery of the sultan, Muhammad al-Hafsi. He would do the same to his son and successor Hassan.

Sidi 'Arafa's uprising against Hassan began after the Spanish expelled Khayriddine and the Turks from Tunis on July 14, 1535. After having signed a treaty with Charles V, Hassan delivered his capital, over the course of three days, to Spanish soldiers, who were allowed to run roughshod over the city.

Recounting the sacking of Tunis, Ibn abi Dinar wrote:

> When Hassan had returned to the Kasbah, every artisan had resumed his work, the merchants had opened their shops, and security was reestablished, the Christians attacked by surprise in the early afternoon. They took all the goods, killed the men, and captured an enormous number of people. Those who were able to flee with their families went toward Zaghouan. The Great Lord of the Christians promised to reward the Arab Bedouins for every Muslim they caught as a fugitive. And so they began to hunt down the Muslims on the mountain paths and in the rivers, delivering them to the Christians. Some of the Muslims succeeded in paying the Bedouins a ransom, sometimes reaching 1,000 dinars. Those who could not escape the infidel Muslims [the Bedouins] fell into the hands of the infidel Christians. On this fatal Wednesday, a third of the inhabitants of Tunis died, another third were taken prisoner, while the final third fled. I heard it said by elders that each third represented sixty thousand souls. Al Hassan opened the city to Christians over three days.[4]

Ibn abi Dinar was writing in 1660, a century and three decades after the events, and the memory still seems painful. Why had the sultan sacrificed his own city, allowing it to be pillaged by Christian soldiers? To punish the population for their ties with the Turks? To satisfy the Spanish? Or to set an example for the territories he still controlled? At this time, the regions under Moulay al-Hassan's rule had shrunk to Bizerte, Béja, and some areas surrounding the capital. The rest of the region had slipped from his grasp. Powerful men carved out villages in those areas which became fiefs over which they exercised authority.

From then on, Sousse was ruled by a man about whom little is known: Abu Slama al-Kli'i, a figure powerful enough to subjugate the city and establish important matrimonial alliances that we will return to later in this chapter. Whatever the cause, the sack of Tunis had the effect of making Hassan appear as an enemy of Islam. Sidi 'Arafa gauged that the moment was right to spread his *da'wa*, the precursor to seizing power. He mobilized his men and his beasts to save the fugitives who had fled the city and led a propaganda campaign against the Hafsid sultan. His political aspirations now in the open, he began to search for alliances. Sometime between July and October of 1535, he married his daughter to the lord of Sousse, Abu Slama al-Kli'i. Strengthened by al-Kli'i's support, he was able to set off to conquer Kairouan, knowing that the region of Sousse was protected.[5]

The Hafsids, the Turks, and the Shabbia Fight over Kairouan

In August 1534, Kairouan was occupied by the Turks, after Khayriddine sent a garrison there. This occupation lasted from August 1534 to April 1538. During these four years, it is not easy to tell who was the true master of the city: the Turks or Sidi 'Arafa. We suppose that the Turkish garrison—made up of about forty men and their *agha*, cut off from the hinterland where the Bedouins were prevalent—was sustained by the support of the people of Kairouan, who seemed to prefer the Turks to the Shabbia.

As for the Shabbia, they were not, at this time, in a position to expel the Turkish soldiers. They lagged behind when it came to equipment, for they did not possess firearms. It would seem that, despite the reputation he had won after the sacking of Tunis, Sidi 'Arafa did not exercise real power, except over some groups of Bedouins whom he influenced by virtue of his spiritual authority.

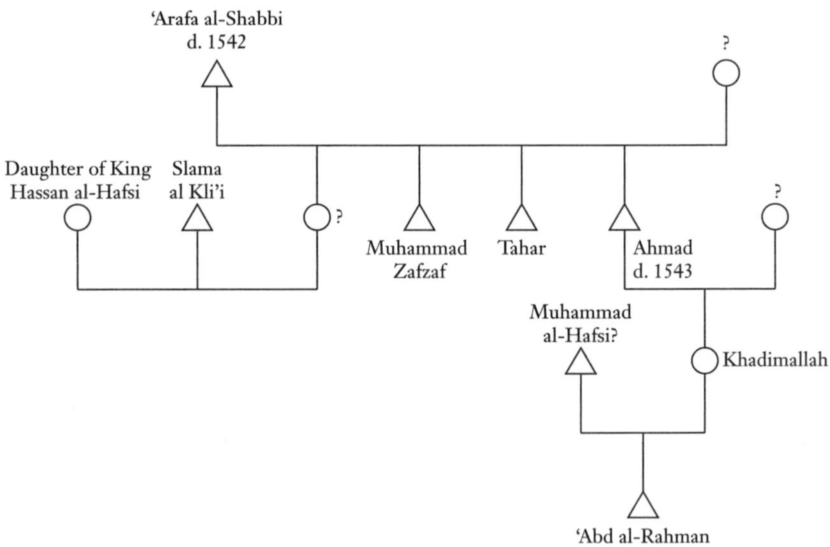

1. Alliances among the Shabbia, al-Kli'i, and the Hafsid king

Al-Hassan Takes Back His Throne: 1535–42

As for al-Hassan, he was able to regain the throne of his ancestors thanks to the intervention of Charles V himself. In exchange, Charles V expected al-Hassan to help him recapture the coastal cities and ensure the security of the Iberian fleet, which was menaced by corsairs who used points on the Ifriqiyan coast to attack the islands of the Mediterranean and the Italian coastline. Bizerte returned to the control of Charles V in December 1535 after a heavy siege. But many other ports and cities escaped his grip and organized themselves into independent cities, submitting to the Turks or to local leaders: Hammamet, Sousse, Monastir, Mahdia, Kélibia, Sfax, Gabes, Tajoura, and Djerba ceased to be part of the Hafsid domain. From 1535 to 1574, these cities were contested by the Spanish fleet, which wanted to reconquer them on behalf of the Hafsids; the Turkish corsairs, who wanted to use them as bases from which to attack the Maghreb; and the Shabbia, who could no longer be contained to the steppes and were drawn to the sea. Only al-Hassan did not look to the coasts: his objective was land, and his means the Bedouins, to borrow an expression from Monchicourt.[6] For the moment, his target was Kairouan, and his enemy was 'Arafa al-Shabbi. But to achieve this goal he would have to rely on his own forces, for the Spanish were reluctant to come to his aid.

Al-Hassan Attacks Kairouan

'Arafa Shabbi had consolidated his power in Kairouan after al-Hassan was discredited following the sacking of Tunis. The ousted sultan decided to liberate Kairouan and reestablish his authority there. He led an army of Bedouins still loyal to him and a small contingent of Christian mercenaries. In September 1535, he arrived outside Kairouan and set up camp in a place called Baten al-Garn, ten kilometers from the city. There, he was attacked by Ibn 'Arafa's troops at night. Caught by surprise, his army was quickly defeated and some of his men joined the enemy. Al-Hassan swore to take revenge; he would subject Kairouan to the same fate that Tunis had suffered a few months prior.

The defeated al-Hassan returned to his capital, more committed than ever to expelling the Shabbia and taking revenge on Kairouan. In 1536, he raised an army of European mercenaries to attack the city again. He was stopped by a Turkish unit and returned to Tunis, defeated once more. Al-Hassan understood that he could not fight the Shabbia and the Turks simultaneously, as they were united by an ambivalent relationship—albeit one that would break down shortly thereafter. Al-Hassan begged the Spanish to come to his aid. They ultimately lent him the support of the Marquis of Terranova, Admiral of Sicily, who arrived at the Port of Sousse with his flotilla in April 1538 as al-Hassan was attacking Kairouan with his cavalrymen. But this campaign failed to oust the Turks. At the end of April, the Turkish unit of Kairouan was attacked, and forty soldiers and their *agha* were killed. This information was sent to the new Governor of La Goulette by the caid of Tunis, Farhat, in the name of the Hafsid king. The sources do not specify whether this anti-Turkish campaign was incited by Sidi 'Arafa or by the people of Kairouan, tired of the Turkish presence.

Reconstructing these events, which vary according to the sources, lends some clarity to this period. We learn from the Caid Farhat that, following al-Hassan's defeat at Sousse and the anti-Turkish uprising in Kairouan, the Hafsid king moved to Kairouan to negotiate with Sidi 'Arafa.[7] One does wonder how such a reversal could have taken place: Abu Slama al-Kli'i, 'Arafa's son-in-law and master of Sousse since 1535, who was probably driven out by the Turks, was the intermediary between 'Arafa and al-Hassan, and was also al-Hassan's son-in-law.[8] Al-Kli'i tried to build an anti-Turkish front by bringing his people together with the Shabbi and the Hafsids, all victims of the Turks. The united front did not last due to 'Arafa's outsized ambitions: we can speculate that he hoped, with the support of the Hafsid king, to become Governor of Tunis, but that the Hafsid king refused to cooperate, thereby preventing this first rapprochement between the Hafsids and the Shabbia. While the Hafsid sultan turned once again toward the Spanish, 'Arafa, whose legitimacy was still not acknowledged by the Kairouan elite, resorted to subterfuge. He pretended to give his *bay'a*, his oath of allegiance, to Yahya, a Berber of Lemtouna who was a descendant of the Hafsids. But Yahya was only kept in Kairouan to provide a veneer of legitimacy; he was a puppet king controlled by Sidi 'Arafa. This subterfuge reveals the obstacles faced by the brotherhood's leader in his attempts to claim power and to rule in the name of Hafsid legitimacy.

While 'Arafa had barely taken control of the city of Okba, what were Hassan and the Spanish doing? In May and June of 1540, an expedition commanded by al-Hassan's son failed, again, at the doors of Kairouan. From then on Sidi 'Arafa appeared to be the true master of Kairouan, following the eviction of the Turks and the defeat of al-Hassan. Meanwhile, the Spanish, understanding al-Hassan's ineffectiveness, opened negotiations with Khayriddine.

The Negotiations with Khayriddine

The secret dealings between Khayriddine and the Spanish are revealed by the Spanish correspondence between the authorities and Juan Gallego, who acted as their intermediary with Khayriddine, in March and April of 1540.[9] These negotiations proved unsuccessful, as had earlier attempts in 1538 and 1539. In April 1540, Khayriddine issued his conditions: he demanded that the Spanish guarantee him possession of Algiers, Bjaïa, Bône, Tunis, La Goulette, and Tripoli. In exchange, he would supply Charles V with fifty or sixty galleys to use against the Venetians, the King of France, and even against the Ottoman sultan. Khayriddine would send his son Hassan to Spain as a hostage to assure them of his loyalty. He would disarm his ships, and his *rais* would become caids of the cities. Christians would be permitted to fish for coral in Tabarka and La Calle. Citizens from the two kingdoms would be able to trade freely.

But Charles V had several demands of his own that would eventually derail the negotiations. He wanted to maintain control over two of the cities Khayriddine also claimed: Bjaïa, because it had historically belonged to the Spanish Kingdom, and Tripoli, because it belonged to the Knights of Malta. He also demanded that Khayriddine deliver him the units of the Ottoman fleet in addition to those of the pasha. It seems that Khayriddine, a man of honor, refused to betray the Ottomans in this way.

The failure of the deal brought the Spanish back into Moulay al-Hassan's camp between September and November of 1540. Three Spanish regiments, those of Sicily, Naples, and Hungary, escorted by galleys under the supreme command of Fernand de Gonzagues, left their homeports and headed toward the coasts of Ifriqiya. In September 1540, they took over Monastir, and then thanks to the help of Bedouins loyal to Moulay al-Hassan, they took Hammamet, Sousse, and Sfax. Following this easy victory, the fleet quickly returned to Messina, in Italy, before the winter. They left behind a garrison at Monastir to help protect the sultan and build confidence among his supporters, planning to return the following year to take Kélibia, Djerba, and Tajoura, and even to march on Kairouan. But events would unfold differently due to the Hafsid sultan's eagerness to finish off his enemies.

The confrontation between al-Hassan and the Shabbia took place shortly after the departure of the Christian units. Was it Hassan who was eager to start fighting earlier than planned? Or did the Shabbia strike first? The commander of the garrison of Monastir mobilized two thousand of his soldiers, promising them riches and captives. Al-Hassan himself led sixty thousand Bedouins, among them women and children who swelled the ranks. The Shabbia army was made up of 22,000 cavalrymen, 15,000 infantry, and six hundred Turkish musketeers (holders of firearms), led by a renegade. The encounter between the two armies took place in a marshy area. The Shabbia army was led by the son of 'Arafa and his second in command, a renegade from Malaga named Cachazo. Al-Hassan was ambushed soon after the clash began and forced to flee, first to Sousse and from there to Tunis. He abandoned most of the Bedouins, many of whom perished in the marshes. The Spanish troops were able to return to their headquarters without losses. The Shabbia victory occurred on November 12, 1540, and became known as the "Victory of Jammal," named after a small town in the Sahel. A consequence of the Shabbia victory was that the recently subjugated coastal cities revolted against al-Hassan. Only Monastir would remain, for eight more months, in Spanish hands.

This last defeat did not discourage al-Hassan, who went back to the Bedouins to recruit more soldiers. He sought the help of Ahmad al-Ghariana, the leader of a segment of the Ouled Said and a declared enemy of Sidi 'Arafa's. He begged the Spanish authorities to give him the troops of La Goulette and Monastir to use in his attack on Kairouan. His supplications were ignored, and indeed the viceroy of Sicily decided to repatriate the unit based in Monastir. Before setting sail, al-Ghariana took Kélibia from the Turks and, after evacuating the population, gave it back to the fallen king. In May 1541, the detachment from Monastir embarked for Trapani. Moulay al-Hassan gave up hope that he would succeed in taking back Kairouan. Those hopes were crushed once and for all in October 1541, when the fleet of Emperor Charles V met with disaster at the gates of Algiers.

During the year 1542, al-Hassan, with his typical persistence, returned to the charge. He kept up a regular correspondence with Fernand de Gonzague and informed him of the advance of the Turks toward his frontiers, at Tajoura and at Bône, and of their complicity with the Shabbia. But Charles V, preoccupied with the war against France, placed less importance on the Maghreb. Al-Hassan therefore decided to travel to Europe to plead with the emperor in person to intervene and help him expel the Turks. But Charles V had left Barcelona on May 1, 1543. Al-Hassan decided to try to meet him in Naples before he crossed the Alps, but he did not succeed. It was at this time that the Governor of La Goulette informed al-Hassan of his son Ahmad's uprising. He decided to return to Tunis after having been authorized to raise a small army of Italian mercenaries.

The Fate of al-Hassan

When he learned that his father had decided to reconquer Kairouan and make it suffer the same fate as Tunis, Ahmad secretly returned to Tunis (we don't know where he was), determined to overthrow his father. He was supported by 'Amor Jbali, sheikh of the quarter of Bab al-Jazira, and the notables of Ariana. He presented himself at the Kasbah, where he settled.

On returning to Tunis, al-Hassan fought his son and those who rallied around him under the banner of the saints Sidi al-Jbali and Sidi Abdallah bin Dawoud. According to Ibn abi Dinar, Dawoud had killed so many unbelievers that his hand was permanently fixed to the handle of his sword. Al-Hassan and his Italian mercenaries were vanquished: the sultan fled toward the island of Chikli, but he was caught and returned to his son. After having consulted those close to him on the appropriate fate for his father, Ahmad Sultan decided to blind him.

The correspondence between Ahmad al-Hafsi and Fernand de Gonzague, reconstructed by Monchicourt, allows us to follow the main events occurring after the fall of Sultan al-Hassan. Thanks to some accomplices, the defeated sultan took refuge with the Spanish at La Goulette. He then left the fortress in the autumn of 1545 to recruit Arabs and attack Tunis, all while continuing to receive support from the Spanish and Francois de Tovar.[10] But in February 1546, Francois de Tovar betrayed al-Hassan—he locked him in the fort and stole a large part of his fortune.

The Spanish had a stake in the fate of the Hafsid sultans. They only agreed to help them in exchange for payments, all while considering them a stopgap in the face of the Turkish threats. To ensure that the Hafsids honored their financial commitments, the Spanish always kept one of their sons as a hostage. Al-Hassan's second son, Muhammad, had been detained at La Goulette probably since his father's first departure for Italy in 1543. When the eldest, Ahmad, rebelled, his younger brother Bakkar took refuge at La Goulette. Muhammad was therefore liberated and became his father's main supporter in the recapture of the throne.

Meanwhile, changes were underway in the fort of La Goulette. Francois de Tovar was called back to Europe. His replacement, Louis Perez de Vagas, landed on February 17, 1546. His first action was to sign a truce with Sultan Ahmad. Suddenly, the presence of al-Hassan and his son Bakkar in La Goulette became problematic: the Spanish couldn't support both parties at once. The young Bakkar was thus sent to Palermo, and al-Hassan went to Kairouan. Was he sent there by the Spanish on a diplomatic mission to negotiate with the Shabbia, as Monchicourt suggests on the basis of the Spanish archives? Or did he take refuge in Kairouan with the help of his son-in-law, al-Kli'i, as Ibn abi Dinar writes?[11] When does the marriage between Sultan al-Hassan's daughter and al-Kli'i date to? What is the link between al-Kli'i and the Spanish? Many questions remain. What seems certain is that al-Kli'i was playing the role of intermediary with the Shabbia.

Rapprochement Between al-Hassan, the Shabbia, and the Spanish

In the second half of 1547, the Governor of La Goulette sent the Sharif Bouzaiane, a relative of al-Hassan, to Kairouan to negotiate with the Shabbia. The Shabbia had made contact with the Spanish, and the Spanish felt no threat from these nomads lacking both firearms and access to the sea, so did not oppose their advance toward the Sahel.

Al-Hassan stayed in Kairouan between 1547 and 1550. Ibn abi Dinar reports that during this sojourn the following event took place: While he was taking refuge in the *zawiya* of Sidi al-Jdidi (today Sidi 'Abid), the fallen sultan was stopped by a group of young children who asked him to play a musical instrument. The sultan, aware that he was being humiliated, cast the instrument aside and declaimed the famous verses: "We were lions and men respected us, and now the time has come when we fear hares."

During this stay in Kairouan, Prince Muhammad, son of al-Hassan, married the young daughter of Sheikh 'Arafa, Khadimallah. The marriage signaled an alliance between the Hafsid sultan and the new Shabbi chief, Muhammad ibn abi Tayyib. However, this alliance did not last long, and al-Hassan soon departed again for Europe in search of Charles V. A note from the Vatican, dated January 26, 1548, reported:

> The king of Tunis in Barbary, on his way to Germany to see the emperor, stopped first in Rome and visited the palace of the pope. A small white band concealed where his son had torn out his eyes. He was dressed in an African style. Two Barbarian stablemen, dressed in Barbary clothes, accompanied him to Rome by horse. He continued his ascent toward Germany, passing through Mantua, Milan, and Augsburg. He arrived there on May 8, 1548, where the diet of the Holy Roman-Germanic Empire had been convened since September 10, 1547, and where Charles V tried to reconcile the

> Protestants and the Catholics. Moulay al-Hassan complained of the thefts committed against him by Tovar and the usurpation of his throne.[12]

By al-Hassan's account, the theft was of four large precious stones estimated to be worth 225,000 ducats, twenty-six diamonds, one hundred rubies, four hundred sapphires, a quantity of emeralds and pearls worth a million pieces of gold, a chest containing 800,000 gold doubloons (Spanish gold coins), and furniture and various other objects worth 90,000 ducats. These vain complaints did not seem to move the emperor. In Augsburg, the arrival of the King of Tunis was barely remarked upon: "The prince was carried in a litter and accompanied by his son Bakkar and a small group of servants, half of whom were black and whose dress resembled that of the Turks."

Charles V, persuaded to support the fallen king's political goals, asked that he be kept in Sicily. Al-Hassan refused. The Spanish authorities ultimately offered to help the king in one last attempt at taking back his throne. This is how, in 1549, the sultan and his son Bakkar came to be embedded in the fleet of André Doria. Doria sailed along the Tunisian coast trying to persuade the cities to accept the sovereignty of King Hassan, but his efforts were in vain, for they all aspired to become city-states.

Since the political unrest had begun, a wind of freedom had been blowing through the port cities, which did not recognize Hafsid or Turkish claims, and even less those of the Shabbia. The appearance of a new Turkish leader, Dargouth Rais, changed the dealer and shuffled the cards. Alliances unraveled more quickly than they were formed.

The Shabbia were establishing themselves as a true power in the interior. But they were increasingly drawn to the coasts, hoping to escape their seclusion in the steppes. They had amassed enough power to enlarge their tax base to include the coastal towns and the market of the arquebuses. We don't know exactly how much power Sidi 'Arafa and his followers had, though the Spanish compared him to the pope, and the locals considered him a savant. His successor, Muhammad ibn abi Tayyib, was designated caliph of the Shabbia community and challenged the declining Hafsid king.

The Shabbia state was rudimentary. They governed with a *djem'a* that counseled the family, the brotherhood, and the state simultaneously. The Shabbi leader was at once imam, caliph, and grand master of the brotherhood and ran a large part of Ifriqiya from his base in Kairouan.[13] If his authority was guaranteed in the city, it was looser among the tribes, where he was represented by his disciples. But the real center of Shabbia influence was the great confederation of the Hnansha.

Would the Shabbia succeed in transitioning from a spiritual power to a political one? This disappointingly brief transition was the work of Muhammad ibn abi Tayyib (1543–57), a somewhat controversial character because his orientation was more political than spiritual. *Al-Fath al-munir* hardly speaks of him, suggesting that he was not entirely respected. His aunt, 'Arafa's daughter, refused throughout her life to eat meat, for it was a symbol of illicit riches and of estrangement from the brotherhood's austere foundation.[14] As tensions simmered between the Shabbia and other maraboutic families, politics dominated the house of Muhammad ibn abi Tayyib, who seems to have been somewhat removed from the brotherhood's spiritual roots.

The coastal cities were driven by the spirit of autonomy, for they had prospered ever since Muslim and Jewish traders from Spain and Portugal had established themselves there. The cities had also become ports of anchor for Levantine corsairs, who brought with them profitable trade. All other protagonists disrupted this balance, as happened with the appearance of a new corsair leader, Dargouth Pasha.

7

Dargouth and the Ottoman Breakthrough in the Mediterranean

Dargouth Pasha was among the great Turkish corsairs who rose to power in the sixteenth-century Mediterranean. Born in Anatolia as a peasant by the name of Torghudce, Dargouth Pasha joined the ranks of the *levend* sailors, Muslim and Christian mercenaries who had been recruited in the Aegean Sea and attached to the service of the Ottoman fleet. In the context of the bitter struggle between the Turks and the Spanish for coastal dominance, Dargouth was taken prisoner by André Doria's nephew in Corsica on January 15, 1540 during a mismatched battle between Dargouth's thirteen galleys and his adversary's eighty.[1]

After being freed, he settled in Djerba and married the daughter of Salah, an Ottoman dignitary and governor of the island. Several years later, he gave his own daughter in marriage to the son of Khayriddine. He began to covet Mahdia, which he occupied for a short period in 1544 before the Spanish intervened. Then he resumed his activities, using Djerba as a base, taunting the Genoese admiral, André Doria. In early 1551, his island was besieged by the Genoese fleet. He was saved thanks to his own ingenuity: Unbeknownst to his enemies, Dargouth dug a canal, transported his vessels by land to another point on the island, and took to sea by night while the Genoese were still laying siege to the island, hoping to starve him out.

During this period, Dargouth placed himself in the service of the Ottoman fleet and participated in naval operations, notably those conducted against Malta and Tripoli. He was thus appointed Governor of the Karlielli region, whose principal port was Prevesa.[2] His real goal, however, was the city of Tripoli, then occupied by the Knights of Malta, so he returned to the Mediterranean and resumed his efforts to occupy Mahdia.

For some time, Mahdia had been governed by a Turk, Hassan Shalbi, who some sources present as the nephew of Khayriddine Barbarossa.[3] In

1548 the Shabbia tried to occupy the city. Unable to maintain a maritime siege, they instead signed a truce with the Turks, who were beginning to run out of supplies. The following year the inhabitants of Mahdia, represented by their council, the *djem'a*, decided to expel Shalbi from the city, along with all the Turks and their families. The city hoped to become an independent city-state, and its traders to form an autonomous port town. But Dargouth succeeded in entering and occupying the city, and Mahdia became a base for his fleet and for his incursions against the Italian coastline. Charles V reacted promptly to this occupation.

Occupation of Mahdia by the Spanish: 1550–54

A fleet departed from the south of Italy. The viceroy of Sicily, Jean of Vega, took Sousse and Monastir. On June 28, 1550, he began an attack of Mahdia that lasted until he subjugated the city on September 10, 1550. Moulay al-Hassan and his son Bakkar came with Vega on his ship from Sicily. Meanwhile, his other son, Moulay Muhammad, and his relative, Bouzaiane, arrived from La Goulette. Sometime between July 11 and July 25 of that year, at the start of the siege of Mahdia, Moulay al-Hassan died of a fever. He was between sixty and sixty-five. He was buried in Kairouan in the *zawiya* of Sidi al-Ghariani. His son, Muhammad, became King of Tunis. Muhammad, remember, was married to a cousin of Muhammad ibn abi Tayyib, head of the Shabbia brotherhood. This marriage aligned the Shabbia with the Spanish, particularly between 1550 and 1554.

The Marabouts and Spanish against the Turks

Muhammad ibn abi Tayyib—master of Kairouan, supporter of the late King al-Hassan, and relative by marriage of the newly appointed King Muhammad—supplied the Spanish with foodstuffs with the support of his Bedouin allies and refused to help Dargouth. In recognition of his support, the Spanish ceded Sousse and Monastir to him. He installed a mounted unit made up of Bedouins in Monastir. Meanwhile, the Shabbia, Muhammad al-Hafsi, and the Spanish were all on the same side. But the Spanish were torn between the two brothers: Muhammad al-Hafsi, the legitimate king, and his usurping brother, Ahmad. Ahmad brokered a truce with the new commander of La Goulette, Alonso de la Cueva, who had taken up his post in September 1550, after his predecessor was killed during the siege of Mahdia. The Spanish, conscious of their precarious position, said this:

> The lord of Kairouan having been and being a servant of his majesty, it is recognized that if he participates in the present truce, he does so under the provision that if the truce fails between his Highness of Tunis and the said lord of Kairouan, it would not result in a breach of the present truce, agreed upon between his Highness and don Alonso.[4]

This rapprochement between Muhammad al-Hafsi, the Spanish, and the Marabout endangered Dargouth's position, but Dargouth had an unexpected ally: Sultan Ahmad. The two men sympathized with one another, and in 1548 Dargouth offered the king a beautiful captive from Castellamare. After being driven out of Mahdia, Dargouth found himself in an uncomfortable position. Between September 1550 and April 1551, he faced serious challenges. He was poorly received by the Djerbians, who feared that his presence would precipitate a Spanish raid. He lacked supplies and capital. His brother-in-law, the son of Sheikh Salah, sent aid that allowed Dargouth to take to the seas again and resume his threats against the Spanish.[5] In 1551, Dargouth failed to take Gafsa and was tracked by Doria to Sirte. He found himself caught between Mahdia, under the control of the Spanish, and Tripoli, under the control of the Knights of Malta. He took refuge in Istanbul in the spring of 1551 and remained there until 1556. With Dargouth temporarily ousted, old alliances in Ifriqiya were renewed.

A piece of correspondence from June 6, 1552 between the Governor of Mahdia, Sanche de Levya, and the Hafsid pretender, Moulay Muhammad—writing both in his own name and that of his father-in-law, the King of Kairouan—reveals an agreement on trade and good neighborliness that regulated the movements of men and merchandise. Prince Muhammad, now a vassal of Charles V, was obligated to pay a tribute of 4,000 gold crowns in kind, six horses, six falcons, six greyhounds, and six Christian slaves.[6] This pretender, who represented Hafsid legitimacy, was supported by Hammamet and by various Bedouin factions, including the Ouled Yahya, kin of his grandmother al-Jaziya. Challenging him was his brother Ahmad Sultan, the usurper of Tunis, who had not abandoned his plan to reconquer the entire territory. He attacked the Shabbia army in December 1552, defeated them, and got one step closer to Sousse. The Shabbia found themselves in a difficult position, for their Spanish allies evacuated Mahdia on June 4, 1554.

The Return of Dargouth

In 1556, Dargouth's retreat ended with his appointment as Governor of Tripoli. During his time in Istanbul, he had occupied several important positions, but his career there was impeded by the powerful Rostom Pasha. Dargouth had hoped during his years of retreat to obtain the rule of Algiers, but he was denied it. He had also coveted the admiralty but was refused that, too, despite having effectively led the Ottoman fleet from 1552 to 1554. The title of admiral was instead bestowed on Sinan Pasha, brother of Rostom Pasha, even though he was not a sailor. And so Dargouth sought to govern Tripoli. The city was held by Mourad Agha, who had been loyal to Khayriddine since he had defeated the Knights of Malta in 1551, when the knights decided to save their lives by ceding the city to their Turkish enemies and boarding a French ship. In May 1556, after Mourad Agha's death, Dargouth was appointed Pasha of Tripoli. This new post allowed him to take part in the assault on Oran led by Hassan Coursou, Pasha of Algiers, but the attack failed.

Under the leadership of this great corsair, the Kingdom of Tripoli grew in the image of Algiers. He led several offensives to enlarge his territory. On December 20, 1556, Dargouth finally took Gafsa, where he set up his own caid and imprisoned the caid of Djerba, who was allied with the Shabbia, and killed him shortly thereafter. Concerned by these successes, Philip II, emperor of Spain, tried to negotiate with Dargouth as his father, Charles V, had done several years earlier with Khayriddine. But Dargouth had another plan: to use his momentum to conquer Kairouan.

The Conquest of Kairouan: December 27, 1557

After bringing the sheikhs of Djerba and Gafsa under his control, Dargouth sent seven families from Sfax to Tripoli (including that of al-Mokni, its sheikh) because he feared a rear attack. A Spanish source describes the capture of Kairouan, which the Turkish troops, the Bedouins, and even the wandering King Muhammad al-Hafsi took part in (not having gained anything from his alliance with the Shabbia, the latter had aligned himself once again with the Spanish).[7] The Spanish documents describe the ease with which the Turks took Kairouan and the escape of Muhammad ibn abi Tayyib. Dargouth imposed a heavy fine on the city and demanded that the property of the Shabbia be returned to those who had just won, that is to say the Turks. The flight of the Shabbia allowed the ancient brotherhood of the Ghariani to regain its prestige and to benefit from the support being provided to the Turks of Kairouan.

What became of Ahmad Sultan in this new political situation? He did not break with Dargouth, against the advice of the Spanish, who told him to support the Shabbia, considerably less dangerous to them than the formidable Dargouth. Dargouth, for his part, counseled Ahmad Sultan to break with the Spanish of La Goulette. Ahmad Sultan ignored the advice of both sides, choosing a prudent neutrality instead.

In March 1558, Dargouth left Kairouan. There were two reasons for his hasty departure: a conspiracy against him that was brewing in Tripoli, and news from Istanbul of an imminent Spanish attack being prepared by the Venetians, who had recently broken ties with the Sublime Porte. Before leaving Kairouan, Dargouth appointed his ally Muhammad al-Ghariani as sheikh of the city. He placed at his disposal a contingent of Turkish troops commanded by the son of a renegade, the caid Shatmane bin Muhammad.

Kairouan Under the Rule of the Turks: 1557–60

After having fled Kairouan, Muhammad ibn abi Tayyib tried to establish contact with the Spanish, suggesting that they attack Djerba and Tripoli to drive Dargouth from the city and promising to pay the costs of such an operation. The Governor of La Goulette, refusing all interventions in the region's interior, instead advised Muhammad ibn abi Tayyib to increase the suffering of the Turks in Kairouan by preventing them from resupplying. Recent information from Kairouan indicated that dozens of Janissaries were fleeing the city's misery. The Spanish also encouraged Ahmad Sultan to attack Kairouan and reestablish himself there. But the king refused, instead maintaining good relations with the Turks: he welcomed the deserting soldiers and offered Dargouth valuable gifts.

In February 1560, the Christian states united against Tripoli. The Gâteau-Cambrésis Peace Treaty signed between France and the Spain of Philip II made possible an expedition that brought together the pope, the city of Florence, and the Knights of Malta to take control of Tripoli and drive out the Turks. The campaign succeeded only in occupying Djerba. Muhammad ibn abi Tayyib went to meet the Spanish, hoping that a joint attack with the Bedouins would liberate his capital Kairouan. But his hopes were dashed, for an attack led by Dargouth and Piali Pasha retook Djerba. Muhammad ibn abi Tayyib fled once and for all into the steppes. Another branch of the Shabbia, active in the southeast, took up the torch with Zefzef, the son of 'Arafa, who was less of a politician than his departed cousin and who opposed both the Turks and the Hafsids.

The region of Gafsa had been under Ottoman control since 1556, while the oasis of Tozeur was under the authority of Sultan Ahmad, who maintained strong ties with the Turks. All around, this tribal world was shared among the defenders of the Shabbia and those who remained neutral and placed themselves at the service of the highest bidder. Tribal groups allied with the Shabbia reasserted their loyalty to the wandering prince Muhammad, who was united with the powerful brotherhood through marriage. Did the Shabbia hope to help Muhammad ibn abi Tayyib conquer his father's throne and become a tribe privileged by its proximity to power? Unfortunately for them, this prince was asset-poor, and his aspirations to the throne would never be realized.

Muhammad, a Wandering Prince

Muhammad was the son of al-Hassan and one of his wives, Rahmouna. When al-Hassan was removed from power in 1542, Rahmouna sought refuge in La Goulette. Shortly before that, in 1540, al-Hassan had signed a treaty with the Spanish that required him to give up one of his sons as a hostage. Muhammad thus spent two years in the fortress of La Goulette. He was released in 1542 so that he could care for his blind father, and his youngest brother, Abu Baker, known as Bakkar, took his place until 1547.

Muhammad would become his father's principal source of support in Kairouan, allying himself with the Shabbia and taking part in battles against the Turks. When his father died in July 1550, he found himself exposed and without support. He wandered for several years among the Bedouins and eventually asked the Spanish for permission to return to La Goulette. The Spanish refused Muhammad's request because they maintained good relations with Ahmad: supporting two enemy brothers at the same time was unacceptable. Sultan Ahmad offered his brother a substantial pension if he agreed to go live in the Christian world—in Sicily, for example. Muhammad contacted Philip II and proposed to place himself at his service. But the king of Spain did not have confidence in Muhammad's abilities, and instead gave Muhammad permission to live with his large family in Sicily. Muhammad remained on Italian territory for several years. He was returned to Tunis when Don Juan occupied the city and installed Muhammad on the throne on October 14, 1573.

While the wandering prince had been in Sicily, the situation on the ground had changed. In 1560, the Bedouins had succeeded in expelling the Turks from Kairouan and Gafsa. But the Shabbia did not return to their city because it had come under the control of another Marabout family, the Ghariani. The Bedouins attacked regions under the control of the central power, which allowed Zefzef to recapture Tozeur. Sultan Ahmad was forced to buy them off. The Turks lost territory, especially since the powerful Dargouth was off fighting on another front.

The Siege of Malta and the Death of Dargouth

The Knights of Malta were a thorn in the side of the corsairs and the Ottoman fleet, one that obstructed maritime circulation and communication between Tripoli and Istanbul. At Dargouth's insistence, Sultan Suleiman organized a campaign against the Knights: Mustafa Pasha would lead the army while Piali Pasha would lead the navy. The Sultan recommended that when meeting 'Ilj 'Ali, who was coming from Alexandria, his troops take advantage of Dargouth's experience; he had recently arrived from Tripoli at the head of a large force. It was a bitter contest. During the siege of the fort of Saint-Elme, Dargouth suffered a blow to the head from a projectile. He died on June 23, 1565. The Ottoman campaign continued until September but failed to drive the Knights from their island.

The history we have just traced shows the profound complexity of the period that preceded the establishment of the Ottomans in Tunis. Multiple players harbored claims to the region. Alliances were formed and dissolved just as fast. Groups changed camps according to their interests of the moment, creating an impression of anarchy. In fact, many different powers emerged over a territory that did not recognize the authority of any one central power. Paradoxically, the Ottoman state did not appear to be interested in the Maghreb. Instead, it was the great corsairs, in the service of the Ottomans, who wished to establish themselves and build bases in the region. Therefore, it is important to read the occupation of Tunis and its surrounding territory not through the prism of a central state, but rather from the perspective of dynasties founded by these men of the sea. Khayriddine Barbarossa, his descendants, his adopted son al-Hassan, and his renegades—still powerful in Algiers—nurtured ambitions for control of the coastal cities of Ifriqiya.

8

Mediterranean Networks

The occupation of Tripoli by the Ottoman Turks, like that of Algiers three decades earlier, sealed the fate of Tunis: the plan to unite the coast of the Maghreb was coming to fruition. At the forefront of this project were the Mediterraneans, people born of a cosmopolitan world of renegades and corsairs. These were men like Khayriddine Pasha, his son Hassan, his loyal servants, Hassan Agha, Dargouth, 'Ilj 'Ali, and the many others who made up his house. They shared a vision of expelling the Spanish and driving them all the way back to their peninsula, fighting the Arabs and the Berbers, and transforming the social landscape by occupying the cities with people from the Mediterranean and Moriscos from Spain. Algiers would be the springboard and the fallback base in the execution of this project.

Despite Khayriddine's defeat in Tunis by Charles V, he did not abandon his plan to occupy the city and drive out both the Spanish and the Hafsids. But how would he achieve this while far from the Maghreb lands in his new role as Grand Admiral? Following his promotion to Grand Admiral, Khayriddine had left Algiers, even though he remained its pasha for life, and established himself in Istanbul. Nevertheless, he retained influence over the affairs of Algiers, and followed the events that went on there. Identifying the men who reached positions of power and analyzing their rise allows us to better understand how Tunis came to be occupied in 1569 and the city's history during the two decades that followed.

The House of Khayriddine in Algiers

When Khayriddine left Algiers in 1534, he appointed one of his Mamluks, Hassan Agha, to lead the *oujak*. He remained in the post for a decade.[1]

Hassan Agha: 1534–45

Born in a Sardinian village, Hassan (his Muslim name) was captured as a child as part of Khayriddine's privateering exploits on the Mediterranean. Khayriddine made him a eunuch and raised him as his own. During this period, the great corsair was establishing his house in Algiers and surrounding himself with loyal lieutenants. After several years, Hassan Agha was elected to the role of *kahia*, or lieutenant, charged with the stewardship of the house and the care of its master. He was then promoted to a military role and led the army to collect taxes. He thus became Khayriddine's second in command, trusted to carry out important missions and charged with the administration of the city when Khayriddine left to conquer Tunis in 1533. Then, Hassan's appointment as governor seemed natural, for the Janissaries and the rais all agreed on his legitimacy. His government had no internal troubles, for both the Turks and the Arabs feared his severity and forcefulness. It was under his leadership, in October 1541, that Charles V planned a major expedition against Algiers.

Algiers the Well-protected

Charles V decided to get rid of the intrepid corsairs of Algiers. A war against the Turks would only be possible after the destruction of this important stronghold, which disrupted navigation and threatened the Spanish coasts. This African war would also divert the Turks from the Hungarian front, where Charles V had encountered setbacks, and allow him to achieve a victory in the Mediterranean that would improve the image of the imperial armies. The bad news from the east about the capture of Budapest and the Ottoman march on Vienna persuaded Charles V to execute his plan, even though his associates warned that the season was too far along for a maritime campaign. Ignoring their concerns, he prepared a large fleet that would be reinforced by the galleys of the Knights of Malta. With his impressive armada, 516 boats and more than 36,000 men, he set sail for Algiers.[2]

Charles V chose several well-known figures to accompany him on this expedition. Several western informers alleged that Hassan Agha was frightened by Charles V's preparations and planned to leave the city before meeting his enemy. In fact, Hassan Agha was well aware of the imminent Spanish attack and mobilized his Arab and Kabyle soldiers as well as the Turks and renegades. He strengthened the city's defenses and ordered, under the penalty of death, that the inhabitants of Algiers remain in their homes with their belongings, so that they would be compelled to secure their own neighborhoods. Hassan Agha's supposed desertion is denied by many sources, who instead glorify his leadership when Algiers was under serious threat.[3] Haedo also denies the accusation, describing his courage, valor, and generosity throughout this ordeal.[4]

On October 20, the emperor's fleet departed for the raid of Algiers. A reconnaissance mission was charged with identifying the landing point. Before initiating combat, Charles V sent an emissary to Hassan Agha and proposed terms of surrender: he reminded him of his Christian origins, and suggested that, in the event of a truce, the Spanish would guarantee the security of the city and of its inhabitants. But the governor refused. The Spanish army attacked the beaches of Algiers under fire from Arab cavalrymen, who occupied the high points surrounding the beach. The fighting began, and the Arab cavalrymen were pushed back. Meanwhile, many galleys were facing the city. But the weather changed rapidly and a terrible storm broke out. The soldiers deployed on the beaches were subjected to freezing temperatures and a torrential downpour that lasted for several days. The Arab cavalrymen attacked the Spanish troops and tried to draw them away from their camp. Several battles took place at the gates of the city, in which the Knights of Malta distinguished themselves. But the violent storm that raged on October 25 and 26 of 1541 destroyed five hundred boats, as well as equipment and provisions, and so altered the outcome of the battle. A cruel hunger took hold, and the emperor was forced to kill horses to feed his men. The surviving soldiers reloaded the ships in a state of indescribable chaos. What was left of the fleet followed the ship of André Doria back toward Matifou, the most protected place in the bay of Algiers. But there, too, many ships were damaged, and a few sank after another storm.

And so, the great imperial fleet met one of its worst defeats, and Algiers earned its title—"the well-protected." Hassan Agha profited from this victory, which was thanks in large part to Mother Nature. The Kabyle King of Kouko, an ally of Charles V, left his mountains to aid the Spanish, but turned back when he heard of the disaster. In April 1542, Hassan Agha organized a campaign of reprisals against Kouko's territory, which the king preferred to surrender without fighting. He pledged to pay a tribute and offered his son and heir to the throne, Ahmad ibn al-Qadi, as a hostage. The Spanish attack, meant to destroy the *oujak* of Algiers once and for all, ended up having a different result: the submission of a large part of Kabyle. Following this successful campaign, Hassan Agha tried to force the surrender of Tlemcen, but he failed in the face of Spanish intervention. Upon his return from this last mission, he became sick with a cold that took his life in November 1545.

His interim successor was Hajj Beshir, a Turk by birth and the general captain of the militia, who was married to a Morisco from Valencia. During the siege of Algiers, he distinguished himself with his boldness. The Turks and the Janissaries chose him without waiting for a nomination from Istanbul. This transition of power was accompanied by a great Arab uprising led by Sheikh Boutrik, who seriously threatened the Turks in Algiers. Hajj Beshir led an army of four thousand Turks and renegades and five hundred Andalusians and sipahis to inflict a stinging defeat on Boutrik. Shortly after this victory, a new governor arrived from Istanbul and Hajj Beshir ceded his place. He died four months later.

During the period following Hassan Agha's death, two other men made names for themselves in Algiers: the Caid Ramadan (Rabadhan according to Haedo) and the Caid Safar (Saffa according to Haedo). We will return later to the Caid Ramadan, who would come to govern Tunis in 1569. As for Safar, he was a classic example of a poor Anatolian peasant who came to Algiers seeking fortune. He moved up through the ranks in the army and also occupied the well-paid position of Caid. He died in 1561 at the age of fifty-one. He had no direct descendants, so he named his youngest brother, Dawoud, as his heir. Safar had taken Dawoud in as a child, and Dawoud would become the richest caid of his time. He married the only daughter of Hajj Beshir, the interim Governor of Algiers.[5] This arrangement reveals much about how Turkish society was organized in Algiers, with its endogamous matrimonial politics and the many paths to enrichment available to the caid because of his administrative and fiscal responsibilities. The Regency of Algiers was a place of great opportunity for everyone, from the humble soldiers from the east to the great dignitaries of the Ottoman state, who sought to place their men there.

Hassan ibn Khayriddine: June 20, 1545, to September 22, 1551

The new governor was none other than Hassan, Khayriddine's own son. He was born in Algiers in 1517 to a Moorish mother from Algeria belonging to a *shurafa* family about which we have little information. Haedo suggests that she was probably an Andalusian, for her son Hassan spoke Spanish fluently, as though he had been born in Spain. How was he chosen from among the many contenders? Khayriddine Pasha, still powerful in Istanbul, supported his son's candidacy on the basis of the role that he and his brother 'Arrouj played in founding the *oujak* of Algiers. Could this appointment suggest the foundation of a hereditary power in Algiers? There is no doubt that Hassan ibn Khayriddine had many advantages, including his father's legitimacy and his belonging to the local milieu, for he had been born and raised on this territory. Hassan ibn Khayriddine was a *kulugli*, which complicates the picture of Turkish power in Algiers as being exclusively foreign, at least at this point in time. He would govern Algiers for many years. He made it his mission to establish alliances with the Arab population as well as with the king of Fes to attempt a landing in Spain. But in this he was thwarted, as much by the betrayal of the Moroccan king as by the Spanish operation to take back Tlemcen.

Hassan was preparing an offensive against Tlemcen when he learned of his father's death in July 1546. A messenger from the king of France arrived with two galleys to deliver the catastrophic news. Hassan, profoundly upset by this loss, gave up his assault on Tlemcen and made a treaty with the Spanish general, the Count of Alcaudette. We can imagine that Hassan had been counting upon the support of his father, commander of the imperial fleet, to launch an attack on the Spanish coast in due course, but that his plan was aborted after Khayriddine's death.

The loss of Khayriddine sparked fierce competition over the pasha's estate. To defend his father's property—part of which now belonged to him, and the rest to the sultan—Hassan sent one of his men, Ja'far, to Istanbul. But intrigues forced him to leave Algiers himself in September 1551: Rostom, the Grand Vizier and son-in-law of the sultan-caliph was trying to seize the great hammam that Hassan had inherited from his father, and so Hassan returned to the imperial capital to protect it.

Before leaving the city, Hassan had designated the Caid Safar as his deputy. He became the object of conspiracies during his almost seven-year sojourn in Istanbul. They were fomented as much by the Grand Vizier as by French diplomats who suspected that Hassan was working against them. Ultimately, the influential Rostom Pasha blocked him from resuming his post in Algiers.

The Appointment of Salah Rais: April 1552 to June 1556

Rostom Pasha rushed to appoint Salah Rais in Algiers.[6] Salah Rais was a native of Alexandria, and he worked as a corsair under Khayriddine's command. He fought the Spanish numerous times during the early years of the *oujak* of Algiers. A close friend of Khayriddine's, and of the same generation, he belonged to Khayriddine's house and had married the daughter of the king of Kouko. When Khayriddine finally left Algiers, he brought Salah Rais with him to Istanbul and trusted him with many maritime missions. He continued his rise and in 1543 became the helmsman of the sultan, commanding his galliot, a very personal responsibility that made all kinds of scheming possible. On his master's death, Salah Rais was likely placed in the service of the powerful Rostom Pasha. The sultan agreed to give him the governorship of Algiers, and Salah Rais assumed this post in April 1552. His main purpose was to pacify the rebellious regions of the south, Toghourt and Ouargla. In 1554, he succeeded in overthrowing the King of Fes, who was allied with the Spanish, and replacing him with a pretender to the throne who was more favorable to the Turks. Learning of this defeat, the Governor of Peñón de Vélez abandoned his position, which was also then taken by the Turks. Salah Rais replaced him with one of his men, the caid Khidr. On the way back, he visited and fortified many cities. In 1555, he set off to reconquer Bjaïa, following a campaign that lasted four months and during which Salah benefited from the help of the king of Kouko, his stepfather.

Following this victory, he sent his son Muhammad, born of a Kabyle princess, to Istanbul to ask the sultan-caliph for military aid and leave to attack Oran and Mers el-Kebir. In the spring of 1556, Salah Rais directed his fleet toward Matifou while waiting for the forty Turkish galleys the sultan had sent to conquer these two cities. It was during these preparations that he died of the plague in June 1556. His son, Muhammad, would later become the Governor of Algiers.

Caid Hassan Coursou: June 1556 to September 1556

After the death of Salah Rais, the Janissaries decided to appoint a man of his house, a young renegade from Corsica whom he had raised and who served as general of the army: the caid Hassan Coursou. Coursou sent an emissary to Istanbul to inform them of the governor's death and to obtain permission to carry out the attack that had been planned by his predecessor. During the twenty days that the galliot took to travel to and from Istanbul, Hassan Coursou led an army and a sizeable fleet to begin the siege of Oran. The skirmishes had hardly begun when the ship returned from Istanbul, ordering Coursou to stop the campaign and put the fleet in the hands of the admiralty to protect the Bosphorus Strait, which was under threat from Doria. Hassan Coursou immediately lifted the siege and returned to Algiers, where he learned that the sultan had appointed a new governor—Tekeleri Pasha—who was in Tripoli and on his way to Algiers.

Tekeleri: October 1556 to April 1557

To Hassan Coursou's satisfaction, the new governor was not accepted by the militia of Algiers. Orders were given to all the ports to prevent his ship from docking. He was received at Bône and Bjaïa with the boom of a cannon. His arrival at Matifou was not met by the salvos of artillery that were customary for an envoy of the sultan. He only took possession of the city of Algiers thanks to the complicity of the rais, who, not wanting to disobey the sultan's orders, persuaded the Janissaries to allow them to negotiate with Tekeleri. Ultimately, they conspired to allow the governor to enter the port and to take power.

Tekeleri immediately arrested Hassan Coursou and subjected him to the worst sorts of torture, even though Coursou had been cleared of the charge of collaborating with the militias to oust Tekeleri. He subjected the caids of Bjaïa and Bône, 'Ali Sardo and Mustafa the Greek, to similar torture. This violent approach was intended to bring the Janissaries of Algiers into line and prevent them from disobeying future orders. Only Youssef, the Caid of Tlemcen and a Calabrian renegade of Hassan Coursou's, decided to avenge his master: with the help of the militia, he killed Tekeleri in April 1557.[7]

Tekeleri's post was then given to Mustafa Arnaout, who held it for a few days before ceding it to Youssef, a highly intelligent twenty-six-year-old, who began his rule by distributing money to soldiers to gain their support. But only a few days in, he was killed by the plague that ravaged Algiers.[8] The soldiers replaced him with Yahya, Caid of Miliana, who had previously held administrative responsibilities. He governed for several months, from January to June 1557. He was married to the daughter of Hajj Beshir, the former Governor of Algiers. He had a daughter with her, Leila 'Aisha, who married Caid Dawoud, the brother of Caid Safar, who would become the interim Governor of Algiers.[9]

The conflict that accompanied Tekeleri's appointment as governor demonstrated the opposing interests of the rais and the Janissaries. The captains of the galleys, not being dependent on the governors of Algiers, accepted more readily the decisions coming from Istanbul, as they were reluctant to become dissidents of the sultan-caliph for fear of reactions at the top.

The Second Government of Hassan Pasha ibn Khayriddine: June 1557 to July 1561

The latest events in Algiers worried the authorities in Istanbul. They feared the response of the Janissaries, who had developed the frustrating habit of forcefully weighing in on appointments and refusing the governors who didn't suit them. Rostom Pasha, the rival of Hassan, son of Khayriddine, died in 1557, allowing the sultan to name Hassan to the governorship of Algiers. And so, in June of that year, Hassan headed to Algiers at the head of a large navy, anticipating opposition from the Janissaries. But he met no such response, for the soldiers considered Hassan Pasha a legitimate ruler, and he landed there smoothly. He immediately set about enforcing the sultan's orders and combating the Spanish presence. He won a great victory against the coalition of the King of Fes and the Spanish, defeating the Iberians at Mostaganem on August 26, 1558. He took 12,000 Iberian prisoners and subjugated the *qal'a* of Beni 'Abbas, who recognized his sovereignty with a tribute.

His prior experience in the region encouraged him to create alliances with the Kabyles. In 1560, he married a daughter of the king of Kouko. He also arranged a marriage between one of his advisers, Caid Hassan Griego, the nephew of his lieutenant 'Ilj 'Ali, and his wife's sister. The two women were well received in Algiers and the weddings were celebrated with much pomp and circumstance. These marriages highlight a critical aspect of Hassan's politics: he sought to expand his alliances in local society, especially with the formidable Berbers of the mountains. The support of the Kabyles mitigated his dependence on the Turkish Janissaries. These alliances gave the Kabyles the right to parade in Algiers with weapons in hand, something that no one in the city had ever seen before.[10]

Having come under suspicion by the Turkish soldiers because of his many seditions, in 1561 Hassan created another army corps, the Zwawa, made up of Kabyles and designed to neutralize the Janissaries. This measure complicated the relationship between the governor and the Janissaries. The *diwan* of the militia of Algiers, made up of soldiers and Turkish officers, worried that an alliance between Hassan Pasha and the Kabyles could endanger the sultan's authority and compromise his interests. The *diwan* decided to put an end to this budding alliance, which it perceived as an existential threat. In July 1561, the *diwan* forced Hassan Pasha to order the Kabyles to leave Algiers in two hours, and to prohibit the sale of all arms, under the penalty of death. Once these measures had been taken, the *diwan* arrested Hassan Pasha, his ally 'Ilj 'Ali, and his stepbrother Caid Hassan, and sent them to Istanbul in chains. The perpetrators of this plan were the two most important officers in the militia: Hassan, a Bosnian, who served as an *agha*, and Coucha Muhammad, general captain of the militia, a Turk of the kind Haedo described as "jackals and villains."[11] Both were charged with governing the city while awaiting the appointment of a new governor.

In Istanbul, Hassan Pasha, son of Khayriddine, denied all the accusations against him. He defended himself so well that the sultan ordered the newly appointed Governor of Algiers to send the two men responsible for the sedition to Istanbul to be executed. The new pasha, Ahmad, was a *bostangi*, or attendant of the gardens, who had obtained this appointment thanks to Sultan Suleiman's wife, Roxelane.[12] However, he died of dysentery just four months into this role, in May 1562. His *kahia*, Yahya, governed for four months while waiting for a new governor to be appointed. (Yahya participated in the siege of Tunis in 1569 and died on his return in 1570.)

The Third Government of Hassan, Son of Khayriddine: September 1562 to January 1567

Hassan's third return to Algiers was a source of great joy that even the women of the city shared in. Hassan was determined to drive the Spanish from the coasts of the Maghreb. He mustered a great army formed of Janissaries, renegades, and Andalusians, to which were added a thousand cavalry sent by his stepfather, the King of Kouko. He prepared huge expeditions against the cities that were occupied by the Spanish. However, the expedition against Mers el-Kebir failed due to the intervention of a powerful Spanish fleet commanded by André Doria that came to the aid of the city. Over the course of the year 1565, Hassan was in secret talks with the sultan to prepare an offensive against Malta for the following year. When the moment came, he participated with a fleet of twenty-eight galleys and galliots, including three thousand Janissaries, and put himself under the command of the Great Captain, Piali Pasha. At the time of this campaign, Hassan's son Mahmoud informed the sultan of his intention to participate and asked for provisions for his sailors, which were given to him.[13] The assault against Malta failed and half the Algerian contingent perished. It was during this battle that Dargouth Pasha suffered an injury to his head and died.

In January 1567, a new governor was named. Hassan Pasha prepared to leave Algiers for good. He left the great bath he had built as a *habous* (also known as a *waqf)* to profit the future kings of Algiers. He left behind his wife, the daughter of the King of Kouko, and his daughter, who was still young at the time. This surrender symbolized a complete rupture with Algiers. Hassan ended his life in Istanbul, where he died in 1570 at the age of fifty-five.

Hassan's death prevented any further transmission of hereditary titles in the house of Barbarossa. This would have been little contested due to the prestige of its founding fathers and their strong ties to Algiers, but the possibility was realized as Hassan's descendants disappeared. His youngest son, born of a Kabyle princess, left no record. His eldest son, Mahmoud, who had been born in Istanbul, likely to a Corsican renegade, had been well positioned to achieve power in Algiers because of his strong family ties. In addition to his ancestry, after the disaster at Malta, he had married the daughter of Dargouth Pasha, which strengthened his connections and increased his wealth. But Mahmoud was killed by his own Christian galley slaves during the Battle of Navarino. The episode is described in detail by Cervantes, who was a slave in Algiers and participated in the Battle of Navarino in 1572:

> The son of Barbarossa [actually, his grandson] was so cruel, he treated his captives so poorly, that when his rowers saw that la Louve (a Christian galley) was approaching and would soon overtake them, they simultaneously let go of their oars, seized the captain . . . passed him from bench to bench, from the stern to the bow, devouring him in such a way that by the time he reached the great mast, he had already given his soul to the devil.[14]

And so, the last known descendent of Khayriddine Pasha, founder of the *oujak* of Algiers, dramatically perished.

Muhammad Pasha ibn Salah Rais: January 1567 to March 1568

The new governor was a *kulugli*. Muhammad Pasha was the son of Salah Rais and the daughter of the King of Kouko, making him the first governor born to a Berber mother. He set out to reconcile the militias and the sailors, authorizing the Janissaries to board the corsair boats as soldiers of the navy,

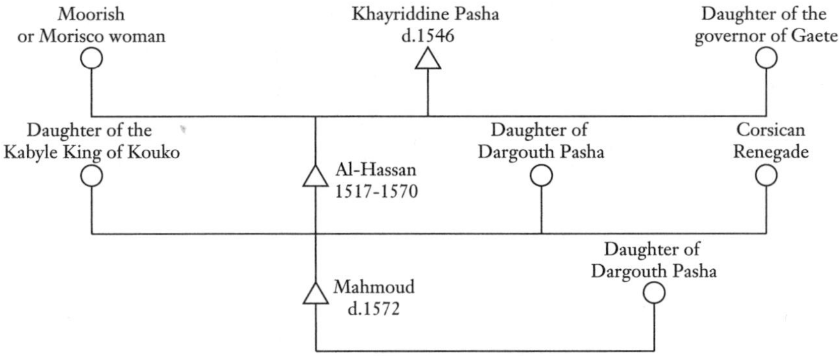

2. The house of Khayriddine

and the sailors, Christian or renegade, to join the militias. This measure should have brought the two forces together, at least temporarily.

But Muhammad Pasha did not manage to rule for long. He was removed from office under a pretext: after a Turkish caid was accused of raping a young woman, the population of Constantine revolted. Muhammad Pasha severely punished some of these insurgents. Others fled to Tripoli by land, and from there to Istanbul, where they aired their grievances to the sultan. He responded by commanding Muhammad Pasha's removal. It would be interesting to know the tenor of these complaints to better understand why they led to this result, or perhaps they were simply a false pretense: the powers of Istanbul would have had reason to fear this Arab-Berber man, born of an Alexandrian father and a Kabyle mother.

Reconstructing the history of the pashas of Algiers between 1535 and 1568 reveals what was at stake in the appointment of governors: the interests of those who occupied the land—that is, the soldiers and the sailors; the legitimacy of the house of Khayriddine and the men that he led; the interests of the powers in Istanbul, who wanted to position their men in Algiers; and the diplomatic constraints imposed on the sultans by their French allies.

It was 'Ilj 'Ali who was appointed by the sultan's decree in 1567. He arrived in Algiers in March 1568, and his installation would have direct consequences for the Ottoman takeover of Tunis. He would take up Khayriddine's project from more than thirty years earlier: the conquest of Tunis.

II. IN THE FOLD OF THE EMPIRE

9

The Battle of Tunis, 1569–74, and the End of the Hafsids

The bringing of Tunis into the Ottoman fold began in 1569 with a clash between two men: 'Ilj 'Ali, a renegade who served the Ottoman Empire, and Don Juan of Austria, son of Charles V and brother of Philip II, King of Spain. Rivalries and personal ambitions intersected in this turbulent Mediterranean context.

'Ilj 'Ali and the Conquest of Tunis

The capture of Tunis in 1569 was the work of 'Ilj 'Ali, a renegade who had become an important dignitary in the empire. He was born in a small town in Calabria, a poor region in the south of Italy whose shores were often attacked by corsairs. During one of these incursions, he was captured and became a galley slave in the service of the rais, his master. To escape this difficult position, he converted to Islam. His new status enabled him to accompany his master on raids, build up a small fortune, and eventually charter a frigate to work for him. In 1560, when the Christian fleet tried to attack the islands of Kerkennah, which were then under the control of Dargouth Pasha, 'Ilj 'Ali was charged with obtaining support from Istanbul. He was very successful: the sultan agreed to send Piali Pasha, his admiral, to join the battle. The two men won a major victory by destroying the strongest Spanish ships and taking more than ten thousand men as prisoners following their capture of the forts built by the Christians on the island. 'Ilj 'Ali's reputation was secured.

In 1565, Dargouth asked for 'Ilj 'Ali's help in the war against Malta. Hassan ibn Khayriddine, 'Ilj 'Ali, and Dargouth besieged the island. The latter died there on June 18, 1565. 'Ilj 'Ali's great courage on the battlefield stood out. Piali Pasha appointed him governor of Tripoli, replacing Dargouth, and charged him with organizing the funeral of the great corsair.

His post in Tripoli, which he held for two-and-half years, allowed him to enrich himself considerably. He amassed fabulous wealth from the Christian ships he continued to pursue in the Mediterranean and also got hold of part of Dargouth's inheritance.[1] However, Istanbul, which continued to oversee the orderly running of its provinces, sent a message to the governor of Algiers (which then included Tripoli) dated November 21, 1565, with the order to relinquish Dargouth Pasha's personal treasury and facilitate its return to Istanbul, leaving both goods and money untouched.[2]

Thanks to his friendship with Piali Pasha, in March 1568 'Ilj 'Ali received the coveted post of Pasha of Algiers. This was a highly sought-after office because of the prestige and riches that it afforded whoever held it. Since January 1567, the *oujak* had been governed by Muhammad Pasha, son of Salah Rais, who had replaced his father when he died from the plague in May 1556 while preparing a major attack against Mers el-Kebir and Oran. To appoint 'Ilj 'Ali to this post, a pretext was needed to dismiss Muhammad Pasha. One came in the form of a complaint brought by the people of Constantine, on whom Muhammad Pasha had cracked down severely after they accused the caid of rape and drove him from Constantine. This proved enough to drive Muhammad Pasha from his post. Thanks to his connections and his wealth, 'Ilj 'Ali now found himself at the head of the richest *oujak* in the Maghreb. He left Tripoli, entrusting it to Yahya.

The Government of 'Ilj 'Ali in Algiers

'Ilj 'Ali, now based in Algiers, was driven by dual ambitions: to weaken the Spanish in the Mediterranean and to bring back as many Moriscos as possible to populate the city with people renowned for their expertise in agriculture and trade. He committed himself fully to the uprising the Moriscos were planning. He set into motion a great force, made up of 14,000 arquebusiers, sixty thousand Arab soldiers, and four hundred camels carrying gunpowder in an attempt to mount a diversionary attack against Oran, a Spanish presidio, and land with his ships on the coast of Spain. On Holy Wednesday, he sent forty galliots to Almería to await the signal that the uprising had succeeded. But the plot had been discovered, and the uprising failed. The Beylerbey of Algiers did not abandon this goal and continued to supply the Moriscos with material support, munitions, and hardened soldiers to supervise them. With his plan for Spain temporarily deferred, he turned his attention to Tunis.

The Overland Expedition against Tunis

This expedition seems to have been part of the larger plan, envisioned by Khayriddine Pasha, to unify the coastal cities of the Maghreb and to weaken the Spanish in the Mediterranean. There are many explanations for it. According to Haedo, who was always well informed, 'Ilj 'Ali was responding to the requests of certain notables who were exasperated by the unfair policies of their sultan. Staying true to his tendency to distort names, confusing official titles with their surnames, the Spanish priest wrote:

> Hamida persecuted his father's supporters, who were unable to suffer his tyranny nor that of his ministers, men of low birth, whom Hamida, in order to take down the nobility, had raised in status and to whom he had given the most important responsibilities and offices, writing several times to Ochali, as soon as he became king of Algiers, asking that he come to Tunis and promising to deliver the kingdom and the city to him. The three main people who made these propositions were Ben Djibara, caïd of the cavalry, secretly in revolt against the king, the caïd BouTaïb, and the caïd Alkader.[3]

In these three characters, somewhat products of Haedo's imagination, I believe I can recognize Abu al-Tayyib al-Khaddar, minister of the sultan of Tunis, and maybe the Caid al-Jbira, a kind of military steward. This version of the facts was confirmed by Ibn abi Dinar, who draws on what he was told by the city's notables to add to what is known about this episode: Abu al-Tayyib al-Khaddar, minister and relative by marriage to Ahmad al-Hafsi, known as Hmida Sultan, had heard it from the mouth of the King of Tunis, who said that if he was attacked by 'Ilj 'Ali, he would be incapable of defending himself. Animosity existed between Hmida and 'Ilj 'Ali, dating back to the time when the renegade was Pasha of Tripoli. Abu al-Tayyib al-Khaddar, who had reason to be concerned about the king's unfair attitude, reported this confession to the Pasha of Algiers, who rushed to attack Tunis.[4] In the Western sources, we learn that 'Ilj 'Ali wanted to drive the Spanish from La Goulette because a major expedition was being prepared against the Turks, and this enclave helped to replenish the Iberian galleys. Together, these two goals justified an attack against Tunis and La Goulette.

In October 1569, 'Ilj 'Ali set out toward the east at the head of an army composed of five thousand musketeers and six thousand Kabyles. In Beja, he encountered Moulay Hmida, Sultan of Tunis, with thirty thousand men, insecure and weak in the face of the Turks.[5] A sham battle occurred in which soldiers in the service of the Hafsid prince abandoned him and rallied behind the Turks, forcing the sultan to take refuge in the fort of La Goulette. The army of 'Ilj 'Ali entered Tunis. He stayed for four months, pacified part of the area, and then returned to Algiers, leaving behind his lieutenant Ramadan with some thousand Turks and as many Zwawa (Berbers from Algiers). Haedo describes the same event but says that there were three thousand Zwawa under the command of the Caid Muhammad, a Neapolitan renegade of Ramadan's.[6] For now, Tunis was partially occupied by the Turks. The Spanish remained in La Goulette.

After having entrusted the city to Ramadan, 'Ilj 'Ali returned to Algiers in April 1570. It was a dark period for him. His relations with the Janissaries were poor. Fearing attack from his own soldiers, he left the palace of Jenina, residence of the pashas, and settled far away in a fort. He spent a year in solitude. In April 1571, he resumed his attacks on La Goulette. He prepared his fleet and headed towards Istanbul to obtain the necessary authorization. On his journey, he encountered galleys of the order of Malta; he succeeded in capturing several, changed course, and returned to Algiers with his ships decorated with flags and great spoils. This money likely allowed him to buy the goodwill of the soldiers and consider another assault on La Goulette. But while he was preparing his fleet for this attack, with his second-in-command, Mami Courso, leader of the rais of Algiers, he received the order to participate in the battle of Lépante.

The Battle of Lépante and the Meteoric Rise of 'Ilj 'Ali

On October 7, 1571, the Turkish fleet found itself facing a coalition composed of the Republic of Venice, the states of Pope Pius V, and Don Juan of Austria, the illegitimate son of Charles V. This was the largest naval battle of the century: nearly the entire Ottoman fleet was annihilated. Over the course of the fighting, during which the Ottoman admiral perished, 'Ilj 'Ali managed to leap aboard one of the galleys of Malta and confiscate the banner of the knights, which he then took with him to Istanbul. This trophy earned him the name Kilidj 'Ali (the sword), and he was granted the high office of grand admiral while maintaining his position as Beylerbey of Algiers along with all its privileges. He established himself in Istanbul and entrusted Algiers to one of his lieutenants, 'Arab Ahmad. The former Calabrian renegade was destined for great things, for the powers of the grand admiral were enormous. Everything connected to the navy fell under the purview of this office: islands, coasts, ports, and arsenals. The revenues were considerable, too, for the grand admiral had the right to one-fifth of everything that was taken at sea.

In the battle of Lépante, the Ottomans lost a large number of their galleys. Kilidj 'Ali responded rapidly by calling on the leaders among his friends to rebuild his fleet, dividing the labor among several shipyards. In less than two years, he was able to present the sultan with a fleet of 240 galleys, better armed than those that had been destroyed. The reconstruction of the imperial fleet facilitated the attack on Tunis shortly after.

Tunis under the Safekeeping of *Ramadan*, October 1569–May 1573

Tunis was controlled by the Turks of Algiers beginning in the fall of 1569. Ramadan governed on behalf of the Pasha of Algiers. Who was this man, the right hand of Kilidj 'Ali? His origins are obscure. We know that he was a young Sardinian captive, sold to a Turk who taught him Turkish and Arabic, which is why some considered him a Turk.[7] Ramadan began his career as a caid and took a Corsican renegade as his wife. When he took charge of Tunis, the city had only recently been conquered and was in a difficult situation, cut off from its hinterland and threatened by the Spanish fort in La Goulette. He did not make any grand gestures, save for a few skirmishes against the Christians of La Goulette. On March 11, 1572, he was appointed *wakil* of Kilidj 'Ali in Tunis, Sousse, Kairouan, Monastir, Djerba, and Bizerte.[8] His nomination was supported by a recommendation from Abu al-Tayyib al-Khaddar and the notables of Tunis. On April 8, 1573, the sultan confirmed his appointment as *mouhafidh*, or governor of the province.[9] Several days later, on April 16, 1573, Haydar was appointed Beylerbey of Tunis. These successive, sometimes even contradictory appointments were likely the result of negotiations in Istanbul amongst the various contenders. Even before Tunis and La Goulette were fully occupied by the Ottoman Turks, Haydar was appointed governor. It was while holding this office that he participated in the siege of the city.

Don Juan Attacks Tunis

After the victory at Lépante, Spain turned away from the Mediterranean. Don Juan received the order to destroy the fortifications at La Goulette and along the entire coastline. But the young Spanish prince had other plans. Upon learning that some of Kilidj 'Ali's galleys had been damaged by a series of storms and were immobilized, Don Juan decided to disobey orders and attack and occupy Tunis. On October 7, 1573, he left Sicily with a strong armada and conquered Tunis without difficulty. The fleet he mobilized was massive: 107 galleys, thirty-one vessels, in addition to the galleon belonging to the Grand Duke of Tuscany and many vessels belonging to wealthy individuals. The soldiers were from different nations: thirteen thousand Italians, nine thousand Spanish, and five thousand Germans. Don Juan is said to have had the intention of creating a Christian state in Barbary. Meanwhile, in Istanbul, Kilidj 'Ali was accused of having supported Don Juan's attack. For this he suffered the sultan's fury and almost lost his life. To wash off the rumors of his treason, Kilidj 'Ali asked permission to set sail for Tunis.

When Don Juan entered Tunis, Ramadan did not confront him, but retreated to Hammamet where he fought several Arab troops backed by the Spanish. Then, he headed to Kairouan. Tunis was abandoned to the Spanish, who, under difficult conditions, began to construct a fortress, which the people of Tunis called a *bastioun*. Work on the fortress began on November 11, 1573. The Spanish lacked proper materials, money, and a workforce. The work was entrusted to Count Serbelloni, who left behind a testimony about life in the fortress, which was hastily constructed in eight months.[10]

In Istanbul, it had long been decided that an expedition would be sent to Tunis. It was preceded by a land attack that began at the end of June 1574. The Spanish learned of the arrival of Haydar, the Governor of Tripoli and Tunis, leading four thousand men, Turks and Arabs; the sheikhs of Djerba and Kairouan with six thousand horsemen; as well as combatants from Constantine and Bône. On July 1, Serbelloni was informed of the approaching Turkish fleet. On July 13, the fleet anchored within sight of La Goulette. It was commanded by Kilidj 'Ali, though the expedition itself was under the authority of Sinan Pasha, general of the land troops. Kilidj 'Ali organized four batteries. The first two were sent toward the bastion; they were led by Haydar and the Caid of Kairouan, both under the command of Hassan Pasha, the Bosnian. The other two batteries were sent against La Goulette, one led by 'Arab Ahmad, and the by Kilidj 'Ali himself.

Once landed, the soldiers began to dig trenches in order to approach Tunis. The general-in-chief commanded the troops that had come by land, under Haydar, to begin laying siege to the city. The Spanish retreated to their bastion. Sultan Ahmad, who was supposed to be responsible for controlling the surrounding countryside with his men, took refuge in the fort of La Goulette instead.

On August 10, Ramadan, who had left Tunis before the Spanish arrived, returned with five thousand men. Serbelloni received the order to reinforce La Goulette, but the fortress was already under fire and it fell on Monday, August 23. The entire garrison was massacred, save three hundred men who were taken prisoner. Serbelloni confessed that several of his men, paralyzed with fear, had defected to the Turkish camp. The Turks began to attack the bastion of Tunis on August 24. On September 6, an all-out assault began, and the fortress fell after a week of resistance. Serbelloni was taken prisoner and brought to Istanbul, where he was exchanged a year later for Muslim prisoners.

The Sad End of the Hafsids

The throne of Tunis had been occupied by Sultan Ahmad since 1543, and he had faced repeated setbacks. He had taken refuge with his family in La Goulette since his defeat by Kilidj 'Ali in 1569. When Don Juan occupied Tunis on October 7, 1573, he installed Muhammad, brother of Sultan Ahmad, on the throne.

The reign of Muhammad, enthroned by the Spanish, was fleeting, lasting from October 14, 1573, to August 23, 1574. Muhammad was the reigning king's half-brother. He had long wandered with his father al-Hassan and had then resided in a fief in Hammamet until his brother, Ahmad, demanded that the Spanish intern him in Sicily. He lived there from 1556 with his family until Don Juan brought him and put him on the throne on October 14, 1573. On August 23, 1574, he was taken by the Turks to Istanbul, where they installed him under honorable conditions. We even find him embroiled in intrigues fomented by the Grand Vizier to discredit Sinan Pasha by accusing him of having concealed a valuable jewel. We then lose track of him in Istanbul. Two of his sons, Nasir and another, were killed during the capture of La Goulette. The youngest, 'Abd al-Rahman, stayed in Palermo and became head of the family, responsible for his mother and the widows of his two dead brothers. His financial difficulties forced him to ask the Spanish authorities for support.

As for Ahmad Sultan, he burst into tears the moment he was told that he must leave Tunis. His son Hmida comforted him and reminded him that he must return himself to God. There are two versions of the story of his

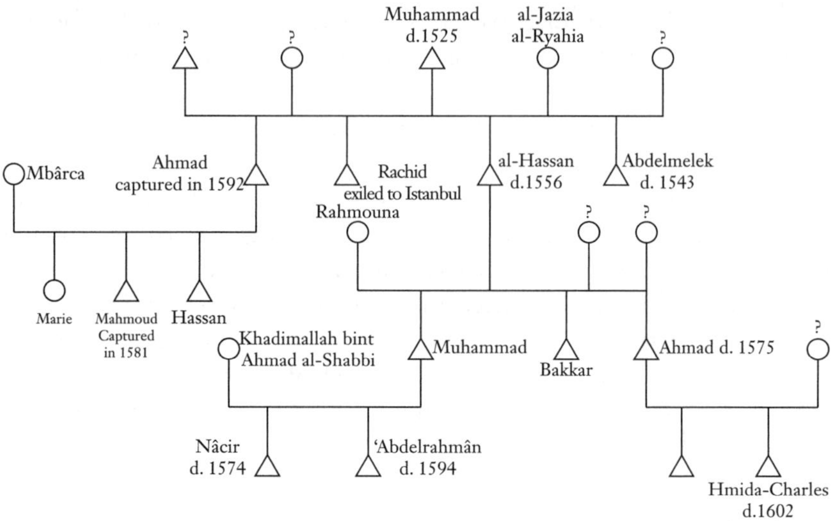

3. Genealogy of the last Hafsids

removal, one from Ibn abi Dinar and one from the Spanish sources. Ibn abi Dinar says that the king went into voluntary exile, for he refused to share power with his brother, in keeping with an Islamic tradition that forbids two kings from meeting except on the battlefield. The Spanish version is summarized in this official letter from Don Juan:

> In order to deal with the government of the Moors, it seemed to me a good idea to leave in Tunis the Infante Mohamed because he is a careful and clever person, qualities that were felt to be missing in King Amida [sic], his brother, who moreover demonstrated neither faith nor gratitude toward S.M.[11]

Ahmad Sultan was ordered not to leave La Goulette until the 13th of October, when the war council decided to intern him in Sicily. The fallen king, discredited and suspected of duplicity with regards to the Spanish Kingdom, was placed along with his family aboard a galley commanded by Don Juan. They landed in Palermo, where they stayed for a few days with his uncle, Ahmad, before continuing with Don Juan to Naples. A witness provided this description:

> He was taken prisoner in the Castle of Saint Elme where I saw him in 1574. He seemed very old, and I judged by sight that he must have been at least eighty. However, the governor of this castle assured me that every day he slept with a Moorish slave who was his concubine. Of his two sons, there was one who was lame, very ugly, and of an unpleasant appearance but whom he loved passionately and whom he always had in his bedroom. He could not tolerate the presence of the other, even though he was good looking, of a pleasant temperament, and knew how to handle weapons perfectly and ride a horse without a saddle or bridle, following the custom of his nation. All of these qualities made it so that he was permitted to wander around town as he wanted to and destined him to succeed Mouhamad: for the hatred his father felt towards him was one reason he attracted the friendship of the Spaniards.[12]

Ever since Ahmad Sultan had ordered his father's eyes gouged out, his cruelty had been legendary. Perhaps what he detested in his father, and later in his son, was their subservience to the Spanish and their lack of Bedouin pride, which he had inherited from his grandmother, al-Jaziya bint Awlad Yahia. His father and son were both perfect servants of Spain, whereas he had tried to use the Spanish to defend himself against the Turks.

Sultan Ahmad, forced to pass time with Don Juan on board his galleys, established himself in Naples for a time. Always under close watch, he then returned to Palermo during the summer of 1574, when the fate of his capital was being determined. Don Juan, warned too late of the imminent Ottoman attack on Tunis, chose to protect the Sicilian coastline and abandon the presidio of La Goulette to its fate. When the Ottoman fleet left the western Mediterranean and headed toward Istanbul at the end of October, Don Juan authorized Ahmad Sultan to return to Barbary to try and recover his throne. With La Goulette and Tunis lost, the return of the Hafsid king was considered preferable to the installation of the Turks, for everyone knew of their special relationship with the corsairs. But Don Juan of Austria's perspective was not shared by the Governor of Sicily, who addressed a letter to the King of Spain informing him that:

> Amida has carried on in such a way that he has persuaded me that his soul and his intentions are overflowing with wickedness

> vis-à-vis the interests of V.M. A shrewd and cunning man, he seeks to conceal it but it reveals itself in the great curiosity he has to inquire. . . . Furthermore, I was warned on several occasions, by different sources, and even by his own servants that as soon as he steps foot in Barbary, he intends to go to the Turks and to make a deal with them. I believe that his reappearance in Barbary would be harmful and as a result I am of the opinion, now moreso than ever, that it is not in the best interest of V.M. to send him back.[13]

In February 1575, the Sicilian governor's suspicion resulted in the transfer of the prisoner-king from Palermo, where he had been free to wander, to Castellamare, a more isolated location. This decision exasperated the king, who threw his burnous on the floor and began to cry out of despair. Then, to calm himself, he drew upon his string of coral and shells while muttering a few prayers. In his new residence, he was set up comfortably with his wife, his servants, and his favorite son. He was allowed to take part in the life of the city, for example, by attending the Easter celebration in the cathedral. This was a prudent decision by the authorities, who wanted to treat him decently in case they needed him later.

However, fate had decided otherwise. The plague arrived in Palermo in June. Moulay Hassan was transferred, along with the entire government of Sicily, to Termini. He died there suddenly in August 1575, and without the sources that announced his death specifying the cause. His embalmed body was returned to Tunis in November. He was buried in the mausoleum of Sidi Qasim al-Jalizi.[14]

Moulay Hassan's death did not go unnoticed: the Pasha of Tunis had his remains displayed, probably to show that the Hafsid dynasty was definitively over. But was it really? The fallen King of Tunis left behind a wife and two sons, one of whom, 'Abd al-'Aziz, who was "lame, weak in content and form," was allowed to return to Barbary. The second son, unloved by his father, established himself in Naples. He had a unique destiny: he soon embraced Christianity under the name Charles of Austria.

A Hafsid Converted to Christianity

How was Hmida introduced to Catholicism? During his Neopolitan sojourn, he frequently visited the Carthusian monks of the monastery of Saint Martin. He was baptized in the chapel of Castel Nuovo and spent the rest of his life at the hospital of the Franciscan fathers, though it is unclear whether he was there to be cared for or to care for others. He died there in 1601.

On his tombstone was inscribed:

> Here lies the son of the king of Tunis Amida, who became Charles of Austria by virtue of the holy water. In his tenderness for this monastery, he bequeathed it all his possessions, so that his prayers opened the kingdom of heaven to him. Magnanimous heart, marked by piety and tears, he lived and died under the habit of the Friars Minor. In the year of our lord, 1601.[15]

The son of the King of Tunis lived for more than a quarter of a century and died as a Christian. His conversion to Christianity was a sober decision that marked a total rupture with his past. In becoming a Franciscan monk, Hmida-Charles opted for the cloister and celibacy, concluding his life among the sick and leaving behind the court and its splendor. The news appears to have destroyed his family, and one cannot ignore the strange concordance between the date of Hmida's conversion—August 11, 1575—and the sudden, inexplicable death of his father some days later. Hmida's conversion must have been an emotional shock to a person already psychologically drained by exile and constant surveillance. Moreover, Hmida's repudiation of Islam was not just a private ordeal, but a drama that discredited the ruling family and extinguished Sultan Ahmad's hopes of retaking the throne of his ancestors.

The era of the Hafsids was ended, although from time to time claimants to the throne would resurface. All traces of them had disappeared completely by 1593.

As for Kilidj 'Ali, this young, scrappy man, spitefully known as the *fartas*, continued his brilliant career until his death on June 27, 1587 at eighty years old. He was a strange and melancholy figure. Was it his repudiation of Islam that tortured him? The bishop of Dax, François of Noailles, who knew him in Istanbul, claimed that he remained Christian his entire life. Nevertheless, Kilidj 'Ali refused Philip II's offer to govern over Sicily or another province in exchange for abandoning Algiers.[16]

10

The Age of Uncertainty: 1574–87

The victory against the Spanish brought the conquered territories into the fold of the empire. After the long crisis of the sixteenth century, a new period began, during which populations witnessed a centuries-old dynasty disappear in turmoil. The Spanish soldiers' three-decade presence in La Goulette and their yearlong occupation of Tunis were harshly felt. Would Turkish power bring stability and security and do away with the unjust policies of the last Hafsids? Was the military victory of 1574 a rupture in the history of Ifriqiya, the abrupt beginning of the Ottomanization of the land? Or was it the beginning of a long process of political change and social reconfiguration, in which the Turkish element would be central? The first thirteen years of the Ottoman occupation of Tunis and of some of the Ifriqiyan territories was a period of great instability, unrest, and uncertainty about how the province would be managed: administrative, judicial, and military institutions were being painstakingly assembled.

Sinan Pasha had been authorized to grant senior positions to those who deserved them and who were distinguished by their heroic deeds or support for the Ottomans. Acting in the name of the sultan—and with urgency, for the fleet needed to return to Istanbul before the fall storms—Sinan Pasha trusted the new conquest of Tunis to a beylerbey, a provincial governor with the rank of "pasha of two *tugh*" (ponytails). This senior official occupied the middle of three ranks in the Ottoman administrative hierarchy. The sultan appointed him as his representative for one year, with the possibility of renewal. He had significant civil and military responsibilities.

And so Tunis became an *iyala* made up of multiple *oujak*s (regions or houses), in which garrisons were established. The titles held by the senior officials vary in the documents: they are called *wali*, or *beylerbey*, or *mirmiran*, or *amir al-umara*. Leading the provinces were governors called beys, amirs, or caids.

The First Pashalik of Haydar: May 1573–75

Before setting sail, Sinan Pasha charged Haydar with governing the province. In many ways, Haydar seemed to be the right man for the job. He knew the Maghreb well and had played a prominent role during the decisive battle of July and August. We don't know whether the new pasha had instructions to follow or if he was authorized to act as he saw fit given the particular circumstances of the new conquest. The pasha had established his own council, or *diwan*, a true place of power, in which local men, notably *ulama* and jurists, governed alongside the Turks. All the policies of the regency were formulated and carried out under the authority of this council.

The interior territories, meanwhile, submitted to the caids, officials designated by the pasha, who purchased their goods, maintained order, and levied taxes. A new judicial system was created in parallel: A Hanafi *qadi 'askar* accompanied the army. Hanafi jurists were later sent to develop new laws, resolve disputes, and dispense justice. The new judicial system established by the Ottoman Turks would continue after the end of the Hafsids. The Hafsid sultans held much of the power: they dealt with many matters themselves and delegated the rest to the *qadi*s. There were four judges in Tunis. At their head was an important figure—the great *qadi*, called *qadi al-jama'a*. Then came a judge of equal importance, *qadi al-ankiha* or the judge of marriages, followed by the *qadi al-mu'amalat* and *qadi al-ahla*.[1] In the provinces, the judges, considered deputies of the Ottoman Empire, were given the title of *na'ib*. The judicial system was complete with *mufti*s or juris consults to whom everyone could appeal for a judicial opinion.

Every Thursday, for one hour, the Hafsid sultan had presided over a judicial council made up of *qadi*s and *mufti*s to debate contentious issues. The Ottoman Turks did not alter this system much. However, they gave the Hanafi judge seniority of rank, followed by a Malaki judge, called a *na'ib*. In addition to the judges, *naqib al-ashraf* (or the trustee of the descendants of the Prophet) would attend. Before his return, Sinan Pasha designated a high-ranking judge, the *qadi al-qudah*, Hassine Effendi, to monitor the legitimacy of the measures being applied to Tunis and to determine the salaries of the Janissaries, judges, scribes, and civil servants of the diwan. Hassine Effendi moved to Tunis and put down roots there.

Haydar, who oversaw the implementation of all these measures, had extensive experience in the Maghreb. He had come from Tripoli in 1557 with the unit of Dargouth Pasha, who was fighting the Shabbia. He served as Governor of the city of Kairouan from 1557 to February 1560, when the Turks abandoned it under pressure from the nomads of the surrounding steppes and because of the great misery that hung over the city. Many Turkish soldiers deserted Kairouan. On many occasions, Haydar himself was tempted to abandon the city to its decay, before he was driven out, probably by Arab warriors loyal to the Hafsid sultan.[2] We do not know Kairouan's fate in the decade that followed, but it seems certain that by 1569, it was again in the hands of the Turks, led by Haydar: he issued a currency bearing his name, the haydari dinar, which remained in circulation until the seventeenth century. As soon as the high powers decided to undertake the expedition to Tunis, Haydar set off overland. His soldiers contributed effectively to the siege of Tunis and of La Goulette (from July 13 to September 13, 1574).

The choice of Haydar as the first governor may have seemed wise, but his management style proved to be ineffective. The administration of Tunis was not functioning properly, and difficulties quickly arose. The new province was ungovernable, both because of the Janissary army—guaranteed impunity by its geographic distance from Istanbul and the strong-headed men who composed it—and deprivation, diversion, and greed practiced by various officials and their subordinates. Furthermore, the province was neither completely pacified nor clearly delimited. The governors of the neighboring provinces of Tripoli and Algiers each tried to subsume the territory and subject to their authority the recalcitrant populations, whose main objective was to avoid paying increasingly cumbersome taxes.

During his first two years as governor, Haydar Pasha busied himself with reestablishing order and checking the power of the Janissaries, all while working to assure his personal fortune and that of his acolytes. Complaints began arriving at the top, accusing Haydar of colluding with his *defterdar* Muhammad, the official charged with controlling the regency's imports and expenses. It seems that both men had pocketed considerable sums belonging to the state, including all the provisions left by the Spanish after they abandoned La Goulette and the bastion of Bab al-Bhar. A comptroller, the *defterdar* Mustafa, who was sent to Tunis to investigate these numerous complaints, accused Haydar of forgery and embezzlement. His damning report went unanswered. Haydar was unconcerned, and even charged with governing Tripoli as well as Tunis after the death of his pasha Mustafa in 1575. He was removed from his position as governor of Tunis not long after, but remained Governor of Tripoli.

The Government of Rajeb Pasha: 1575–76

The arrival of Rajeb Pasha was welcomed in Tunis, but he too quickly became the subject of complaints from a Tunisian notable, Abu al-Tayyib al-Khaddar, Governor of Kairouan. In a long letter, Abu al-Tayyib enumerated all the abuses for which he considered Rajeb Pasha liable: confiscating and selling goods belonging to local proprietors, whom he imprisoned; misappropriating tax revenues for his own profit; reclaiming real estate owned by Hafsid sultans; selling oil at prohibitive prices; misappropriating revenues from the *habous*; colluding with the caids; and trafficking in agricultural products with "the infidels." He had even, according to Abu al-Tayyib, gone so far as to devalue the currency by coining a new, worthless one, using the expertise of a Jew named Moussala. These maneuvers profited Rajeb Pasha while impoverishing a population already under strain. The pasha carried out these fraudulent moves with the help of a number of accomplices, whom he paid with public money even though they exercised no official function.[3] Finally, the complaints against Rajeb Pasha were heard and resulted in an order to demote him and to bring him and his accomplices to justice.

The Second Government of Haydar Pasha, August 1576 to October 1577

In August 1576, Haydar was again named Governor of Tunis. In his correspondence with the imperial capital, he complained constantly of the poverty of the province and proposed solutions to remedy it. The Spanish attacks against Kerkennah and Mahdia in June 1576 forced him to recruit new soldiers even while the insecurity was interrupting tax revenues. Foreseeing more enemy attacks, he also proposed to fortify the ports of Bizerte and Tunis. To address the scarcity of resources, he asked that the cities of Kairouan and Monastir, both under the control of Tripoli since 1571, be joined to Tunis.[4] Istanbul granted him this request.

If we are to believe the repeated warnings sent by Istanbul, Haydar Pasha's management from 1576 to 1577 was disastrous. Throughout these first years of the Turkish government, complaints against the different pashas and their associates proliferated. We can assume, based on the established facts, that these denunciations also served as a pretext to undermine the senior officials in power and support other candidates. It is hard to believe that integrity alone motivated the plaintiffs, who were often local notables or Turkish officials, to appeal to the high court that represented the Great Diwan of Istanbul, in which each party had its supporters. Despite the grave malfeasance of which he was accused, Haydar Pasha, who was probably supported in the imperial capital, remained in power. Once again, he governed Tunis and Tripoli. This joint stewardship enlarged the scope of his post, even though the regions over which he exercised authority were discontinuous: many caids enjoyed considerable autonomy and the interior areas were not completely pacified. These difficulties did not discourage the pasha, who had his heart set on carving out a province that united Tunis and Tripoli. But Haydar's grand plan was thwarted when Abu al-Tayyib al-Khaddar—former minister of the Hafsids and Governor of Kairouan since the arrival of the Turks, known for having played an important role in establishing the Turks in Tunis—was appointed the new Bey of Tripoli.

Abu al-Tayyib al-Khaddar: A Turkophile Notable

Abu al-Tayyib al-Khaddar belonged to a prominent old family. As the minister of Ahmad al-Hafsi, with whom he was allied, Abu al-Tayyib had been closely involved in 'Ilj 'Ali's arrival in Tunis in 1569. A powerful man, he traveled often to Istanbul and we can follow his trail from the sultan's firmans, where he is mentioned as a key figure in the campaign of 1574.[5] He was clever, and well established in Istanbul, where he was considered a vital partner and enjoyed a comfortable pension, a *ma'ash*, in exchange for services rendered. He was even approached to oversee record keeping and the control of *miri* land (land that had been returned to the state) once the conquest of Tunis had been achieved.[6] This cadastral system was never established, which made possible the rampant corruption by officials in positions of power. Abu al-Tayyib al-Khaddar was part of the network of 'Ilj 'Ali and Ramadan Pasha, and he put his talent and his position as a local notable at their service. In a letter addressed to the sultan, he raved about Ramadan Pasha, praising the governor's good policies and his honorable behavior toward the local population.[7] It was following this letter that Istanbul accorded to Ramadan all the territories then occupied by the Ottomans: Tunis, Sousse, Djerba, Kairouan, Monastir, and Bizerte.

Throughout this period, Abu al-Tayyib was Bey of the *sanjak* of Kairouan, a post he had held since the arrival of the Ottomans and the appointment of Haydar, who then held the post, as first pasha. Did Abu al-Tayyib plead the city's case to Istanbul? A firman dated August 1576 recommended to the Beylerbey of Tunis that he oversee the security and repopulation of Kairouan; the completion of various public works in progress, notably at the citadel; and the payment of the Janissaries' salaries. The Ottoman state was even ready to pay the deficit, if necessary.[8]

Can we see behind this interest in Kairouan a particular bias from Abu al-Tayyib, who planned to carve out an independent territory? That's what the order of events suggests. On October 18, 1576, he was designated the new Bey of Tripoli, and the admiral was ordered to facilitate his voyage. Haydar was also ordered to prepare for the arrival of the new bey and establish good relations with him in the interest of the state.[9]

What happened between the two men? Did Haydar Pasha worry about the rise of a Tunisian notable close to 'Ilj 'Ali and Ramadan Pasha—one who, moreover, had a network in Istanbul? On July 29, 1577, Abu al-Tayyib was killed and his belongings were confiscated by the *makhzan*.[10] It seems likely that there was a link between Abu al-Tayyib al-Khaddar's appointment to the head of the beylikat of Tripoli and his assassination, but no source describes the circumstances of the murder. No one alleged that Haydar was involved, although he continued to be accused of many other wrongdoings (including claiming Abu al-Tayyib's estate, selling the assets of plague victims for his own profit, and seizing goods destined for the state).

Abu al-Tayyib al-Khaddar's Estate

After the death of the *faqih* Abu al-Tayyib al-Khaddar, his palace was confiscated by the state. It was a big house in Tunis comprising a *sabbat*, a *diwan*, and a *makhzan* (warehouse). In August 1577 (the owner was killed on July 29), it was estimated to be worth 100 dinars *nwacirs*. Four people, not identified by the document, immediately bought the house for a sum of 300 dinars. On the same day, a new buyer presented himself: Muhammad al-Harrar al-Yamani, known as 'Abid, who acquired the house for 450 dinars.[11]

This document seems to exonerate Haydar, whose name does not appear in any of the transactions, but it also shows profits from quick successive sales. It was probably this capital gain that was diverted to profit the governor, and not the building itself. Following these sales, the affair was brought in front of the courts: Abu al-Tayyib's brother brought documents showing that he was the owner of half the palace, and on the basis of this

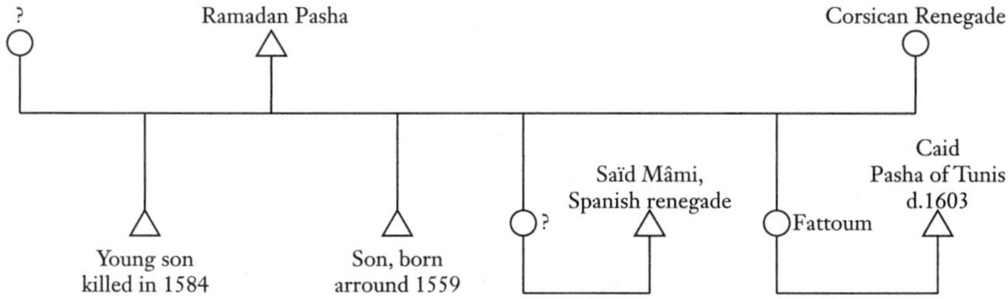

4. The house of Ramadan Pasha

title, he asked for his right to the other half. He was told that sales made to profit the *makhzan* were final and not open to appeal.[12]

Did this all take place because of the pasha? As a result, Haydar was effectively demoted from his duties as the Pasha of Tripoli, and, in August 1577, the Great Diwan named a new pasha to lead Tripoli, Tshakarji Hassan. He was unable to govern the province because it was plagued by disorder and insubordination.[13] A short time later, Haydar departed Tunis, leaving it again to Ramadan Pasha.

The Government of Ramadan Pasha: October 1577 to May 1579

Ramadan Pasha knew Tunis well, for he had already governed it on 'Ilj 'Ali's behalf from 1569 to 1573. At that time, Don Juan had occupied the city and Ramadan had retreated to Hammamet, where he successfully prevented the landing of Prince Muhammad al-Hafsi, who was backed by several Spanish galleys. He also joined armies with the Turkish Janissaries of Kairouan under Haydar's command in preparation for the assault on Tunis. He ultimately did not take part in this attack because he was appointed to govern Algiers as pasha, a post he held from 1573 to 1577. In 1575, he came to the rescue of the King of Fes, who had been dethroned by a usurper. Ramadan helped him win back his throne and returned with considerable plunder. Shortly thereafter, the sultan had him replaced by Hassan Pasha, one of 'Ilj 'Ali's Venetian renegades, who arrived in Algiers on June 29, 1577. Ramadan left for Istanbul on August 19, and the sultan quickly granted him the pashalik of Tunis. He arrived there in October 1577.

Meanwhile, Haydar pleaded his own case so well in Istanbul that he was again made Governor of Tripoli. He would do everything in his power to expand the territory that he governed. In 1578, he persuaded the central administration to link together Kairouan, Sousse, and the region from Gafsa to Tripoli. However, this decision was not implemented because of opposition from the Janissaries.[14] Ramadan went on to govern Tunis for two years, where he was very well liked. He then left Tunis to govern Tlemcen, and was replaced by Ja'far Pasha.

The Government of Ja'far Pasha: September 2, 1579 to March 3, 1580

Ja'far Pasha was a eunuch of Hungarian origin who belonged to the house of the sultan. He was captured as a young child along with several members of his family. Because of their good looks they were offered to the mother of the sultan. Ja'far therefore grew up close to power and benefited by being appointed to many pashaliks. Known for being just and righteous, but also firm, he was probably sent to Tunis to reestablish order there.[15] Ja'far Pasha tried to fix the chaos created by Haydar's poor management, but he failed to do so and asked to be relieved of his post in March 1580.

At the same time, Haydar, still Pasha of Tripoli, was called to Istanbul. As for Ja'far, after a period in the imperial capital he would be named Pasha of Algiers. He arrived there in August 1581 to replace Hassan Veneziano, the subject of numerous complaints. Ja'far Pasha remained in Algiers until May 1582.

The Return of Haydar, 1581–84

Haydar, who had been serving in Tripoli since 1578, continued all sorts of abusive practices. An investigator sent by the sultan issued a damning report on his rule, so bad that the pasha was summoned by the Great Diwan in 1580. Before this highest authority, he dismissed the charges against him and claimed to have executed his duties loyally. The Diwan accepted his defense and named him Governor of Kafa, on the Black Sea, which was evidently not his wish. Thanks to his contacts in the sultan's entourage, he instead secured an appointment to Tripoli and Tunis in 1581. The Ottoman archives show the sums that he paid to obtain this post: the pashas, when they were named to a post, paid a senior imperial official who brought them the news—a "royalty for good news," *halwane bshara.* Haydar was allowed to return to Tunis, accompanied by his treasurer Muhammad and his brother Ahmad, who had been named Governor of Kairouan, Gabes, and Fezzan.[16] It was through his brother that Haydar, more powerful than ever and driven by great ambitions, took back the Maghreb. Without harboring pretensions for the pashalik of Algiers—the turf of the great admirals—he hurried to construct a beylerbeylik that would regroup the pacified territories stretching from Bizerte to Tripoli. To achieve his aims, he would inform the sultan of the troubles that plagued the cities administered autonomously by the caids in an attempt to make them look incompetent. He wrote to the Sultan that Kairouan, Sousse, and Gafsa, leased by the caids 'Ali, Muhammad, and Mourad for the sum of 70,000 gold coins, were experiencing problems and that a group of five hundred Janissaries had seized the taxes due to the state. But if the soldiers had confiscated state taxes, it was because the pasha and the caids were not paying them their salaries.

The Attempt at Hafsid Restoration

Haydar Pasha faced many challenges during his third mandate, notably the attempt to reestablish the Hafsid dynasty. A decade after the installation of the Ottoman Turks, some Hafsid pretenders, encouraged by the Spanish, still sought to take back the throne. In the years 1582 to 1583, the pretender Ahmad ibn Muhammad al-Hafsi tried to take back power with the help of twenty thousand Arabs. After having left his family in Palermo, he would roam the desert for a dozen years.

During the same period, Gafsa was revolting. Reinforcements were sent: a thousand soldiers came overland from Tripoli and artillery arrived by sea. The former pasha Rajeb (supposed to have been condemned for embezzlement some years prior) appeared before the city leading his cavalrymen. The forces assembled by Haydar Pasha quelled the uprising and retook the city of Gafsa. Meanwhile Mahmoud Bey, Governor of Fezzan, and his cavalrymen succeeded in occupying several villages in the south and reestablishing order there on behalf of Haydar Pasha. Haydar wanted to carve out a vast territory encompassing the south up to the region of Djebel Abiadh and Barca to control the trade routes between Tripoli and Egypt.[17]

However, this ambitious plan could not be realized because of the difficult Maghrebi terrain and the rivalries between the different governors and their houses. Successive appointments and dismissals highlight the lobbying that went on in Istanbul, where each high official was attempting to place his men in positions of power. In 1584, the aging Haydar left Tripoli and Tunis for good. His departure momentarily put Kilidj 'Ali's men back at the head of the Maghrebi provinces.

The Fleeting Return of Kilidj 'Ali's Circle, 1585–87

After Haydar's departure, a pasha by the name of Ahmad ibn Ali was appointed. He left behind an inscription in the mosque of the Kasbah, dated to 992 of the Hijra (1584–85), which gives the order to construct a minbar in the mosque, which had since become Hanafi.[18] But this pasha would not remain in Tunis for long. The year 1585 saw a power vacuum develop, for the pasha's *diwan* had suspended its meetings. The local population sent a delegation to Istanbul asking that judges, jurisconsults, and *ulama* be permitted to meet every Saturday to hear their grievances.[19]

Meanwhile, the province was auctioned off: a candidate for the post of pasha offered to pay Istanbul 18,000 florins in addition to the salaries of the Janissaries in exchange for Tunis, Sousse, Monastir, and Kairouan. After consulting the notables in Tunis, the Ottoman authorities refused, for they feared the stress the sale would place on the taxpayers.[20] This is one version of the story: it is more likely that Kilidj 'Ali Pasha, aging but still officially the Governor of Algiers, was working in Istanbul to place men from his house in the provinces of the Maghreb.

At this time, Kilidj 'Ali was still powerful. As well as being Captain Pasha, he was the third most powerful man in the Ottoman state, meaning that he had control over all maritime territories, including Algiers; this brought in substantial revenues, and explains his strategy of putting his own renegades at the head of the provinces of the Maghreb. The Janissaries wanted to disrupt this practice; their interest was in independence from Ottoman officials, which allowed them to shamelessly exploit the local populations.

Among Kilidj 'Ali's men was Ramadan Pasha, whose path we have followed up to October 1579. Now he was named Pasha of Tlemcen and ordered to wage war against the newly dissident King of Fes. The story that follows, told by Haedo, reveals the stakes of the appointments of high officials and the dangers faced by these men, who were frequently accused of conspiracies. On his way to Tlemcen, Ramadan arrived in Bizerte, the usual port for the departures and arrivals of pashas, to board the galley that would take him to his destination. While he prepared for his departure, a galley arrived from Algiers carrying several local people and the primary *bulukbashi* officers on their way to Istanbul to file complaints against their pasha Hassan Veneziano. Ramadan asked them not to continue their journey toward Istanbul, for fear that Kilidj 'Ali might suspect him of having instigated the complaints. Ramadan thus remained in Bizerte for five months, until March 15, 1580, when he went to Algiers to await his official appointment. But this never arrived, and Ja'far was named in his stead. On September 19, 1540, Ramadan left Algiers for Istanbul with Hassan Pasha, the Venetian.

In April 1582, Ramadan returned to Algiers. His mission was to return two French vessels captured by one of the great captains, Mourad Rais, despite the agreements prohibiting all attacks against the ships of friendly countries. Ramadan was not able to carry out this mission, for the corsairs opposed all negotiations with France. The rais greatly respected Mourad—the old sea dog—and did not want anyone to interfere with his interests. Ramadan left Algiers in August 1583 for Tripoli, where he was named governor. He was appointed at a time of unrest, and was ultimately unable to reestablish order. He died in 1584, poisoned by the ambassador of France—or, according to a more plausible theory, killed by Janissaries.[21] Kilidj 'Ali lost in Ramadan Pasha a loyal man who had served him for decades and built a network of alliances in the Maghreb.

Unlike Kilidj 'Ali, who does not seem to have left any descendants, Ramadan had a family, some of whom lived in the Maghreb. During his time in Algiers, he married a Corsican renegade who gave him a son, who was twenty-one years old when his father left Algiers (he was born in approx. 1559), and two daughters, one of whom married a rich Spanish renegade, Caid Mami, and the other Caid Khidr, the son of a Neapolitan renegade, himself Caid of Constantine.[22]

In September 1586, Caid Khidr would become Pasha of Tunis. Our source, Haedo, does not address the fact that Ramadan took another wife while he was in Tripoli. After Ramadan's death, his widow headed back toward Istanbul carrying an immense fortune of 800,000 ducats, four hundred Christian captives, and forty young slave girls. Arriving in Zakynthos, she was welcomed by the island's authorities. She continued on after a stopover, and during the next leg of her journey, her ship was attacked by the admiral of the Venetian fleet, Emo. He had two hundred Turkish soldiers on board killed, slaughtered the son of Ramadan in his mother's arms, had the young girls who accompanied the widow raped, and after cutting off their breasts, threw them into the sea. This event almost reignited the war between the Sublime Porte and Venice. When news of the attack reached Istanbul, the Venetian ambassador would have been imprisoned if not for the intervention of Sultan Safia, who was of Venetian origin and saved him from a certain death. Venice accepted all of Istanbul's terms of compensation, executing Emo, and bringing back Ramadan Pasha's widow along with her belongings and four hundred African slaves to replace the freed Christian captives.[23]

After the death of Ramadan, Tripoli was given to Ilyes, who governed it for several months without succeeding in restoring order.

Mustafa Pasha the Greek: 1585–86

Mustafa Pasha was a Greek renegade from the island of Xilo who had arrived in Algiers accompanying Hassan Pasha Veneziano, who had been appointed governor in 1577.[24] He therefore knew the region fairly well. Named Pasha of Tunis in 1585, Mustafa Pasha so abused his authority that his appointment lasted only months. He was replaced by Hassan Veneziano.

Hassan Pasha Veneziano: 1586 to June 1587—The Last Attempt to Unify the Oujaks of the Maghreb

Hassan Pasha successfully plotted to obtain the coveted post in Tunis. He received orders to investigate his predecessor and prevent him from leaving for Algiers before paying the soldiers and his taxes to the state. He arrived in Tunis to find chaos due to the complete insubordination of the Janissaries, who intervened in all political affairs. Throughout 1587, the sultan threatened to punish the Janissaries if they did not end their abuses. The same year, responding to a request made by the local populations, the sultan ordered the construction of a fort at La Goulette to protect the port.

In June 1587, Kilidj 'Ali died. The sultan eliminated the position of beylerbey and instead named a series of pashas with a temporary mandate of three years each. Hassan Veneziano Pasha permanently left Tunis at the end of 1587. He was named Pasha of Tripoli and shortly thereafter followed in the footsteps of his old master, becoming grand admiral. He died several years later after being poisoned by his rival Cigala.

The loss of Kilidj 'Ali and his men halted the dream of unifying the *oujak*s *of the* Maghreb. With the deaths of Kilidj 'Ali, Ramadan, and Hassan Veneziano, the era of the great corsairs—who came from poverty and rose to power as governors of the provinces, and even grand admirals—came to an end. These men, driven by great personal ambition, also had a political vision for the world around them and pursued their plans in the context of the Spanish–Turkish conflict. Beginning in 1587, new characters presided over the region's fate.

Fifteen years after the Ottoman victory, their conquest was not yet complete. The Hafsid pretenders were still at large, nurturing hopes of recovering their throne. The Shabbia were far from the scene and did not constitute a threat, but another brotherhood leader, Abu al-Gaith al-Quachach, rose to prominence in Tunis at the same time as the Turks and presented a powerful challenge to their authority. The Ottoman Turks were less concerned with pacifying relatively unfamiliar territory than they were with appeasing various social groups and involving them in the occupation. Everything would be decided on the ground, where new instruments of power were being put into place.

11

Instruments of Ottoman Occupation: The Army of Janissaries

The Turkish soldiers who made up Sinan Pasha's expedition, along with reinforcements from Algiers and Tripoli, were the main instrument of Ottoman presence in Tunis. These soldiers, commonly known as Janissaries, were in fact made up of many different recruits, and seldom came from the prestigious military imperial corps of the same name.

The Origins of the Turkish Janissaries: An Iron Discipline

The Janissary corps are intimately linked to the emergence of the Ottoman Empire. Created in 1362, they were blessed by the mystical Sheikh Hajj Baktash who baptized *yanitcheri*, or the new soldiers, a name that would later be translated as *inkishari* in Arabic and *janissaire* in French. This elite corps was distinguished by the way they were recruited: it was made up exclusively of young Europeans who had converted to Islam and been uprooted from their homes. They had only their master, the sultan, as a protector; he in turn relied on the Janissaries for all his military operations and administrative responsibilities. These young Christians were Greek, Albanian, Armenian, Polish, Hungarian, and Caucasian. The system of kidnapping children for military service, known as the *devshirme*, was a regular feature of imperial orders. Recruiters would travel through the Christian provinces, convene fathers and sons between the ages of five and twenty, and choose the most handsome and robust among them. For the fathers, the pain of separation was tempered by the hope that their sons would rise to the highest levels in the imperial administration. Sometimes Muslim fathers even tried to pass off their children as Christian during the recruitment process, so desirable was this career as a Janissary. Once chosen, the young children were initiated into their new religion, taught Turkish, and given special training that was intended to form them into seasoned, disciplined soldiers loyal to their sultan and their spiritual master, Hajj Baktash. Their honor code, which dates to the era of Mourad the First (1359–89), stipulated absolute obedience to their officers and other authorities, the renunciation of luxury and lavishness, and celibacy. It prohibited having a trade, and specified that soldiers could only be recruited through this system.

The Janissaries were, by necessity, affiliated with the mystical order of the Bektashi. They cohabitated with the dervishes, who taught them austerity and helped them to endure celibacy. The Janissary corps resembled the soldier-monks of medieval Europe, for the bektashi dervishes would hear the confessions of the initiated men and share bread, wine, and cheese with them.

The Janissary troops obeyed the orders of the general, called the *agha.* During times of war, the soldiers took part in conquests along with other army corps, and during times of peace they served the palace, acted as street police, guarded the consulates, and accompanied travelers in unstable regions. This elite force had its own set of symbols, of which the pot, or *kazan*, was the most emblematic. It was the symbol of food: the Ottomans' ancestors, nomads from the steppes, used to gather around the *kazan* at dusk to share warm meals. Each unit had its own *kazan.* Every day, groups of soldiers armed with enormous wooden spoons would march in a procession carrying brimming pots from the barracks to the Janissaries on duty. When the soldiers passed by, people would stop to pay their respects. No one dared laugh, out of fear for their lives. The pot also served a protective function: any person in danger would be safe as soon as they placed themselves in proximity to the *kazan*, for then the Janissaries would be called, on their honor, to protect the fugitive. When they were unhappy, the soldiers would overturn the pot to signal that a mutiny had begun. The Janissary corps was distinguished by their uniforms, which western travelers described as picturesque.

Over time, the Janissaries' discipline faded and the rigor of their early years gave way to insubordination and disobedience. The Janissaries become more deeply involved in politics, going so far as to depose the sultans. Suleiman al-Qanouni (1520–66) removed the marriage ban and allowed the soldiers to marry after seven years of work. He also authorized them to practice a trade during peacetime. By the time the Ottoman Empire began to expand into the western Mediterranean, the Janissary corps had already strayed far from its origins. The men sent off to the new Maghrebi provinces were no longer a flawless, professional army, but rather mercenaries who had been softened by family life and reduced to scrabbling for means of subsistence. The soldiers sent to the Maghreb would distort this depraved model even further, at a moment when the empire was struggling with economic problems and was occupied in fighting a costly war against Iran. Under these conditions, the empire was reluctant to weaken the frontlines by sending away its best men.

The Turkish Soldiers Sent to the Maghreb: A Cosmopolitan and Undisciplined Corps

When Khayriddine Barbarossa requested the incorporation of Algiers into the empire and military aid against the Spanish, the Ottoman sultan answered his call. He sent a corps of Janissaries and ordered that Turkish volunteers be sent to Algiers and enjoy the same privileges as the Janissaries. Thousands of volunteers went free of charge. The soldiers sent to Algiers, Tripoli, and later Tunis were not Islamicized Christians, coming from the *devshirme* and raised to respect the institution, but men from Anatolia and other regions of the empire. Among them were the *sebkhans*, Turkish Muslims, who were occasionally recruited on a need-only basis and sent home at the end of each campaign.[1] Oftentimes, these men ran rampant after returning to their regions, joining organized bandits who threatened the security of the countryside. By sending them far away, the sultan managed to get rid of these young troublemakers and mitigate the pressure on the rural areas. The volunteer recruits had no ties to the military profession. They were peasants or poor artisans who were afforded privileges that, up until that time, had largely been reserved for non-Turks. The town criers were responsible for rounding up recruits in the port of Izmir by calling out: "He who wishes to die without suffering, and he who wants to enrich himself without fatigue, come enlist under our banner."[2] It was thus that troops of soldiers and oarsmen were assembled over the winter of 1573 to 1574, when the grand vizier began calling for an expedition to Tunis.

This recruitment strategy encouraged all sorts of people to join the new regencies in the hopes of improving their lot. Even petty criminals went: in June 1584, prisoners in Rhodes were sent to Tripoli with orders to settle there.[3] The Maghrebi provinces became a place of exile for outlaws and an opportunity for poor people hoping to enrich themselves. As in other Arab provinces, there were two categories of soldiers, one more prestigious than the other. This was the case in Egypt, where we find two corps: the prestigious *mustahfidhan*, and the unmarried *'azaban*, who were responsible for guarding the coastal garrisons. The term *'azaban* was altered to *zbantut*, a word with a pejorative connotation that harkens back to delinquency and banditry. This tension created a rivalry between the two armies and also neutralized any hint of insubordination among the Janissaries, who were becoming more and more aggressive—even in Istanbul, where they sought to dethrone the sultans.

Similar rivalries could be found in the Maghrebi provinces, where the Janissaries did not share a group identity or an *espirit de corps* with the assimilated soldiers. The men primarily identified in terms of their geographic origin, which meant that each barrack carried the name of the city its occupants came from: the Anatolian plateau, Ankara, Sinope, Bodrum, Boughaz, or some other Mediterranean province such as Rhodes, Chios, or Thessaloniki.[4] Regional solidarities shaped the identities of these groups and the rivalries that divided them. It was an unwritten law that during recruitments, volunteers from the same village left in groups, sometimes more than one from each family. These men were placed under the authority of one of their own, who they affectionately called *dey*, or their maternal uncle. Before becoming a political institution, the function of the *dey* was to reconstitute familial ties to lessen the pain of exile.

Very little united the Janissaries from the *devshirme*, who were deployed to the Maghreb, and the Anatolian village volunteers, who were deployed in groups. Disagreements erupted between them, notably between the Janissaries and the *'azaban*, who were generally recruited from the coasts of the empire. In Algiers, the rivalries were so intense that the sultan ordered the beylerbey to ensure that in the *diwan*, the Janissaries would sit on the right and the *'azaban* on the left.[5] The Janissaries' privileged status was also likely to have influenced the need for this distinction within the council's forum.

The forces sent to conquer Tunis in July 1574 were estimated at seven thousand infantrymen, seven thousand *sipahis* (cavaliers), and six thousand volunteer soldiers. In addition, there were the soldiers that Kilidj 'Ali left behind in Tunis in 1569. The estimates of his troop numbers vary, but Ibn abi Dinar estimates there were about eight hundred Turks and eight hundred Zwawa, or Kabyle soldiers.[6] There were also soldiers from Tripoli, under Haydar's command.[7] At the end of the expedition, it was estimated that of the soldiers who chose to stay in Tunis, around five hundred were Janissaries, 2,500 were *sebkhans*, the volunteer Anatolians, and a thousand were men joined to the contingents based in Algiers and Tripoli.

These four thousand soldiers were divided into groups, or *odha*, of a hundred, each under the authority of one *bulukbashi*, or superior officer. These forty officers formed the Janissaries' *diwan*, under the command of the *agha*, their general. The *agha* was assisted by one representative of the sultan, eight *chaouchs* (bailiffs) responsible for keeping order during gatherings of the assembly, two *khuja* (Turkish language secretaries), and an interpreter, (the *turjuman*).

The military thus constituted was the principal instrument of the Ottoman occupation. Its relationship to the local populations was complex. By joining the professional army, most of the volunteer recruits hoped to become lords or effendis. But because of their rustic and Turkish origin, they were mocked and called the "cows of Anatolia." According to the hierarchical Ottoman system, one had to come from outside the local society, even be a slave of the sultan, to join the political and military elite. Departing for a faraway province was an opportunity for the *sebkhan* or the *'azab*, free men of inferior status to the Mamluks, to begin a process of ennoblement and enrichment that would never have been possible in their regions of origin, which offered no opportunities for upward mobility.

Methods for Replenishing the Army

The army had to replenish itself after soldiers died, whether in combat or of natural causes, or returned to their homelands. The Regency had two pools of recruits available to it. The first category consisted of "natural" Turks, to borrow the term European writers used to describe those who were native to the Anatolian plateaus. The second category were Christians from conquered lands who had converted to Islam and joined the militia as "Turks by profession." Salvago, a Venetian interpreter working in the Ottoman Empire, refers to peasants who abandoned their ploughs and went to ennoble themselves in Barbary, where they married local women and enrolled their sons in the military. According to this same account, this militia was defined by who was excluded from it: Jews, Tzigane, Moriscos from Spain, and indigenous people.[8] In other words, the Turkish army kept its distance from the society around it, which was characteristic of the Ottoman Janissaries. This emphasis on foreignness formed the basis of a military corps that was privileged, closed to local populations, and could only recruit from outside. In the Maghreb, this policy created an opposition between the two "military societies"—the Turks, on the one hand, and on the other the Arabs, who came from rural areas and were chivalrous warriors. As for the urban dwellers, they constituted a world apart: they were not concerned with the use of arms, and observed without reaction the establishment of a new social order, one in which the Turks sought to take the lead.

This somewhat unnatural policy enshrined the domination of a minority group by banning all mixing with the local populations and replenishing itself from the exterior. For soldiers, these rules proved difficult to follow. The single soldiers did end up marrying native women and had children who were characterized as *kuluglis*, children of slaves, a word that harkened back to the presumed origins of their fathers as Mamluks of the sultan. How was this new category of "creoles" perceived—as Turkish or as indigenous?

In Algiers, this question was resolved by the Janissaries' *diwan*, which forbade the *kuluglis* access to military positions on the grounds that the ban came from 'Arrouj, the founding father, and even the saint 'Abd al-Rahman Thalbi. The Turkish army of Algiers was concerned with distinguishing itself from the native populations and accepted all volunteers from outside.[9] In Tunis, however, the council of the Janissaries acted differently.

The Career of a Turkish Soldier in Tunis

The soldier, *yoldach*, of Muslim origin or recently converted, was incorporated into a battalion called an *ourta*, and received a salary every two months. He was also entitled to food as payment in kind while based in the garrison or in column. After three years, he became *aski yoldach*, then *bach yoldach*, and would command a group of sixteen to twenty men called a *khba*. By seniority, the soldier became *oukilhardji*, sergeant-major; *odabashi*, lieutenant; *bulukbashi*, captain; then *aghabashi*, commander. The most senior became *kahia* and then *agha* of the *diwan*. These were all temporary positions with a duration of four months. When the soldier had passed through all the ranks, he became *agha mansul*, or veteran, and was an ex-officio member of the *diwan*, the militia's council. He could then participate in civilian life while also enjoying his salary, which enabled him to live with dignity. If the soldier was homesick, he could take a three-month break. If he did not return after this break, he would need to restart his career from the beginning.

Absent or Poorly Applied Rules

The career of a soldier unfolded within a democratic system that allowed anyone to ascend the ranks. To assure more mobility within the army, it was important to change the *agha* every three to four months. In practice, this rule was not always implemented, and some held the post for five to ten years.

The absence of regulations, and the poor application of the ones that existed, transformed the Turkish *jund* into a brutal and undisciplined occupying force. The populations of the three regencies of Algiers, Tripoli, and Tunis suffered greatly under them. The soldiers enlisted to get rich, or at least to be guaranteed a regular salary. Their actions were widely felt. In Algiers, the troops did nothing unless they were assured that they would receive substantial revenues. They sent emissaries to the Sublime Porte to defend their interests. For example, in Algiers in 1567, soldiers complained that the indigenous populations were competing with them for the position of the *yasakcilik*, guardians of the buildings and public monuments, which were traditionally reserved for soldiers. The sultan ordered the Pasha of Algiers to make sure that this rule was respected.[10]

The soldiers' abuses were many: they looted the orchards, confiscated products in the markets, molested young boys, and harassed women. The local administration punished neither the soldiers' petty thefts nor their more serious infractions, for it benefitted from these exploits. When the local populations had finally had enough, they would send written complaints to Istanbul. But the Janissaries and volunteer recruits were stubborn and did not listen to the veterans, their officers, or even the *agha*s. In May 1577, the sultan ordered the Pasha of Algiers to intervene and reestablish order among the officers.[11]

Officials in various positions acted with the same impunity as the Janissaries. For many of them, the *oujaks* of the Maghreb promised quick fortunes: for example, the interpreter Darwish Muhammad stayed in Tripoli for fifteen years and confiscated huge amounts of goods. Responding to the complaints of his victims, the sultan ordered Darwish to return the land he had stolen to its proper owners, dismissed him, and appointed another interpreter. In September 1571, the Istanbul authorities informed the Pasha of Tripoli that the emirs of the *sanjak* were not paying royalties to the state. The sultan ordered that from now on the *chaouch*s, or the *bawab*s, Ottoman officials, would fulfill the duties of the bey or caid, positions occupied most often by the renegades. The Pasha of Algiers was asked to collect state revenues and send them to the imperial capital.[12]

The Payment of the Janissaries

The pasha was responsible for paying the militia and any late pay was a serious threat to order. The money paid to the soldiers came from the various taxes that the pasha collected. In case of financial difficulties, the pasha could borrow from the public treasury, but if he did not repay the loan, he could in theory be imprisoned and his goods sold. In the Maghreb, no pashas were seriously punished for failing to pay.

This system worked so poorly that the soldiers decided to take justice into their own hands and seize their pay directly. Algiers, Tripoli, and Tunis would suffer from the same problems—the diversion of state revenues and the dispossession of the local people—for several decades. These complaints addressed to the Sublime Porte are an important source of information for historians. In 1568, the Beylerbey of Algiers was informed that one of the leaders of the *sanjak* was diverting funds intended for the state; he ordered that the man be arrested and the money returned.[13] Due to the irregularity of taxes, paying the salaries—the responsibility of the provinces—became an endemic problem.

How much did a soldier cost? One document supplies some details. On October 18, 1576, the *defterdar* Muhammad, who oversaw the finances for the three provinces, informed the pasha of the arrival of eighty new soldiers who had to be paid from the treasury of Tunis. The expenses were estimated at 150,000 okjas per year. The salaries were to be paid every three months and were determined after consultation with the *qadi* of Jerba at 84,000 okjas. In addition, 75,000 okjas had to be deducted from the revenues of the *mhalla* to pay for their food and supplies.[14] These heavy expenses pushed the governors to look for alternative sources of funding. In April 1583, the Pasha of Tunis had to borrow 2,500 crowns from French merchants to pay the soldiers' expenses.[15]

Unpaid salaries were an endemic problem and contributed to the relaxation of military discipline. To relieve some of the pressure on the governors, the soldiers were authorized to practice various trades, which gave rise to further institutional degradation. A satirical song describing the soldiers of Algiers sums it up:

> I looked at the army, it's a market, a bazaar. Your soldiers have become merchants of marmalade . . . merchants of rotten milk . . . Your soldiers are spice dealers. . . . Know this, my Padischah.[16]

Different travelers observed, alongside the military's qualities, all forms of ignominy, cruelty, greed, and moral depravity among the Turkish soldiers of the Maghreb. The decay became widespread, and the indigenous populations suffered all kinds of injustice. In the face of these allegations, the sultan wrote to the pasha:

> Information reached me from the beylerbeylik of Tunis of actions that differ from those that occur in others of my well-protected kingdoms and that we have invented many blameworthy innovations *(bida')*. All taxes enter into the pockets of those who collect them and none are arriving to the treasury. The janissaries take by force the land of the indigenous populations which they cultivate and harvest without paying a dime. They enroll their sons and their renegades in the registries of the soldiers even when these youth are not apt for service, and receive their salaries three months before the deadline. They benefit from unnecessary advances, squander the treasury's money, and treat subjects unfairly.[17]

Later, he writes:

> the janissary corps are filled with the miserable and the rebellious, who don't listen and do not execute the orders of the beylerbeys and carry out all that is against *chara'* and the law.[18]

In 1579, either to contain the excesses of the Janissaries or to enforce the law, the sultan appointed Hassan Zoghraji, from Istanbul, to be *Agha* of Tunis. Several months later, another *agha* was appointed. On October 4, 1579, an edict was issued to the Janissaries informing them that Hussein, originating from the cavalry corps, was appointed *Agha* of the city of Tunis. He was told to work in collaboration with the beylerbey, not to contradict his directives, and to obey the orders of the sultan. In addition, he was ordered to punish the rebellious soldiers and establish order among the armies.[19] The appointment, five years after the Ottomans' arrival, demonstrated their desire to bring order to a province that had been administered haphazardly and in which governors had become hostages to the army and completely lacked authority. Hussein established himself in Tunis and became pasha, as we will read more about later.

The Rise of Rebellion

Although the organization of the army was democratic, given the speed with which people could climb the ranks and the rotation of officers in commanding posts, men who joined to enrich themselves were disappointed by the poverty of the land and its lack of resources. What little was available was exploited by the officers and senior officials. In 1588, the soldiers announced that they were no longer content with their salaries of 20 okjas and demanded 22 instead.[20] Correspondence between the sultan's *diwan* and the Pasha of Tunis indicated that there were insufficient revenues to pay the army. At the same time, the beylerbeys raised the officers' pay from 30 to 40 *okjas*, even for those who were no longer active.[21] In certain cases, the salaries were replaced by *za'amat al-iqta'*, tax concessions from the agricultural land. These state-owned lands were not revitalized "dead lands," but properties exploited by families located in the wealthiest regions.

The sultan, concerned about the strength of the army, ordered the pasha not to allow himself to be led by the Janissaries but to request a *qanunama*, a regulation that established the rights of troops and their officers. He also ordered a reduction in the army's responsibilities and decreed that Tunis no longer had to deliver horses and barley to Algerian officials.

In the three *oujak*s of the Maghreb, the unsatisfied soldiers became a threat. Each province identified its own remedies. In Algiers, the soldiers were authorized to work on privateering vessels, which substantially augmented their revenues. In Tripoli, the soldiers looted with impunity. In Tunis, beginning in 1588, the council of Janissaries gained more and more power. This *diwan* was probably composed of officers coming from the ranks of the Janissaries and excluded the corps of the *'azaban* and the *sebkhan* from positions of power, considering them second-tier soldiers. Such exclusion was probably the source of the military putsch of 1591.

12

Land and Men: Patterns of Land Appropriation

In the Ottoman Empire, the question of land in the newly conquered regions linked the political, economic, and military domains, and was one of the issues that concerned the sultan personally. The Ottomans had to address the distribution of land and taxes to guarantee revenue and pay soldiers and civil servants without overburdening the local population. Even though the Ottoman administration was experienced in these matters and had dealt with them successfully in other Arab provinces, it failed to do so in the Maghreb. Looking at what unfolded in the Arab provinces sheds some light on what happened in Tunis beginning in 1574.

The Question of Land: The Center of the Ottoman System

In the conquered provinces, the state, as embodied by the sultan, automatically became the owner of all land. Under this system of appropriation, a plot of land could be granted to a designated beneficiary, who would sow it and plant it in exchange for a tithe. This direct mode of exploitation, generally applied to uncultivated land ("dead lands"), was known as *silyane.* In another, indirect mode, the land remained in the hands of its original farmers, who would pay a tithe to the state. In turn, the state ceded to senior officials or troops the right to collect a tithe as a replacement for their salaries. This concession took three forms.

The first kind of land concession was called *al-khas*. Some lands earned revenues of 100,000 okjas or more and were given to very senior officials for as long as they were in office. In exchange, the recipients were required to contribute to military campaigns a unit that included one well-equipped rider for every 5,000 *okjas* collected. So, for example, someone whose land earned one million *okjas* would be obliged to contribute five hundred combatants.

The second category of land grants was called *al-za'amat*. Their revenues were between 20,000 and 100,000 *okjas*, and they were given to mid-level officials, such as the *defterder*, who was in control of state revenues, or the high secretaries, who, unless they did something seriously wrong, would profit from the land for their whole lives. In exchange, they were required to contribute to military operations in the same way as described above.

The third category was *al-timar*. These lands earned revenues between 3,000 and 20,000 *okjas* and were given to the Janissaries and the sipahis. In exchange, they were required to live in the province where the *timar* was located and contribute one fighter for every 3,000 *okjas*, collected from the first 3,000. So, for example, a *timariote* who received 6,000 *okjas* was required to contribute one fighter.

The lands occupied by the Ottomans were thus categorized into two types: the *silyane*, in which the properties were used directly by their beneficiaries, who paid taxes to the state; and the lands subject to the *timar*, *za'amat*, and *khas*, from which the governor and his treasurer collected taxes, distributing the earnings among the beneficiaries and sending the rest to the treasury. Whether the provinces were organized according to one system or the other—or both, in some cases—it was necessary to carry out a general census before establishing such a laborious distribution scheme. Typically, the officials in charge of the census would go from village to village, counting the people, houses, lands, forests, pastures, and rivers. Based on their reports, a tithe would be calculated and distributed to the designated beneficiaries. Thus, the tithe of one village estimated at 10 million *okjas* could be broken down as follows: two million *khas*, one million *za'amat*, four million *timar*, two million *waqf* (to benefit a religious foundation), one million *oujaklek* (specific expenses for the maintenance of the fortress garrison or a specific population or the armory). It was not the Ottoman state that was obligated to pay the salary of the Janissaries, but rather, the beneficiaries of the land concessions.

Each time they pacified a territory, the Ottomans granted rights to the high officials charged with administering it and to the Janissaries who were established there. But the land concessions they gave away varied according to the two models described above, as well as the region and the time period. When the Ottomans conquered *Bilad al-Sham*, the sultan considered the land to be his property; on the basis of this proprietary right, he then distributed the land in the form of *iqta'*, or fiefs, to his Janissaries. In the Balkans, *sipahi*s (cavalrymen) were given *timar* for life, in exchange for raising an army on behalf of the sultan when necessary and paying taxes to the central authority. During other periods, Ottoman soldiers obtained the title to vacant lands: Sultan Selim I gave *temlikname* (property certificates) to Janissaries who were able to dispose of the *mawat* land and become owners. In this case, the appropriation was justified on the basis that the Janissaries were revitalizing "dead land."[1]

This system of giving property rights and revenues to soldiers and officials had, up to a certain point, guaranteed the smooth functioning of the army and of the provincial administration of the Ottoman Empire. When troubles broke out in Egypt, Sultan Suleiman al-Qanouni ordered his minister Ibrahim Pasha to personally oversee the census of land and peoples before granting the *iqta'*, *timar*, or *za'amat*. In the provinces of Egypt and *Bilad al-Sham*, as in all the other provinces, land was distributed following a vast survey to gather accurate information and quantify the different areas and rights that could be distributed. This fieldwork could take place due to the Ottomans' rapid victories in many of these regions. The Ottomans captured *Bilad al-Sham* after a decisive battle against the Mamluks on August 24, 1516, which resulted in Sultan Selim being given the keys to all the Syrian cities. He was received triumphantly everywhere he went. The Mamluks resisted in Gaza, but they were subjugated quickly; it was a major setback. The great Arab leaders declared their submission to the sultan, who resided in Damascus for close to a year and reinforced the position of the new Ottoman dignitaries in charge of their regions. Several provinces or *sanjak*s were also accorded to the old Arab families, who became administrators on behalf of the empire by assuring the security of their regions, notably along the pilgrimage route, and collecting the taxes owed to the state. These regions also declared their vassalage by delivering the Friday prayer in the sultan's name.

After having subjugated all the Arab and Bedouin leaders, Selim I began his campaign against Egypt. This would prove to be more difficult than expected, as the Mamluk Sultan Touman Bey resisted for a long time. He took refuge among the Bedouins, but they ultimately delivered him to the sultan, who ordered his execution. The victorious campaign against the Mamluks resulted in the complete occupation of *Bilad al-Sham*, Egypt, and the Hijaz. Money flowed into the coffers of the Ottoman state, including the royalties that Venice had previously paid to the Mamluks and all the profits from commercial transit. The subjugated Mamluks secured positions in the regions; the most recalcitrant among them were exiled to Istanbul. The sultan ordered the leaders who had just been placed at the head of the *sanjaks* (regions) to supply him information about the distribution of and income from Mamluk land, which became *miri* property (belonging to the state) and was distributed to new beneficiaries. Egypt thus became the first *silyan* province, where officers and high officials were granted land for life. The sultan named a loyal minister, Younes Pasha, to govern Egypt, but removed him quickly because he coveted goods belonging to the wives of the Mamluks. Selim I then appointed a Mamluk leader named Khayrbek as Governor of Egypt—but not before taking the precaution of bringing his family to Istanbul and putting in place a garrison of four thousand men in the qal'a of Cairo. He also gave the Arab leaders many responsibilities to counterbalance the power of the Mamluks. On his return to Istanbul, Younes Pasha observed that there was no point in waging a war of conquest at the cost of many lives if it would only result in the old elites maintaining their power. Selim I, shocked by the minister's arrogance, ordered his immediate execution. Younes Pasha had not recognized the sultan's pragmatism in drawing on local leaders to administer provinces of whose traditions he was ignorant.

At the time that the Arab provinces were being occupied, the Ottoman Empire was at the height of its power. The empire was treating the regions of *al-Sham*, Tarablus al-Sham, Aleppo, Baghdad, Mosul, Basra, Yemen, Egypt, and the Hijaz more firmly and leaving fewer liberties to the provincial pashas responsible for managing the occupied regions.

The conditions under which the Ottomans took control of the *oujaks* of the Maghreb were quite different. What legal methods did the Ottoman Turks use to appropriate these lands? What status did they give to these territories after seizing them?

The Oujaks of the Maghreb

When the Ottomans turned toward the Maghreb, the empire was facing financial difficulties. The sultans Suleiman al-Qanouni (1520–66) and his successor Selim II (1566–74) lacked the authority of their predecessors and were subject to the strong influence of their viziers. Financial needs among the high officials led to *rashawat*, or bribes, being common across all levels of government, especially under the vizierate of Rostom Pasha. The administration of the Ottoman provinces suffered under these campaigns of influence, promoted by senior officials of dubious morality.

The first indication of these problems in the provinces of the Maghreb was the absence of legislation, *qanunama*, defining the systems of land and financial distribution. To understand this lacuna, exceptional within an otherwise meticulous Ottoman bureaucracy, we must return to the conditions under which the Maghrebi cities were seized, from Algiers and Tripoli to Tunis. The various expeditions led by 'Arrouj only pacified the coastal regions, without ever managing to control large swathes of territories in the interior. The alliances with the local leaders were never durable and were subject to many reversals. The expedition of Sinan Pasha did not pacify the entire territory—only the city of Tunis and the fort of La Goulette, which had been occupied until then by the Spanish, along with several other points along the coast. The rest of the territory sank into what the Ottomans called "anarchy," unable as they were to recognize all the small local powers that had been in place since well before their arrival.

Establishing a new administration and cadastral system required a pacified territory and collaboration with the local notables, leaders, officials, and legal scholars, to resolve the thorny issue of land. These conditions were absent in the territories of the Maghreb, as much in Algiers as in Tripoli and Tunis. The Ottoman administration and army thus encountered novel difficulties there; they would be forced to work with unexpected partners and to do battle on several fronts.

The Land, Contested by the Pashas, the Janissaries, and the Marabouts

The many Janissaries and officers who were not receiving their salaries regularly would change the nature of the *miri* land by treating it as *za'amat* and *timar* land, which they appropriated and derived substantial revenues from. They even succeeded in obtaining documents confirming this appropriation.[2] Some pashas, such as Rajeb, had taken up the habit of refusing to pay soldiers' salaries and instead sending them to extort harvests and livestock from the local populations. Embezzlement hurt both the people and the Ottoman state. Employees of the administration, officers, and even soldiers pocketed royalties that were supposed to go to the treasury. These misappropriations began among the governors in the first weeks of the occupation of Tripoli and Tunis, and eventually came to be practiced by ordinary soldiers.

The spoliation of land increased after 1587. More and more soldiers diverted *miri* land and made it into *za'amat*, without having received any orders to that effect from the sultan. In Tripoli, for example, in the time of Mourad Pasha, only four *za'amat* were distributed for the profit of the high officials; the rest of the lands went to pay the salaries of the Janissaries. In stark contrast, the governors who came after Haydar diverted the land from its intended purpose so that thirty *miri* lands became *za'amat*, which considerably reduced state revenues. The sultan ordered the return of four *za'amat* and did not offer any justification.[3]

In the Regency of Algiers, in 1582, the beneficiaries of the *za'amat* and the governors of the *sanjak*s refused to pay the soldiers their salaries.[4] In Tripoli, some governors re-registered the lands as *za'amat* and *timar* and confiscated them. In July 1585, an order was given to restore the lands that had been listed as belonging to the state and to set aside their revenues to pay soldiers—this despite the landowners brandishing certificates of ownership. Did this signify that the Ottoman state granted property titles to the Janissaries and their officers, then retracted them after observing the abuses? What seems likely is that the Janissaries had been fabricating land ownership laws, *temlikname*, ever since they had taken control of *bayt al-mal* (the treasury), which had previously been controlled by the governor.[5] This was how they managed to profit from the sale of goods. The Turks and the Arabs, who had bought these lands from *bayt al-mal*, refused to pay taxes to the state on the grounds that these lands belonged to them, for they had purchased them with their own money.

This thirst for land characterized the first era of the Turkish occupation and recalled the agricultural origins of a large part of the Turkish military. In Tunis, similar abuses took place: soldiers there also confiscated lands, probably with the complicity of the locals. For this, we have the example of the lands belonging to the saints, including Abu al-Gaith al-Quachach.

The Confiscation of Abu al-Gaith's Lands

In their unbridled quest for revenue, the Turkish pashas did not hesitate to claim the belongings of the *zawiya*s. The instigator of this practice was Othman Dey, who began his career in Tunis as a Janissary. He believed in the *baraka* of the saint and so put himself in the service of the *zawiya* as a courier, charged with carrying bread to the oven. However, his respect for the saint would eventually become a rivalry. Then Othman proposed to the *diwan*, which was struggling to pay its soldiers, that it confiscate the territories and livestock of the great saints of Tunis: Sidi Mansur, Sidi Mahriz, Sidi Bin 'Arous, Sidi Abu al-Gaith, and others. The owners of these *zawiya*s appeared before the diwan to try to regain possession of their belongings, but they were driven away.

It is said that only Abu al-Gaith sought nothing from the Turks. According to his hagiography, he continued to feed his disciples and organize soirées of liturgical song that lasted long into the night. But these claims of his *zawiya*'s abundance are disputed by other reports, which recount the difficulties it faced after the requisitioning of its property. The members of the *diwan* worried about Abu al-Gaith's silence, which they interpreted as malevolence. They summoned the saint, but he refused to appear. He responded that his *zawiya* was kept alive by God and the Prophet, not by land and beasts. The Turks saw in his response a forewarning of divine punishment and prepared to restore his property. But he refused to accept it until all the other *zawiya*s also had their goods returned. The Turks ultimately agreed to his demand. This uplifting story was reported in his hagiography for the purpose of demonstrating the saint's capacity to make the Turks bend to his will, but it also teaches us about the process of the confiscations practiced by the army, which went so far as to include goods that were considered sacred.

We have less information about the Hafsids' possessions and their likely confiscation by the Turks. What remained of their belongings once the ruling family had scattered and insecurity reigned in the countryside? We can assume that many of the abandoned Hafsid domains had fallen into ruin well before the Turks arrived, and that no one thought of exploiting them.

The period from 1587 to 1591 witnessed, in the *oujak*s of Tunis and Tripoli, a real reduction of Ottoman authority. Legal changes, the abandonment of the plan to unify the three provinces, and the departure of the great governors paved the way for the insatiable ambitions of the Janissary officers. In Algiers, the situation was different: two powerful bodies, the Janissaries and the rais, ruled together for a long time and checked one another's power. A great deal of animosity existed between the soldiers and the sailors. Corsair activity, which accompanied the founding of the *oujak* of Algiers, was very dynamic during the period of Khayriddine Pasha. It was dominated by the group of renegades, who, unlike the Anatolian Turks, were experts in navigation. These two groups were antagonistic toward each other, and disagreed over many things, including the appointments of pashas: a governor who appealed to the corsairs would not necessarily have the approval of the soldiers. They might have reconciled in 1568, when Muhammad Pasha, son of Salah Rais, Pasha of Algiers, authorized the renegades and the corsairs to integrate, if they so desired, into the Janissary corps. The Janissaries would be allowed to participate in piracy just like the sailors of the navy.[6] This generous offer even extended to the Jews who had converted to Islam *(slami)*. The animosity between the two groups—the *ta'ifa* of the rais and that of the soldiers—was temporarily alleviated, but it resumed in 1580, when Ja'far Pasha forbade soldiers from engaging in piracy. The Janissaries and the corsairs nonetheless managed to maintain equilibrium at the head of the province, which they mutually controlled. Their disputes were resolved in Istanbul.

Tunis and Tripoli found themselves in a completely different situation due to the absence of a navy and a rais corps. No alternative power checked the authority of the Janissary officers, who committed all sorts of injustices against the local populations and their own soldiers. The soldiers, discontented with their lot, abused the locals in order to improve their own day-to-day lives. But in time, they turned against their own officers: a mutiny began to foment.

13

Algiers, Tripoli, and Tunis, 1587–99: A Decade of Turbulence

The end of the period of the beylerbeys marked a reduction in political authority, the proliferation of abuses by officers, lack of discipline among their men, and Istanbul's powerlessness to control the provinces. The rebellion spread to Algiers, where soldiers and sailors had imposed their laws for decades, and to Tunis and Tripoli, where the army acted with impunity.

The Invincible Militia of Algiers: A Model to Follow?

By the time Hassan Veneziano left the Maghreb at the end of 1587, the situation had radically changed and the *oujak*s seemed to have escaped the control of the Sublime Porte. In Algiers, the militia and the corporation of the corsairs chose a governor who would act in their interests and did not hesitate to contravene the sultan's directives. The council of the "Invincible Militia" determined matters of war and peace, worrying little about conforming to the foreign policy of Istanbul. They attacked the vessels of friendly countries, refused to return the cargo they stole in these raids or punish the perpetrators, and expelled the sultan's emissaries. During this period, the rais, the captains of the ships, were at the height of their power, bringing in fabulous riches they collected in the Mediterranean or off the Atlantic coasts. Almost all these rais were renegades, such as Mami Corsou, Mami Napolitano, and Mami Arnaoute, just to cite the most illustrious, who gave corsairing a considerable dynamism.

The first "triennial" pasha appointed to Algiers was Daly Ahmad, who governed from 1587 to 1589 and left Algiers at the end of his mandate with many riches. He was assigned to Algiers just as Sidi Yahya's uprising was beginning. Sidi Yahya claimed to be the *mahdi*, who had come to revive religion and guide men back to the righteous path. Aided by the cavalrymen of Malta, he gathered the populations of Tajoura around him, roused the island of Djerba, and encircled Tripoli. The Turks prepared a major offensive in which the soldiers from Tunis participated. It ended with the death of Daly Ahmad, who was killed by a spear.[1] The Grand Admiral, sent from Istanbul to quell the uprising, conducted an immediate investigation and determined that it had been caused by the abuses of the Turkish soldiers. In Algiers, Daly Ahmad was replaced by Khidr.

The First Government of Khidr Pasha in Algiers: August 1589 to August 1592

The new pasha was a native of the Maghreb, the son of a Neapolitan renegade in Algiers.[2] Before reaching this high office, he had held the lucrative position of caid. In 1586, he even became Pasha of Tunis. Introduced into the circles of power, he married Fattoum, the daughter of Ramadan Pasha, the former Governor of Tunis and Algiers who was killed in Tripoli in 1584.[3] A man of experience, Khidr would face many uprisings among the Kabyles. The insurgents refused to pay the taxes that the Turks demanded. Several times, they blocked the route of the *mhalla*, isolating Algiers from its hinterlands and leaving the city completely dependent upon revenues from piracy. Khidr also had to put down the uprising of the qal'a of the Beni Abbes, to which he laid siege in December 1590, forcing its surrender.

However, the pasha still clashed with the *diwan* of the Janissaries, who decided to lodge a complaint. The *bulukbashi* officers, accompanied by Mami Arnaoute, the patron of the corsairs, went to Istanbul at the head of four galleys, two of which carried Khidr and his family. The delegation was not heard by the high authorities, given the deplorable reputation of the *oujak* of Algiers, and Khidr was left alone. In August 1592, he was replaced by Sha'ban Pasha.

Sha'ban Pasha: 1592–95

Sha'ban Pasha took power during a difficult moment. Disease and famine were spreading in Tunis, the Kabyles were rising up, and the routes of the *mhalla* were cut off once again. Overwhelmed by these challenges, Sha'ban returned to Istanbul before the end of his mandate, leaving his lieutenant, Mustafa, in charge of the *oujak* for four months. Meanwhile, Khidr Pasha, having been exonerated of the charges brought against him by the rais Mami Arnaoute, resumed his position as the Pasha of Algiers.[4]

The Return of Khidr: December 1595 to September 1596

Khidr Pasha returned to Algiers determined to take revenge on the militia. To that end, he supported the uprising of the *kuluglis*, who were born of local families and Turks but had long been excluded from power. He furnished them with arms that allowed them to do battle with the Janissaries for several months. He also supported their alliance with the *baldis* of the great cities. As a result, Khidr was accused of wanting to bring an end to Turkish authority in the region by reinforcing the power of the local populations. He soon became the victim of a campaign mounted against him by the Ambassador of France in Istanbul, who was concerned about the Francophobic sentiments of the pasha. The ambassador succeeded in having Khidr replaced by Mustafa, who governed from 1596 to 1599. Mustafa took vengeance on Khidr by confiscating a large portion of his property.[5] In response, the Kabyles, whom Khidr had supported, mounted a siege against Algiers. Mustafa was not able to quell the uprising and was recalled to Istanbul and imprisoned.

Next, Daly Hassan Bouricha was appointed pasha, at the recommendation of the French. He was tasked with liberating several French sailors who were imprisoned in Algiers. But he failed to persuade the *diwan* to set them free, and Henry IV's official envoy was flouted and insulted. He was replaced by Suleiman Veneziano.

The history of the pashas of Algiers at the end of the sixteenth century, better known than that of Tripoli and Tunis, reveals the many issues complicating the appointment of governors in the provinces. Two contradictory pressures influenced these appointments: decisions made in Istanbul and the interests of the powers in Algiers. In the imperial capital, a candidate had to satisfy both the high officials, who wanted to position their men in power, and the ambassadors from France, who advocated their country's interests. In Algiers, the pasha had to obtain the approval of the Janissaries and that of the powerful corporation of the rais, both masters of the land.

These competing pressures explain the complicated choreography of appointing rulers, as well as the constant circulation of the pashas among the three provinces of the Maghreb: a ruler who was not suited for Algiers could be put in charge of Tunis or Tripoli while awaiting an intervention from the high officials that would eventually lead him to the coveted post in Algiers. The Janissaries in Algiers enjoyed privileged roles, calling themselves the "Invincible Militia" and acting without respect for the diplomatic rules of the Sublime Porte. The riches accumulated through piracy were at the root of the *diwan*'s arrogance vis-à-vis the local population, foreign powers, and Istanbul.

The situation in Tripoli and in Tunis was quite different. These two regencies had neither fleets nor powerful captains. Their revenues were modest in comparison with the fabulous riches of Algiers, which compelled the military to extort the local populations, who in turn had no means of protecting themselves other than lodging complaints with the central power. But even when they were heard, such grievances were rarely dealt with effectively.

In this way, a style of governing emerged in the Maghreb based on the model developed in Algiers. The Turkish soldiers held power to the exclusion of all others, even their own children born in the region. But this model was not imposed in Tripoli, and even less so in Tunis, where the Turks chose to integrate into local society through a set of political and social processes which we will try to identify here.

1588: The Beginning of the Rebellion in Tunis

In Tunis, the *diwan* exploited the Ottomans' preoccupation with their Asiatic ambitions and used the situation to distance itself from Istanbul's control. Did they push the limits of their insubordination so far as to envision the creation of an autonomous state? We cannot be certain. During a short period when the *bulukbashi* (senior officers) were the masters, the military authority was more powerful than the pasha.[6] Before they too lost power, the officers were freed from the political authority of the pashas. The first Hayder governors, Rajeb and Ramadan, were powerful. They exploited the riches of the land for their own profit, excluding the soldiers and their leaders, who were forced to pillage to supplement their earnings. The exit of the great beylerbeys in 1587 and the ensuing power vacuum in Tunis, where Istanbul had not appointed a pasha for some time, created an opportunity for the officers to consolidate their power and establish themselves as an authority over the governors. Embezzlement was widespread among politicians and military officers, who were all broadly implicated in the dispossession of the local populations. The frustrated locals filed complaints against those who stole their harvests, ripped the clothing off their backs, forced them to work without pay, and disrupted commerce by buying up all the imported merchandise at a pittance and reselling it at prohibitive prices.[7] The central state issued warnings to those responsible but did not stop the abuses, as it had done several years earlier, when it had recalled the officers accused of embezzlement or injustice. In 1579, for example, the *bulukbashi Qasim bin 'Abidine* was removed from his post and called back to Istanbul because of his reprehensible behavior.[8]

Strengthened by the indifference of the central power, officers and soldiers continued to oppress the local populations. They imposed a new tax, the *diyafa*, on all the regions they passed through. As soon as the administration caught wind of this extralegal practice, it demanded that the officers end it.[9] In fact, the pashas of Algiers had agreed to pay this tax, upon their arrival, as a fee for taking office. After falling into disuse, it was reinstated in 1580 at the request of Ja'far Pasha. The army generalized it for its own profit.[10]

More and more, the troops acted with no accountability to the political authorities. To restore order, the sultan decreed that from now on, the appointments and the determination of ranks for the *aghas* and the officers would fall within the sole jurisdiction of the beylerbey, who would ensure that the *aghas* rotated every year, or whenever he deemed it necessary.[11] These measures were imposed in 1588 and were meant to reestablish an administrative hierarchy in which the *diwan* was subject to the power of the pasha. In reality, they had the opposite effect: the rulers increasingly appeared to be the hostages of the military council.

Despite the military's growing strength, the sultan continued to issue directives. He forbade appointing more guards *(nubatji)* than necessary, to keep the budget under control, and commanded that the political authority not allow itself to be controlled by the Janissary corps. He also created a code to regulate the Janissary corps and subjected the troops to it. The absence of legislation was one of the lacunas in the administration of the Maghreb, and the primary cause of the Janissaries' excesses. The Turkish documents enumerated all the abuses, notably the corrupt judicial appointments and the unjustified salary increases, which undermined the regencies' budgets and left them unable to pay their other expenses. The sultan recommended that the beylerbey confront the soldiers, not cater to them, and punish the offenders.[12] But the pashas had no intention of cracking down. Not only did they lack the means to do so, but the troubled situation served their economic interests: all of them were implicated in the flourishing business of trading goods and slaves.

Beginning in the 1580s, Ottoman foreign policy was oriented away from the Mediterranean and toward Asia. The empire no longer considered the Maghreb to be a central priority and was therefore indifferent to the insubordinations there.

In Tunis, from 1587 onwards, the real power was held by the council of the Janissaries. The officers who comprised the council worked to consolidate their interests—not to the detriment of the pashas, but in collaboration with them. Along with the local populations, a portion of the occupying troops was excluded from the benefits of this collusion between the political and military authorities. Herein lies the root of the uprising of October 1591.

The Uprising of October 1591

This event is considered decisive in the fall of the pashas and the rise of the deys. It is celebrated in Tunisian historiography, yet scarcely recorded. Ibn abi Dinar, seventy years after the event, devotes a few lines to it. He attributes responsibility for the uprising to the *bulukbashi* officers. In his florid style, he leads us to understand that the officers were unjust and violent toward their subordinates, the *yoldachs*.[13] The officers had under their command young boys, the *azria*, whom they likely abused both physically and sexually.[14] The soldiers who were appointed to be *azria* were probably young Turkish volunteers belonging to irregular troops that the officers of the prestigious Janissary corps disregarded and treated as second-tier. However, they were the essential first recruits sent to the Maghreb. After emigrating to distant lands to improve their lot, they found themselves confined to inferior ranks and denied opportunities to move upward, which were monopolized by the Janissaries. The uprising of 1591 was not a mutiny of soldiers against their officers, but of a second-order corps against their superiors from the elite Janissary corps.

We know little about these young men, some of whom arrived with the first unit as early as 1574. Many were probably married to local women and joined the military service, along with other activities. Those who remained unmarried lived in the barracks in rooms organized by place of geographic origin, under the moral authority of the "maternal uncle," the dey. Grouped as such, they developed fraternal ties based on regional solidarities, even inscribing the names of their cities and villages on the doors of their rooms.[15] Prevented from rising in rank or attaining command posts, the soldiers decided to act.

The Mutiny

The soldiers prepared their coup in secret. They had won over a sergeant-major *(wakil al-kharj)*, Tobbal Rajeb, who was in charge of the hall of arms.

On the day of the coup, Rajeb abandoned his post so that the officers could not access weapons to defend themselves. On Friday, just as the *diwan* was meeting, the armed soldiers attacked the officers, killing all of those present and following others to their homes, assassinating eighty troops in total. After the massacre, they organized "parties," putting one of their own, a dey, at the head of each group to advise them. The conspiracy seems to have been a spontaneous expression of anger on the part of the soldiers, fed up with the vexations of their superiors. Once their plan had been executed, they looked to the deys, who seemed to have functioned as a committee of experts, for direction.

This period of installing a new authority is not thoroughly explained in the sources. Ibn abi Dinar's account of events does not allow us to determine what happened between the mutiny and 1598, when Othman was made dey (which had meanwhile become a political office). According to this version, three hundred conspirators chose the oldest of the deys, Ibrahim Rhudisli, to be put in charge of the soldiers. He was not able to impose his will. At the end of three years, he asked to go on pilgrimage and never returned. Moussa Dey was appointed in his place. He governed for one year and was no more able than his predecessor. He left for Mecca, and the soldiers assumed he would never return. Two deys, Safar and Othman, fought to fill his position. Othman prevailed, although he was the less supported and the lesser known of the two. He took up residence in the Kasbah with his supporters and demanded that his rival go into exile. Safar acquiesced and departed without a fight. This is the summary of events reported by Ibn abi Dinar, who is said to have met Safar when he returned from exile in Algeria during the time of Youssef Dey. Safar married in Tunis and lived there until 1640.[16]

The historiography saw in this mutiny the rise of an egalitarian military republic in which the highest authority now resided with the dey, who was beholden to the troops. The Mediterranean renegades took possession of a country, and found in Othman Dey the instrument of their policy.

14

Between Myth and History: Othman Dey and Saint Abu al-Gaith

To understand Othman Dey's trajectory, we must also understand that of Saint Abu al-Gaith al-Quachach (1550–1622). The settling of the Ottoman Turks in Tunis was concomitant with the appearance of the saint whose *zawiya* had expanded for half a century until the death of its founder on February 15, 1622. His son-in-law, Zine al-'Arifine al-Bikri, inherited the *zawiya* because the saint had no male heirs. Matrilineal descent was one of the many special attributes of the *Zawiya Quachachia*, which had a radiant presence during the lifetime of its founder. The *zawiya* would have been a serious competitor of the Ottoman Turks.

The saint's life was related in a hagiographic work, "*Nur al-armash fi manaqib Abu al-Gaith al-Quachach*," written by one of his disciples from Gafsa after the saint's death.[1] The work is notable from a symbolic point of view (for the miracles and extraordinary acts it attributes to the saint) and for the historical perspective, given its portrayal of an exemplary personality in the midst of the Turks' settling of Tunis.

Abu al-Gaith was born sometime in 1550 or 1551. He was already an accomplished man by the time the Ottoman army arrived in Tunis in July 1574. But he did not witness these events because he had been away on his *rihla*, or his "initiatory journey" in the east, for part of the year. He established contact with the Turks upon his return, a relationship that seems to have begun fraught with conflict.

A Journey in Raptures

In Tunis, the saint appeared suddenly as if by a miracle. There are no allusions in his hagiography to any premonitory signs during his childhood, which is customary in this genre of literature. The author of this work does not seek to situate his master's life in the family tradition of the saint, who was the manager of a *zawiya* and had a saintly aura from an early age. Abu al-Gaith's appearance at the same time as the Turks in Tunis and his individual experience are the first symbols the author highlights in the saint's life. From there, his career progressed as a series of ruptures: interrupted studies, an unfinished *rihla* (he did not complete his pilgrimage to Mecca), a rather formal *hijba*, and conflicts that were always resolved. Abu al-Gaith seems to have been half ordinary man and half saint, somewhere in between an *'alim* and a mystic, charitable yet thrifty, spiritual but without disdain for the pleasures of life. The hagiography describes his day-to-day life: baths in his private hammam, lavish clothes, perfumes, a well-stocked table, but also the nights of *dhikr* and the suffering and fainting during moments of possession.

He was an ordinary man, a head of household who had three successive marriages. He repudiated his first wife (his first cousin) the day after the marriage without consummating the union. He also repudiated his second wife, Hyzia bint al-Koshbati, also from a maraboutic family. Before agreeing to the marriage, she had insisted on retaining her freedom of movement and the right to ride a horse, but the saint did not keep his promise. Hyzia could not tolerate being forcibly secluded and demanded a separation. His third marriage occurred around 1592 to a woman who had been captured by corsairs. Converted and baptized as Mariem, she was a caring woman and the saint was happy with her. This third wife bore him two sons and one daughter. He raised them royally, along with the son that Mariem had with her first husband, a Christian whom Abu al-Gaith treated like his own son. Abu al-Gaith was deeply fulfilled until the plague of 1606 carried away his two sons, the apples of his eye. His life does not resemble the typical life of a saint—ascetic, unmarried, and living in abstinence and poverty. Instead, the *zawiya* was enormously wealthy. How had he amassed this fortune?

The Growth of a Fortune

The *zawiya* of Abu al-Gaith was able to claim revenues from the *habous* that had benefited mosques, *zawiya*s, and madrasas since the Hafsid era. The eleven most important mosques, eleven madrasas, twelve *zawiya*s in Tunis and its surroundings, fifteen others in the towns and interior regions, and eleven wells and fountains all came under the saint's control. These *habous* foundations represented considerable sums of money and agricultural goods each year, which the original *zawiya* and its annexes used to feed the thousands of visitors that passed through. It was estimated that livestock and other animals comprised two hundred horses, for breeding and traveling, a thousand heads of cattle, three thousand heads of sheep, and five hundred camels.[2]

How did the *zawiya* gain control of the usufructs of these *habous*, normally entrusted to *bayt al-mal?* The hagiography does not say. It only lists the particular conditions in Ifriqya since 1535 that led to the destruction of buildings, the depopulation of the territory, the abandonment of land, and the overall slowdown of economic activities. There are indications of this general decrepitude in juridical and literary sources, which often include questions about the *kharab* (ruins) and the accumulation of trash. Abu al-Gaith amassed the fortune of his *zawiya* from private donations, but especially from the revenues derived from public *habous*. How did he manage to redirect these funds? Had he succeeded in placing one of his men in a Hafsid institution, that of the *nadhir fi shuglay al-zakawat wa-l-mawarith*, and diverting the services of the tithes and estates that were collected when property fell into disrepair? The answer is probably yes, because there was no other way for him to have gained access to public *habous* revenues. At one point, Othman occupied this position.[3]

While things deteriorated around him, Abu al-Gaith al-Quachach profited hugely in ways both symbolic and material. His spiritual radiance stretched well beyond the regency: Cairo, Alexandria, Damietta, Syria, Medina, and even Malta all had *zawiya*s connected with the sheikh's. On the material plane, Abu al-Gaith was, above all else, a prolific builder who was able to channel the energy of his followers into massive works of restoration, beautification, and garbage collection. We might consider these actions as part of a larger project to revitalize "dead" lands, given his other efforts to restore places of worship, most of which were in ruin due to poor maintenance. The initiatives he undertook upon his return from the East certainly contributed to the renewal of the urban landscape.

For example, he had a monument built, by night, to the saint Sidi Hdhifa, whose tomb was in the street facing Abu al-Gaith's house. Passing city dwellers commented that this was strange. A little while later, he integrated the tomb of Sidi Hdhifa, now beautified by his care, into the domestic space of the *zawiya* without opposition from a single authority.[4]

Throughout his life, al-Quachach's power as a saint gave him access to a workforce that would work for free or charge a fee, as appropriate. The finished work was always admirable because he employed specialized craftsmen. He entreated Andalusian artisans to adorn numerous monuments that he wished to restore, notably the *zawiya* of Sidi Qasim al-Jalizi. During the restoration of al-Hwa mosque, he called on the populations of Bab Souika: two hundred people arrived to help.

These properties brought in considerable revenues that the *zawiya* used to support its work serving the disciples from Tunis and from the provinces, as well as students and beggars. Four thousand men and women were affiliated with the brotherhood. The saint organized them like a small state, modeled after that of the Turks. He surrounded himself with countless servants and put into place a column, just like the *mhalla*, that went out twice a year to collect royalties from his disciples. When his affiliates died without leaving any heirs, Abu al-Gaith would inherit their wealth.[5] When the Andalusians arrived en masse in 1609, the sheikh received them and set many of them up in the mausoleum of Sidi Qasim. He fed them for an entire year, supplying them with 1,200 pieces of bread per day, two *kfiz* of wheat semolina for couscous, two cows, and carob tree milk. He employed many of the Andalusian artisans to work on the restoration of places of worship.

From its inception, the influence of the *zawiya* alarmed the Turks. Abu al-Gaith appeared on the Ottomans' radar because they feared a dangerous competitor: the *shurafa*, descendants of the Prophet, had the power to galvanize crowds and undermine a military power made up of foreign Janissaries. The Turks were aware of this because in Morocco a Sherifein power had curbed many Ottoman attempts to occupy the land. For several years, the Turks worried about Abu al-Gaith.

The saint decided to test his new power and see how he measured up against the Turks. On one occasion, he ordered several of his disciples to walk around naked in the souq. This moral transgression provoked the wrath of the city dwellers, who complained to Ramadan Pasha. He sentenced the offenders to be caned and summoned the saint. Ramadan Pasha wanted to be sure that Abu al-Gaith did not take himself to be a *mahdi*, and that he did not intend to declare a religious war against the Turks.[6] Abu al-Gaith defended himself and specified that his men had misunderstood his orders; he had only asked them to remove their sins that they wore like clothes.

This event probably took place at the end of Ramadan's term as governor in 1579. The Turks' worries about Abu al-Gaith dissipated; they no longer opposed the influence of the *zawiya* and instead maintained good relations with it. When subsequent pashas came to take up their posts, they would dock in Bizerte and continue overland to Tunis. Along the road, they were royally received in the *zawiya* of Nouina, which belonged to the saint. By offering hospitality to the representatives of the sultan, Abu al-Gaith established a sense of reciprocity between himself and his guests.

For several years, relations between the saint and the Turks were close and Abu al-Gaith was able to build his fortune without interference from the authorities. As he began to obtain the *habous* of religious institutions abandoned by the Hafsids, the Turks were seeking their fortune elsewhere. They were focused on farming and exporting agricultural goods, but also diverting all kinds of royalties intended for the state treasury. When these resources proved insufficient, they turned to the properties belonging to the *zawiya*s.

The military leaders were well informed about the opulence of the *zawiya* because Othman frequently visited it. He proposed that the pasha confiscate certain plots of land belonging to the saint and use the revenue to pay the soldiers. The pasha quickly sent a *chaouch*, accompanied by a notary, who took for the *makhzan* 100 henchirs for every 130 owned by the *zawiya*.[7]

Othman Dey: 1554–1611

Before he became the providential leader who promoted corsair activities and the rise of the renegades, Othman was an obscure soldier. He started out among the troops and became dey by violently imposing himself on his peers. Within fifteen years, he had succeeded in reestablishing order in the land. He used force and persuasion to control the soldiers and pacify and subjugate recalcitrant tribes on the periphery. During his first tour in Tunisia he tried to integrate into the local milieu by frequenting the *Zawiya Quachachia* until he discovered the world of the renegades and their activities at sea.

Othman was an Anatolian by birth, who arrived with Sinan Pasha's contingent in 1574. Ibn abi Dhiaf considered him to be *a'yan jund al-turk*, or a notable in the Turkish army—a rhetorical formula that masks ignorance about Othman's origins and fails to tell us how an obscure soldier became such a prominent figure during this period. Before arriving in Tunis, Othman had been a butcher and a shoemaker. He was not a soldier by trade (a Janissary) but a volunteer who came from his homeland along with his younger brother.[8] Like all the Turkish soldiers, he had permission to work outside his career as a soldier.

The first information about his early work in Tunis describes him as often visiting the *zawiya* of the Saint Abu al-Gaith al-Quachach seeking the sheikh's *baraka*. He was responsible for carrying to the oven large loaves that went to feed the sheikh's disciples. This small-scale activity was probably unpaid, except in kind words from the saint, who predicted an exceptional future for him. Because of his frequent visits to the *zawiya*, Othman got to know the society and the various circles within it. This poor man who had arrived at the age of twenty, unmarried and with no intention of returning home, immersed himself in the community via a particularly vibrant institution. He became acquainted with all the people from the provinces who flocked to the *zawiya* for ritual visits, or *ziyara*. Through this immersion, he came to know the local milieu better than other Turks.

The hagiography of Abu al-Gaith al-Quachach is one of the rare sources that informs us about the early Ottoman decades. The author, Ibn abi Louhayya, was a disciple from Gafsa who deeply hated the Turks. The Turks distrusted the saint and his disciples, persecuting members of the *zawiya* in Gafsa, including Ibn abi Louhayya and some of his relatives who were imprisoned by one of the pashas. This text is interesting on a symbolic level for its biased presentation of the Turks as deplorable, and the saint as beatified. According to Ibn abi Louhayya, Abu al-Gaith is single handedly responsible for all the misfortune that befalls the new masters of the land. He recounts the role of the saint in the massacre of *bulukbashi* officers by the soldiers in October 1591. In the face of the officers' abuses, he supposedly predicted the mutiny by asking his disciples to purchase heads of sheep and to cook and eat them. The anecdote plays a word game between *kbach* (sheep) and *bulukbashi*. He encouraged the rebellion to seek revenge on the officers. This incited the anger of the Prophet, who scolded the saint, saying: "You anathematize the people of my *umma* to the point where they kill one another." Ashamed, the saint went into isolation for fifteen years.[9]

The saint also punished Ramadan Bey for having heavily repressed the oasis of Sdada, which lived in poverty in the shadow of Saint Abu Hilal Sdadi. Returning from his tour, the bey was struck by two blows that killed him. Abu al-Gaith's power also made Othman suffer a fatal fall from his horse.

As well as describing the saint's supernatural powers, the hagiography contains much information on the structure of the *zawiya*. Abu al-Gaith, his disciples, and various servants constituted a sort of state organized according to the Turkish model. He used his material resources to help the Andalusians, whom he welcomed warmly. He surrounded himself with their elite and counted within his network eminent legal scholars, such as Sassi Nwina al-Andaloussi.[10] This learned man, held in esteem by the pashas of Tunis, was designated to replace Qadi 'Ali Effendi. Abu al-Gaith founded *zawiyas* in the regions inhabited by the Moriscos. The saint's cordial relations with the new colony did arouse some suspicion: the powerful 'Ali Thabit, a close associate of Youssef Dey, accused Abu al-Gaith of wanting to use the support of the Andalusians to rebel against the Turks.[11]

After a number of conflicts with the Turks, Abu al-Gaith went into a semi-retirement that lasted almost seventeen years, ending in 1606. How do we explain this? Was it Othman Dey who pushed Abu al-Gaith to retire? What were relations between these two men like during the period between Othman Dey's arrival in Tunis and his death in January 1611?

Above all, this relationship was characterized by ambiguity and ambivalence. Toward the end of the saint's isolation, he was once again in conflict with Othman—this time, as part of a somber affair involving women that his hagiographer recounts. Among Abu al-Gaith's closest associates was a man named Nasr al-Dahmani who was responsible for his businesses and finances. He lived near the saint and was married to a beautiful woman. Othman Dey demanded that Nasr repudiate his wife so

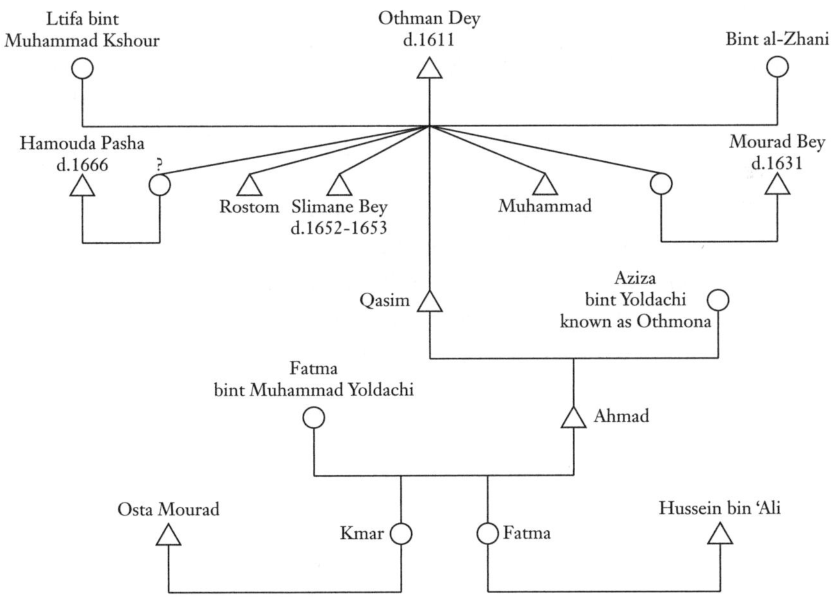

5. The house of Othman Dey

that he himself could marry her. Nasr refused and barricaded himself in his home. Othman nailed the door of Nasr's house shut before the saint could come to his rescue. After some time, Othman proposed that Nasr could either divorce his wife or pay a ransom. Nasr chose the latter and paid 2,300 dinars. His wife died not long after. Abu al-Gaith took it upon himself to marry Nasr al-Dahmani to the daughter of the mufti Muhammad Kshour, a Maliki legal scholar, who was part of the saint's inner circle and was known to have taken part in the system of spoliation that the Turks had put in place.[12] This marriage was witnessed by Ibn abi Louhayya, who was present during the signing of the marriage contract in the saint's own home. This second wife also soon died. Her estate passed to her husband, but also in part to the state, as an agnatic heir. The saint negotiated with the state, which renounced its part of the estate in exchange for 6,000 dinars compensation. Thanks to this inheritance, Nasr became very rich.[13] Furthermore, a *habous* document refers to Ltifa bint Muhammad Kshour, who distributes some of the *waqf* property to the *zawiya*. Grandchamp's documents cite Ltifa as "the wife of the King of Tunis," an intermediary in the business of purchasing captives on behalf of the saint. There is no doubt that this document is referring to the same woman. In other words, Othman Dey married another of Kshour's daughters, probably for her fortune; her father, the judge Muhammad Kshour, had grown rich by working illicitly with the Turkish pashas.[14] This marriage demonstrates the close ties that united Abu al-Gaith and Othman Dey. It also demonstrates the role played by women in the circulation of property and in the integration of the Turks into Tunis.

The life of Abu al-Gaith and his difficult relations with the Turks were symbolically interpreted as a local, or even "national," response to a foreign power. But there is also another way to interpret his life: one that considers the saint as an ordinary man, focused on amassing his fortune and earthly possessions, who cut deals with the Turks more often than he fought them.

15

Othman and the World of the Renegades

Around 1590, Othman began to move in the renegades' circles. We can trace him in the sources of the French consulate in Tunis, where traders, tax farmers, caids, corsairs, and all those who were involved in economic activities on the Mediterranean Sea went to register their various contracts. The first mention of Othman dates to April 5, 1591.[1] From the *zawiya* and the confines of the medina, Othman finds himself propelled into the world of the renegades and the coral collectors of Bizerte and Fiumara Salata, although we cannot be certain how he first made contact with them. Othman is mentioned in a promissory note signed by Nicollas Borilly, the consul of the King of France, on February 16, 1591. Upon the consul's death, which occurred a few days later, a group of Janissaries pursued Jacques Ballue, who led the coral company, and presented him before the *diwan*, demanding that he pay them what they were owed. According to the transcript of the event, the men involved were Mami de Coagio, Ossain Boulokbashi, Razouan Boulokbashi, Ossoman Coadgio Dey, Morat Mailhorquin, and Fouquet Clerici, a Frenchman employed by the company. These men, all involved in the coral trade, held a promissory note for 1,454 crowns, signed by the consul, probably in the name of the company. In it, Othman is referred to as "*khoadja*" and "*dey*": army writer, and leader of a barrack of soldiers.

Othman's entry into the cosmopolitan world of port cities and maritime traffic slightly preceded the putsch of October 1591. We cannot be certain whether he participated directly in the uprising or what the connection was between the conspirators and the world of the renegades. But in the medium term, Othman was the principal beneficiary of this event: all indications suggest that he was backed by a dynamic group that controlled the activities of the corsairs.

One of Othman's captives explained better than anyone the secret to his rise in a letter, written in Provençal. A passage is reproduced here:

> He is a Turk by nationality, around fifty-five years old; a swarthy, strong, and powerful man, who was a soldier for the great sultan in the kingdom of Tunis. This so-called Garaosman, being a native of the city of Tunis [a false assertion] and a janissary soldier, was so well established that after fifteen years he had secured the allegiance of all of the notables of Tunis. Only twelve years earlier, he had possessed just two slaves: one being François de Croissy, who remains in his power, and now he has seven hundred slaves to himself, Italians as well as French, Spanish, and Flemish, as well as well-armed galleys, in addition to six large vessels, the smallest of which is three hundred tons and has two tenders.[2]

After having enumerated the dey's riches, Captain Foucques explains how corsairing operated. His report is damning. He breaks down the mechanisms of piracy and the complicity that the corsairs benefited from: downstream, in the construction of vessels and furnishing of amenities, and upstream, in the resale of stolen merchandise. Piracy was not simply a barbary activity, but an extensive traffic that included many European ports and senior officials from different maritime services. It was thanks to this support that piracy became an extremely lucrative enterprise. It was also a dangerous one, for the renegades engaged in it at the beginning of the seventeenth century risked being burned at the stake if they fell into the hands of the Inquisition.

The merit of Foucques' report is its examination of the activities of Othman Dey as they appear in the consular archives: the sale of all kinds of seized goods, boats, merchandise, and slaves. As the man became powerful, his sailors scoured the sea and brought back all kinds of riches. English and Flemish corsairs collaborated with him. "Ossoman dey, governor and protector of the militia of the kingdom of Tunis," became a powerful personality, but his transactions remained those of an insatiable upstart who did not hesitate to swindle merchants. On June 15, 1609, the businessman Francesco Estelle and his associate revealed to the consul of France that Othman had forced them to take several barrels of herring that the inspectors had declared rotten.[3]

The purchase of captives tapped into considerable revenues. The captives paid ransoms, which ranged in value according to their status. Bizerte became a flourishing port. It housed the rais of the two regencies, Algiers and Tunis, who organized common expeditions. The corporation developed, the number of galleys grew, and a commander of the fleet was appointed.

But piracy and legal commerce were not compatible, and the interests of certain great powers were soon affected. The political authorities became involved, especially since France and the Ottoman Empire had maintained amicable relations for some time.

Local Politics and French Interests

In the middle of the sixteenth century, a major diplomatic event occurred: the signing of the first peace treaty between François the First and Suleiman the Magnificent in 1535. In fact it was nothing more than a truce that could be broken at any moment. But by virtue of the accords, commercial relations between the two states became privileged.

Before that, the sultan-caliphs and the Christian kings, considered irreducible enemies by their respective religions, maintained no diplomatic relations. These first accords ignited a scandal in the Christian world. France justified its policy as commercially necessary for Provence and Languedoc, which, thanks to the stipulations in the treaty, were authorized to acquire products from Aleppo and resell them throughout Europe. By virtue of these same stipulations, the French could move around or live within the Ottoman Empire under the jurisdiction of their own consuls.

Savary de Brèves (1560–1628), an ardent defender of this friendship with the Ottomans, justified it on religious grounds. He argued that many monasteries and colleges belonging to the orders of the Cordeliers, the Jacobins, and the Jesuits could be opened in Istanbul and attract converts to Christianity.[4]

The 1535 treaty opened up promising opportunities for the traders from Marseille. Business between Tunis and Marseille flourished. But this commercial activity proved to be disproportionately difficult because of piracy and the indiscipline of the captains of Algiers, Tripoli, and Tunis, who did not respect the treaty, which should have protected the French boats from attacks. Due to these violations, relations between the French and the Turks of the Maghreb became more complicated, comprising both agreements and ruptures, friendships and animosities. To advance the interests of the Marseille merchants, consuls were appointed as official intermediaries with the local authorities. The first French consul in Tunis was appointed in 1577, barely three years after the arrival of the Ottomans, which demonstrated the influence the French diplomats exercised in Istanbul. They rushed to occupy the terrain, jostling ahead of other European states. The consulate was established in a *funduq* at the entrance to the city. The consuls quickly realized the difficulty of their situation: often lacking authority, they were bullied by the pashas, the council of the Janissaries, and even by the deys and beys, who impeded their efforts. After several years of cohabitation, certain consuls adopted local traditions. Despite the problems among the three regencies, commerce in Marseille prospered. In the consulate of Tunis, a first notarized register was opened in July 1582. It was made available to traders to permit the notarizing of contracts. Meanwhile, in Istanbul, the ambassador of the King of France attempted, for better or worse, to respect the treaties that protected French commerce and oversaw the establishment of companies. The first companies specialized in the exploitation of coral.

The Coral Companies

The people of Marseille were aware that the coasts of the Maghreb were rich in precious commodities and that the Spanish and Italians had invested in the territory well before them. Beginning in the fifteenth century, the Catalans dealt in coral fishing in the region of Bjaïa. The Genoese came next, and the powerful Lomellini family established themselves in Tabarka. Strengthened by capitulations treaties, the subjects of the King of France, the Provençals in particular, hoped to dislodge the Genoese and exploit the privileges granted by peace with the Ottomans. A wave of naturalizations followed: many Florentines, Genoese, Pisans, Luccans, and Corsicans naturalized as French to profit from these treaties of commerce and cooperation.

In a letter dated August 17, 1553, Thomas Lenche, a sea captain and founder of the coral company of Cap-Corse, obtained permission to sell the product.[5] His business flourished, and he became one of the wealthiest traders in the city of Marseille. He owed this prosperity in part to the networks that he put in place with the help of the renegades of Algiers, which allowed him to negotiate at the highest level: with the sultan himself. In 1572, the company obtained the rights to fish coral on the Algerian coasts, a privilege accorded by the sultan's royal favor. The prosperity of this first

French company was spectacular, and its owner was elected as the second consul of the city of Marseille. In 1575, he hosted the sultan's ambassador in his luxurious home.

This success would fuel the desires of rival companies, jealous of Lenche's exceptional prosperity and wanting to establish themselves on the coasts of the Maghreb. In 1577, an entrepreneur, Jean-Baptiste de Nicolle, arrived in Istanbul, negotiated in high places, and was granted permission to start his own company. Shortly thereafter, a galliot of Algiers carrying a representative of Thomas Lenche arrived in Istanbul. The man held a letter of recommendation signed by a powerful figure in Algiers and also authorization to fish granted by 'Ilj 'Ali, the grand admiral and former governor of the city, whose influence remained strong. The two rival companies did business and, alongside their fishing activities, developed a fruitful exchange with the hinterland, in which the renegades played the role of intermediaries. In 1578, the caid Ramadan and his wife Asnisia, from Nice, provided the companies with oil, probably destined for the soap factories of Marseille. Encouraged by his success, Antoine Lenche, Thomas' nephew, would make use of 'Ilj 'Ali Pasha's friendship to obtain for his brother a sort of monopoly on coral fishing and to open a third company. But the Genoese did not consider themselves defeated, and in 1580 they became involved with the Tunisian fisheries, provoking the people of Marseille, who cried usurpation. The ambassador of the King of France in Istanbul obtained the sultan's intervention on behalf of the people of Marseille. It was heard that an envoy of the sultan in Paris was brought to the Barbary Coast on the ships of the King of France, "to put the new coral company under the reach and authority of Captain Bassa, who owned territory in Cape Nègre and Fiumara Salata, in the Kingdom of Tunis, by dismissing the Genoese."[6]

To avoid the Genoese threat, the two French companies—rivals until then, and both protected by the powers of Istanbul and Algiers—ultimately came together and founded the "Magnificent Company of Coral." From its inception, the new establishment relied on the renegades of Tunis and Algiers for the fishing of coral and the flow of the goods. The fishing spots multiplied: Bône, Cape Nègre, and Fiumara Salata *(al-wad al-malah)* were all exploited from 1584 onwards. The company joined forces with traders from Marseille and obtained patent letters from the king, who authorized them to fish the seas, islands, and coasts of the Kingdom of Tunis, as well as to engage in free trade in all legal and permissible merchandise.

However, the company quickly broke up, and Nicolle became its only remaining leader. In December 1588, a *chaouch* of Istanbul installed Nicolle in Cape Nègre and Fiumara Salata. But the sought-after new company was seized by its rivals, who created a new one in July 1591. It seems likely that this new company, which only lasted three years, had been set up in collaboration with the Turks of Tunis, whose names appeared in the notarized registers. What's more, the company left Cape Nègre and chose for its headquarters and fishing ground the port of Bizerte, which had become the maritime base for all pirate activity since the Ottoman conquest. As a result of this choice, which was likely imposed upon them, the French coral fishers found themselves under the thumb of the rais, and the company would be exploited by the corsairs, the renegades, and the powers in Tunis. It was charged a "*lisma*," or annual rent, of 2,000 crowns, half of which went to Hussein Pasha. The agents of the company were required to give gifts to all the intermediaries, and they were subjected to extortion and usurious interest rates. All the coral was centralized in Tunis and then sent to Marseille after the payment of exit duties, consular duties set at two percent, and the salt tax of one percent owed to Marseille. The new establishment in Marseille had the double disadvantage of being under the control of the *diwan* in Tunis, and the hostage of a turbulent population of corsairs in Bizerte. Its accounts (money paid for bribes) show growing difficulties: the company stopped trading on July 9, 1594, and suffered a loss of 44,791 crowns.

The coral companies came to understand, at their expense, that it was not enough to obtain a recommendation from Istanbul to conduct their affairs. They also had to receive the approval of the local authorities by paying significant sums of money: the consuls, or the vice-consuls, who were charged with protecting the company's interests, had to negotiate on-site to obtain the necessary authorizations for their activities. The negotiations were often fraught, and Savary de Brèves himself had to intervene a number of times to strike a deal with the authorities in Algiers and in Tunis.

As well as serving economic interests, the rapprochement between the Ottoman Empire and France served the latter's foreign policy interests. The French King Henry IV (1589–1610) found himself in a difficult position because he was Protestant. Spain actively supported his internal enemies. Unable to fight the Spanish militarily because of defections in his army, Henry IV planned to weaken them from within. He incited an uprising of Moriscos that began in Valencia and then spread across Spain.

His Muslim deputies went to France to execute the plan. In this war, the French depended heavily upon the Barbary powers, who controlled the Mediterranean coasts with their galleys, to block reinforcements arriving from Sicily to help the Spanish fleet. Philip III, who had acceded to the throne in 1598, was informed of all these secret transactions. To thwart the French plan, he attempted a landing at Algiers, but the operation failed. It was at this moment that Spain decided to expel the Moriscos entirely: at war with foreign powers, she could not keep a million enemies on her soil, ready to conspire against her.

At the end of the sixteenth century, these various political elements changed the situation in the western Mediterranean. France, through the intermediary of its consuls in Tunis and its ambassadors in Istanbul, intervened in local politics. It was important for the go-between to be capable of compromise and reconciling the various parties' interests, while still appearing to be an obedient servant of the sultan. Othman Dey performed this role perfectly, and all while stubbornly protecting his own interests and those of the corsairs. He ceded certain points, avoided rupture between the parties, and preserved the hierarchical relationship between Tunis and the imperial capital. He simultaneously maintained interior order and managed external relations, always seeking equilibrium and a strong understanding between soldiers and sailors. This role made Othman Dey a hugely powerful figure. The position he occupied should not be confused with the typical functions of the dey, which explains why none of his successors exercised the same duties quite so forcefully. It was also not an indication that the institutions had been reversed in favor of the dey: the pashas were always the representatives of the sultan and of Ottoman legitimacy. Before 1574, the position of the beylerbey had been coveted by high officials of the state and negotiated in the sultan's council. But since then significant changes had been made to the way they were appointed. Beginning in 1595, the pashas were recruited onsite from among the men already established in one of the *oujak*s, who were heavily involved in the Mediterranean economy.

16

The Pashas of Tunis, Caught Between Diplomatic and Local Interests: 1586–1631

In the month of August 1581, a dispute broke out between Ja'far Pasha and the *faqih* 'Ali Riahi over whether the *faqih*'s legal analysis was sound. The scholar argued angrily: "Fourteen pashas before you have accepted my word, and now you reject it!" The *faqih* was immediately thrown into prison for his insolence.[1] For us, the remark is evidence that there was a succession of pashas between 1574 (or 1569, according to several sources which consider the arrival of 'Ilj 'Ali as the start of the Ottoman era in Tunis) and 1591.

After the period of the great beylerbeys that closed with the departure and death of Kilidj 'Ali and then, one by one, the men of his house, the functioning of the institution of the pashalik was cloaked in opacity, so much so that it is difficult to write about.

Two modes of recruitment appear to have alternated, demonstrating a rivalry between local interests and Ottoman diplomacy. Local interests were represented by men who were born or lived in the Maghreb—a kind of "second generation," products of the renegades—who knew the land because they had strong family connections and belonged to houses like that of Othman Dey or Mourad Coursou. At the same time, high officials in Istanbul were trying to obtain jobs in the *oujak*s of the Maghreb in exchange for large contributions to the state. Between 1586 and 1598, six pashas are known to have succeeded one another in Tunis.

Khidr Pasha: 1586

Khidr Pasha was born in Algiers, the son of a Neapolitan renegade. In the beginning of his career he held the lucrative position of caid and married the daughter of another celebrated caid, Ramadan. This union, reported by Haedo, was confirmed by *waqf* documents, which indicated that the wife of

Khidr Pasha was Fattoum, the daughter of Ramadan Pasha, who was made Governor of Tunis several times.[2]

This first appointment was the beginning of Khidr Pasha's prestigious career. He did not have to wait long before becoming Pasha of Algiers.

Muhammad Pasha: 1588–89

We know of his journey to Tunis by way of his discussions with the mufti Qasim 'Addoum. The pasha established himself as head of the *diwan* and was surrounded by legal scholars who helped him in matters of forfeiture and misappropriation.[3]

Ja'far Pasha: June 1591 to June 1592

There is little information on this pasha of Turkish origin who oversaw the *diwan* and was responsible for administering justice. 'Addoum specifies that Ja'far was removed from his position on June 25, 1592 and returned to Turkey.[4]

Mahmoud Mami Pasha: 1594

Very little information exists about this pasha, who ruled for several months.

Hussein Pasha: 1595–98

Hussein Pasha began his career as *agha* of the council of Janissaries, sent by Istanbul to restore order among the soldiers. After several years, he was appointed pasha. He never left again and was buried in the mausoleum of Sidi Bin 'Arous. We can hypothesize that Hussein Pasha married a descendant of this saint.[5] He settled in the area, and one of his sons, Muhammad Bey, even became general of the galleys of Bizerte. In July 1598, Hussein was relieved of his post. He died on September 7, 1598. Khidr succeeded him.

The Return of Khidr Pasha: August 3, 1598–1601

This was Khidr's second appointment in Tunis. He was also Pasha of Algiers twice and during his tenure had poor relations with the militia, which earned him two revocations. Istanbul preferred to sacrifice him than risk a mutiny. In September 1596, his successor Mustafa, in an act of vengeance, prevented him from selling his slaves and properties, sequestered them, and imposed a heavy fine. Ruined, Khidr returned to Istanbul, where he negotiated so well with the high authorities that we find him again in Tunis in the position of pasha starting on August 3, 1598.

His journey to Tunis is not well documented. We find a trace of him in the notary archives under the name of Qadir Pasha, engaging in all types of commercial transactions. There is also some information in the legal records of 'Addoum, who attended his councils. Khidr Pasha exercised his duties as first magistrate meticulously.[6] After three years in Tunis, he returned to Algiers in 1601, having been appointed pasha of this city for the third time. Driven by hatred for France, he did all he could to harm its interests and was responsible for distancing Algiers from France. He diverted six thousand sequins sent by the sultan to French merchants as compensation for attacks against their ships. Khidr then led a small fleet against the headquarters of an important coral fishing company from Marseille—a bastion of France—massacred several of their employees, and brought the rest back as captives. Henry IV insisted on immediate reparations. Istanbul urgently sent a new pasha to Algiers, Muhammad Kousa, who in 1603 had Khidr strangled and his property confiscated. This first French intervention ushered in a period of considerable animosity with the Regency of Algiers.

Renegade Pashas

When Khidr left Tunis in 1601, the position of pasha was given to an Italian renegade who inaugurated an "Italian" period. This suggests that networks were being established, made up of merchants, renegades, and corsairs who placed their men in powerful posts to guarantee the sustainability of their interests. But what we don't know is the role that Istanbul played in making these appointments.

Piracy began to intensify in 1589, when the sultan authorized the corsairs to attack ships from Marseille as punishment for the city's participation in attacks against his ally, the King of France. But it was difficult to put an end to their activities when relations with Marseille normalized. The corsairs continued to pursue the French ships despite prohibitions issued by Istanbul.

Savary de Brèves, ambassador of the King of France, was put at the head of a mission to Barbary to negotiate French commercial interests and free the captives held in Tunis and Algiers. On June 17, 1605, he landed in La Goulette, by way of Istanbul, carrying an order from the sultan. He was welcomed by the pasha, but the negotiations with the *diwan* and Othman Dey proved challenging, for they refused to compromise on one specific point: their right to search French ships on the open sea. The corsairs feared that the merchants of other European nations would know that the French vessels were not inspected and would therefore use them to transport their own goods, dooming the corsairs of the Barbary Coast to inactivity.

While Othman Dey was negotiating with Savary de Brèves, the general of the galleys, Muhammad Bey, son of Hussein Pasha, was at sea. When the young man—at the age of 28 already the richest of the rais of Bizerte—returned to Tunis, he clashed with the dey. Although the information available about this disagreement is inconsistent, we can piece together what happened.

Captain Foucques, who was present during the incident, described it as follows:

> And of the largest and most important royal houses in Tunis was that of Maomet Bey [Muhammad Bey], not willing to give up everything that he had made, he said one day in the company of seven or eight notables from the city and his Turkish relatives that it was too much to allow himself to be governed by such a man and that he was determined to kill him. He was the most valiant and the bravest corsair in all the Kingdom of Tunis and a man of means. He had two brothers, and he had to himself one of the most beautiful galleys there was among the six, and two beautiful vessels, and four hundred slaves. One person who he counted and thought of as his friend told all of this to Caraosman. . . . this person went to see him and without saying anything grabbed him by the throat and tried to strangle him, ordering four Italians and French slaves to finish the job, even using a rope himself, in the presence of all the notables in the land who were there, and one of his brothers, who darned not say anything, who he had already submitted to his will. He could have ten months of this.[7]

Cross-checking different sources reveals that there was a disagreement between the two men in the aftermath of Savary de Brèves' request concerning the French captives. Muhammad Bey did not want to free them and was unconcerned about how the Ottoman authorities would react. In contrast, Othman Dey, who was considering the interests of the rais, wanted to avoid provoking a direct conflict with Istanbul: the dey did not want to reproduce in Tunis the same sort of conflict between soldiers, politicians, and sailors that had occurred in Algiers. Things came to a head when Othman, renowned for his physical strength and his violent bursts of anger, strangled his rival to death in a heated session of the *diwan*, which was described by many European travelers. This violent outcome probably arose from a real rivalry between the two men, Othman being concerned about the claims of this rich and powerful young man whose social background was more illustrious than his own. If Muhammad's mother was a descendant of Sidi Bin 'Arous, Muhammad would have benefitted from a degree of legitimacy that would have concerned a Turkish soldier like Othman, who constantly felt threatened by the *shurafa*.

Tunisian historiographers, writing after the fact, recounted this episode differently. Al-Wazir al-Sarraj, whose descriptions are often imprecise, reported that Muhammad Bey's mother was completely helpless after the death of her son and found refuge in the *zawiya* of Sidi Bin 'Arous.[8] However, notarized documents from the consulate of France contradict this assertion, showing instead that the brothers, mother, and sister of Muhammad Bey continued to sell captives after the death of Othman Dey. It is likely, however, that Othman Dey got his hands on a part of his victim's fortune.

Ever since Savary de Brèves had applied pressure in 1603 to assassinate Khidr Pasha because of the violence he had inflicted against French coral fishermen, French diplomats wielded significant influence in Istanbul and believed they could influence the appointment of pashas in Algiers and Tunis. The diplomats thought that by doing this, they could protect their compatriots' interests and enforce decisions made in the imperial capital. But their interventions were unsuccessful, and the pashas continued to be recruited from among the Italian renegades who were established in the country and widely involved in corsair activities. It was difficult to convince them to ban a practice from which they benefited greatly. These pashas proved to be adventurers and rogues, more concerned with protecting their own profits than the interests of merchants from Marseille.

'Ali Pasha Genovese: 1606

He began as caid in Tripoli, working in collaboration with Mourad Coursou. In 1606, he became Pasha of Tunis. He returned to this role in 1609.

Suleiman Catania: 1606–1607

He was a renegade, rais of the "patachio" of Othman Dey, who later became pasha between 1607 and 1608. He claimed previously to have been Pasha of Algiers in May 1602.[9] He drew substantial resources from royalties that the coral company paid him. During his time in Algiers, he received 750 crowns every six months as *lisma* paid by the company of the Bastion of France. Once appointed to Tunis, he continued to collect the *lisma*, payable every two months. When the company's financial difficulties started to become more noticeable and payments were slow to arrive, the pasha did not hesitate to hold prisoner two agents of the coral fishermen: Taverny and Claude Severt. Faced with the silence of their leaders in Marseille, the two men indebted themselves to the corsairs to settle these outstanding payments. Osta Mourad Genovese lent 500 crowns of 24 aspros to Claude Severt, an agent of the company, so that he could pay off the two months of *lisma* owed to Suleiman Pasha.[10]

In 1607, following a complaint lodged by the ambassador of France, Suleiman fled. The sultan searched for him and threatened him for his actions against the French vessels.[11] He was replaced by Mustafa Trapanaisi.

Mustafa Trapanaisi: 1607–1608

Mustafa Trapanaisi, who by his own account had previously been Pasha of Alexandria, held the office during the year of 1607, while the powerful Othman Dey led the militia. The pasha effectively served the interests of the dey, without sacrificing his own.

'Ali Pasha Genovese: 1609

He was pasha in 1606 and then again in April 1609 for an unconfirmed length of time. Later, he became Pasha of Tripoli for two years, from May 1615 to November 1617.

Muhammad Pasha: 1611

According to the chancery sources, Muhammad Pasha, a Calabrian renegade, left traces of lucrative commercial activities.

The Return of Suleiman Catania: October 1611–13

Despite the sultan's threats against him, the pasha continued to arm corsair ships, and his sailors on his galleys had no scruples about boarding French vessels. On June 22, 1613, his galley captured the Saint-Rémond, and as it was at sea without a flag, it was declared a prize. The last trace we find of Suleiman Catania is on September 14, 1613, where he is called "*Serenissimo*

Suleiman Bascia gio Re di questo regno." The flagrant violation of the treaty with the French may have been the reason Suleiman Catania came to understand the ineffectiveness of these appointments, as the renegade-pashas had become merchants involved in major business deals, and they were not very concerned with diplomacy. For a while, the 'natural' Turks (the Turks coming from Anatolia, rather than the Balkans) returned to the scene.

Fadhli Pasha: 1613–23

After Suleiman Catania, Fadhli Pasha was appointed to lead Tunis. He remained in power, probably in intervals, until 1623.[12] The man, described in notarized acts as a Turk of Tunis, did not belong to the world of the renegades. It is difficult to say what changes correspond to his appointment. During his tenure, the three sons of a previous pasha, Hussein (d. 1598), reappeared: Hmida, Mustafa, and Youssef Shalabi. Their brother Muhammad, general of the galleys in Bizerte, had been murdered by Othman Dey in 1608. These young men were probably related to the great Saint of Tunis, Sidi Bin 'Arous, through their mother. They returned to buying and selling captives, a commerce which they had likely been barred from practicing as long as the powerful Othman Dey and his men were in command. We find them at the home of Abu al-Gaith, insisting on seeing the saint and reminding the servants that kept them at bay that the saint was a representative of the sultan and so could not refuse their visit.[13]

Qasim Pasha: 1624–29

The new pasha was at the center of many commercial activities, but he does not appear to have been a very talented negotiator. When the Venetian boats were attacked by the corsairs of Algiers and Tunis, a pasha was sent from Istanbul on a special mission to carry out the negotiations.

'Abdi Pasha (1624) and the Venetian Affair

'Abdi Pasha was a former Janissary of Albanian origin who was "coadja" or secretary of the *diwan* in Tunis. He was also the nephew of Mami Arnaoute, the great corsair of Algiers. 'Abdi was part of the group of Turks who passed through the Maghreb but completed their careers in Istanbul. His knowledge of the land and of the milieu of the corsair captains led the sultan to choose him as an intermediary to negotiate with the powers of Tunis. Appointed in October 1624, he arrived one month later.[14]

The Affair

In June 1624, six galliots from Algiers commanded by 'Ali Mhenni and five galliots from Tunis commanded by Osta Mourad, the captain general of the galleys of Bizerte, stopped near the Turkish fort of Castelnuovo. They obtained free passage after having corrupted the *agha* and attacked the Venetian village of Perasto at dawn. The loot was impressive: four hundred captives and 100,000 ducats. The next day, the corsairs surprised ships in the port of Durazzo, attacking the Ionian islands under Venetian control. They carried out a major raid and then headed toward Prevesa to rest. From there, having strengthened their forces with galliots from Saint-Maure, the corsairs continued toward the island of Thiaki. In the course of looting, they were informed by the watchmen that an impressive Venetian fleet was headed toward them. They left the area, hotly pursued by the Venetians under the command of Antoine Pisani. Pisani caught up with the *fustes mariotes* (small, very fast boats) that had been abandoned by their crews, except for ten Turks who had remained on board and were immediately decapitated. As for the Maghrebi corsairs, after taking a break to put their ships in order at Cape Ducato, they returned to their home ports without further problems.

After this affair, the Venetian Senate lodged a complaint in Istanbul. In the name of the friendship and peace that reigned between these two states, they insisted that the corsairs be punished, the loot returned, and the captives freed. Parallel to this official initiative, two inhabitants of Perasto requested money from the Venetian Senate so that they could negotiate the recovery of their compatriots in Tunis and Algiers. The Venetian consul in Istanbul, bearing the title of *baile*, was responsible for presenting the complaints of the Venetian Senate to the highest Ottoman authorities. These officials responded immediately, calling on the Pasha of Bosnia to severely punish the *agha* of Castelnuovo, who had allowed the corsairs to reach Perasto. But his orders fell on deaf ears. At the same time, a new pasha, Khosrof, was appointed to Algiers. He took up his post, carrying with him two important documents: an order from the sultan demanding the restitution of the loot, and a fatwa from the Mufti of Istanbul declaring piracy against allies of the great lord illegal.

It was in this context that Salvago the dragoman, who had played an important role in this mission, was sent to Algiers and Tunis.

Jean-Baptiste Salvago was a native of Péra, a Turkish subject, and a Christian. He had been working as a dragoman on the *baile* road of Istanbul since 1619, meaning that he interpreted for the consul and accompanied him on his journeys. En route through Venice in 1622, where he stayed for longer than expected due to his patron's illness, he was given this sensitive mission in Barbary. His mission was facilitated by the sultan, who appointed him Pasha of Tunis starting at the end of October 1624. 'Abdi, to whom Salvago had given a *hatti houmayoun*, or a written order from the hands of the sultan, ordered the liberation of all the Venetian captives.

The instructions that Salvago received from his government were clear: dedicate all his energy to executing the orders from Istanbul without explicitly implicating the Republic of Venice; offer expensive garments to the Pasha of Algiers, and discretely promise him that he would be compensated for his efforts. He had at his disposal 3,000 reals that he could offer to the pasha when the Venetian captives had left the area, and 1,000 reals intended for other stakeholders involved in the process of buying their freedom. The same arrangements were to be made in Tunis.

Apart from the negotiations for freeing the captives, Salvago was expected to discreetly collect all of the information he could regarding the Venetians detained in Barbary, the corsairs' activities and the importance of the fleet, the intentions of the rulers of Algiers, the participation of the Ottoman dignitaries and the benefits they drew from piracy, and the distribution spots for goods captured at sea.

After various mishaps, Salvago arrived in Algiers in February 1625. He was received by Khosrof Pasha, who told him to ignore his orders from Istanbul regarding the Venetians, except for those concerning the French and the English, which he would need to reconcile with the powers in Algiers. He also explained that the negotiations with the corsairs would be difficult, as freeing the captives constituted an enormous loss for their owners. Furthermore, the corsairs hated the Venetians, who were accustomed to decapitating the Turks who fell into their hands.

Salvago's mission in Algiers was a complete failure. He was told he would be chopped into pieces if he persisted in demanding that the captives be freed. Khosrof Pasha encountered strong opposition among the rais, who did not want to hear anything about the restitution of captives and asked how they would continue to arm ships if the sultan maintained peaceful relations with the English, Dutch, Venetians, and French. Salvago came to understand that Khosrof Pasha was being manipulated by the rais, who were diverting money to him so that he would derail the negotiations.

Unable to openly contravene the orders from Istanbul, the *diwan* of Algiers, which gathered in a large assembly, deferred, week after week, the discussion of the Venetian captives. They hoped that the plague that was spreading in town would strike Salvago and his companions, one of whom did in fact die in this epidemic. The pasha claimed to have the power to bribe several members of the *diwan* and obtain the captives' freedom if he had the funds, but the dragoman said that he did not have any money and that nothing would be paid before the captives had left. The pasha abruptly lost interest in the affair.

Having failed in Algiers, Salvago headed toward Tunis to negotiate with the authorities. 'Abdi Pasha promised to impose the death penalty on Osta Mourad, for he had done everything in his power to impede the negotiations so as not to ruin the captains. But things took a different turn when the *diwan* of the Janissaries was called to decide the fate of the captives. Youssef Dey found a way to disobey the sultan without causing serious offence: he refused to read the document written by the king and read only orders from other dignitaries whose opinions he cared about less. The captives were not freed, Salvago's mission failed, and 'Abdi Pasha was called back to Istanbul. During this time, Qasim continued to insist on a position as pasha. In 1628, he participated in a delegation whose mission was to work with the Janissaries of Algiers to address the question of the borderlands between the two *oujak*s.[15] He became friends with the Venetians, and in February 1629 he sent three horses to His Highness Sereno of Tuscany. This is the last mention of him.

Bakir Pasha: 1629 to April 1631

Bakir, or Boubakir, another Turk, was appointed to the post of pasha. The notary deeds refer to him as Bequier Pasha and show that he was heavily involved in slave trafficking. He died in April 1631. The post of pasha was once again vacant.

In the first third of the seventeenth century, the mode of recruiting for the position of pasha was transformed. It was held by renegades, corsair captains on the payroll of the deys and beys, who alternated at the head of the three *oujak*s, completely independent from the imperial capital. It no longer resembled what it had been under the reign of Khayriddine or 'Ilj 'Ali, when the rulers had represented the houses of the grand admirals, who were Mediterraneans and renegades, but also men of honor with great political ambitions. After the passing of this first generation, Istanbul no longer held control over the provinces of the Maghreb. The Ottoman administration, for all its meticulousness, did not keep an ordered record of the pashas, according to the Turkish historian Sameh. Certain appointments that had been decided by the *diwan* of Istanbul appear not to have been made. The Maghreb was no longer on "Ottoman time." The archives of the French consulate give us access to only fragmentary clues about the men who held these positions.

Yet despite the weakening of his power, the pasha remained the highest authority in the regency—the go-between for foreign envoys, but also the only recourse for local populations. The pasha was, in theory, the first magistrate. His council would hear the most delicate legal proceedings. One is entitled to wonder how the renegade-pashas carried out this key function in the cases they heard. The mechanisms of justice in this environment probably deserve to be questioned.

European diplomats responsible for negotiating the ransom of the captives affirm the weakening of the pashas, who appeared to lack authority. During these long and difficult negotiations, decision-making was left to the deys and the beys, who were the masters of the pashas: Suleiman Catania was the renegade of Othman Dey, 'Ali Genovese that of Mourad Coursou. Power in Tunis was organized around the dey and the bey, who operated more in collaboration than in conflict. The rest, as described by travelers and diplomats, was a question of concealment and deception. If the pashas always presented themselves as docile representatives of the sultan, it was to keep the strong symbolic connection with Istanbul, which legitimized all the other authorities. Protected under the roof of the empire, the deys and the beys could blend into the local milieu.

17

The First Turkish Houses of Tunis: Matrimonial Strategies and Transmissions of Power

The first two decades of the Ottoman occupation of Tunis suggest a shift toward a military power made up of militia officers, cut off from local society and replenishing itself exclusively with new recruits from the Christian provinces of the empire. This system, which was based on the principle of alienage, was imposed in Algiers. Since the distant period of Khayriddine Barbarossa, attempts to involve the *kuluglis* were destined to fail. To justify the exclusion of the natives of the land, the *diwan* invoked a prohibition formulated by both 'Arrouj and the protector saint of Algiers, Sidi 'Abd al-Rahman al-Thalbi, which freed the *oujak* of Algiers from all forms of "creolization" of power.

The Regency of Tunis seems to have taken a similar path. However, the mutiny of 1591 ruined early plans for an allogeneic military aristocracy. The deys and the beys, and even certain pashas, chose a different path: integration into the local society through marriage and alliances. Othman, "Protector of the Militia" and defender of the *yoldach*, also became the defender of the local populations.

The First Forty Deys: Maternal Uncles and Protectors of the Militia

Before it became an institution, the term "dey" meant maternal uncle. The forty deys who shared the management of the soldiers played the role of protecting the *yoldach* volunteers, who had come from their faraway villages with the expedition of 1574. After the mutiny of October 1591, it was decided that the troops would henceforth fall under the command of one dey, whom the *diwan* would consult before making any decision that concerned them. Initially, the function seems to have been clearly defined as a benevolent protector of the soldiers. Yet starting in Othman's period, the dey became a kind of governor of the capital, charged with maintaining order as the soldiers frequently disturbed the peace in the city. The dey had to transform the brutal occupying force into a regular army under the control of its leaders. The mission was not easy, for the soldiers in the regency had established bad habits, and it was difficult to discipline them while their superiors were implicated in all sorts of corruption.

Othman Dey imposed his decisions by force and introduced important changes in relations between the Turks and the natives. He guaranteed that soldiers would be paid by collecting taxes from among the local population. He did not extort anyone, but he was firm, and he brutally punished every offending soldier. He assured his own wealth through piracy. It was by means of this balance that Othman imposed power on both Turks and locals at the same time.

The regime of the Ottoman Turks was imposed during a period of social collapse and the weakening of a great number of social and religious institutions: How would the population face the brutality of the military presence? With what consistency and momentum would this population, diminished and beleaguered by the events of the sixteenth century, react to Turkish rule?

The Turks of Tunis

As we have seen, the Turks of Tunis were a heterogeneous group, so the term "Turk" is a generic one, attributed to those who were enrolled in the armies or navies of the Ottoman Empire. Some of these men were Anatolians by birth, the others Christian converts from the islands of the Mediterranean. How did this latter group become Turks? A summary ritual, a circumcision, and a banquet offered by the master transformed a Christian captive into a Muslim Turk of the Hanafi school. Some were forced to convert; others did so voluntarily. These new arrivals distinguished themselves from the indigenous population in various ways, including through dress code, language, and rituals. They lived in *funduq*s or in barracks, probably introduced to the lingua franca—the mix of languages spoken in the Mediterranean ports—by those who frequented the same souqs, *souq al-Atrak*, and the same Hanafi mosques. They were also recognizable by their surnames, which often ended with "al-Turki," or "Bin 'Abdallah," or their professional designation: *kahia*, *agha*, *khuja*, etc.[1] During the sixteenth century, the Turkish milieu was a microcosm that snapped up newcomers: Jews and Islamized Christians, or captives wanting to convert. At first, these men shared little but their foreignness, which allowed them to behave like thieves without restraint.

This underworld gradually engendered a new culture, associated in the contemporary collective imagination with a specific ethnic origin and an elite refinement, even though it was originally made up of the dregs of society.

The people of the sixteenth century had a completely different perception. They saw in this cosmopolitan group a suspicious world that it was better to stay away from. The sources attest to this mistrust, provoked by the vulgar actions of the *yoldach*, which ranged from pillaging to drinking. Even at the highest levels, certain representatives of the Turkish religious authority behaved without regard for the local notables: the qadi Kamal subjected a distinguished Tunisian scholar to a beating and exposed his genitals.[2] Yet this world of commoners and adventurers would eventually constitute a new Turkish aristocracy. In a very Arabized society, with a high consciousness of lineage, one did not become a notable if one was not recognized as such by the old elites in positions of power. From this point of view, the social imagination contributed in part to constructing a group's identity. Memory transmitted through chronicles also contributed to the creation of origin myths. Writing of the first forty deys who accompanied the soldiers on the expedition, al-Wazir al-Sarraj referred to them as *al-tabaqa al-ula*, the first generation, comparing them to the first Arab soldiers who came to Islamize Ifriqiya. Later, Ibn abi Dhiaf, referred to them as *a'yan jund al-turk*, or notables of the Turkish army. But these stories do not indicate how the integration of the Turks was achieved.

Integration in the Urban Space

The urban social space was a closed environment. How could a single military man, foreign to the city, socialize beyond the foot soldiers to whom his status confined him? Which urban spaces offered Turkish soldiers the chance to socialize? There were hardly any cafés in Tunis.[3] Wine was sold in taverns, often owned by captives, that also served as meeting places where drinking and brawling were common. Far from the noisy world of the ports and taverns, the *zawiya*s and the religious brotherhoods were the most effective means for the Turks to integrate. We must recall that the Janissaries were closely linked to a religious order, that of the baktash, and that the association of the army and religious order were vital to the celebrated military corps. In addition, the Ottomans were known for the respect in which they held descendants of the Prophet, the *shurafa*, and for sainted men in general. The Turkish leaders thus frequented the *zawiya*s, including the *Zawiya Quachachia*.

Several Turks integrated into urban society through brotherhoods and thereby became established dignitaries. Hussein Pasha was even married to a descendant of Sidi Bin 'Arous. The interment of Ramadan Bey in the mausoleum of Sidi Qasim suggests a matrimonial alliance among those close to the saint. The process of integrating the Turks could not have been achieved without the help of local learned and devout elites who agreed to give their daughters in marriage to these upstarts. A powerful new group was created, accepted, and legitimized beginning in the second generation, with the birth of Turkish children to mothers who belonged to the great local families.

Certainly, not all Turks reached this privileged status. The majority blended into society by marrying locals, or more often, captives from piracy. No source mentions the arrival of Turkish women before the eighteenth century. The Janissaries established themselves in the city garrisons. Wanting to settle permanently, they had no choice but to marry in the locations to which they were assigned. This fact is both obvious and little known. It is not hard to imagine why the families gave their daughters to the *yoldach*s who had regular pay and privileged status as members of an occupying army. Little stood in the way of these unions. The children born to these couples formed a new category: the *kulugli*s. We can assume that this category of persons multiplied. In 1574, the Turkish soldiers left behind by Sinan Pasha were estimated to number four thousand. This is a minimum estimate, if we consider that those lost in battle or to a natural death would have been replaced by new recruits. If we assume that these men married and that each had three children, we can estimate by the beginning of the seventeenth century they would have numbered 12,000, about ten out of every hundred people (the population of the regency was estimated at one hundred thousand).[4] The social landscape of the cities was enriched by new groups of Turks, including soldiers, scientists, and traders, who were constantly being replenished through external flows. Their numbers also grew through the expansion of families and the birth of *kulugli*s, children born to a Tunisian mother and a Turkish father.

The Turks and the Tribal World

When the Ottoman Turks established themselves in city garrisons, the rural world escaped their hold for some time. Their policy consisted of controlling the cities and villages while waiting for the right moment to subdue the nomads or highland peoples, who were resistant to all forms of authority.

Well before the arrival of the Turks, this rural society had been transformed. The groups defined themselves less through their Arab or Berber origins, as matrimonial and political alliances had for a long time mitigated this ethnic cleavage. The Arab populations, distant descendants of the Hilali invaders, were largely mixed with the indigenous Berbers and had helped to Arabize them. By the fifteenth century, the large tribal groups no longer defined themselves exclusively through ethnicity, but through lifestyle—nomadic or mountain sedentary. When the Turks took possession of the land, the term "Arab" was used exclusively for the nomadic, transhumant populations, without ethnic overtones.[5] Over the course of the sixteenth century, the various social components of the old Hafsid Ifriqiya redefined themselves. The northwest was occupied by the Houara, Berbers who were largely Arabized thanks to Ouled Souleym, who had imposed their political authority on this community. From this confederation, one group detached themselves and occupied the western region: the Hnansha, who led the powerful family of the Harar (free men). Their territory was located at the head of the Medjerda and stretched between Constantine and El Kef. Subgroups separated from the mother community, one of which established itself in Tebessa and the other in the environs of El Kef.

We have seen the power of the Hnansha, who were the principal supporters of the Shabbia when they rebelled against the Hafsids. But the Hanansha were defeated alongside the Shabbia, and their hegemony over the region's interior weakened. The failure against the Turks was a momentary setback for the tribal groups who claimed to descend from the Ouled Souleym. But other groups reemerged, notably the Riah, divided into the subgroups of the Ouled Said, Sba'a, and Ya'qub. The Riah were considered turbulent and unpredictable. The Tunisian adage, *illi wrah al-Riah ma yirtah* (the man who tolerates the Riah can never have peace), expresses well the way these groups were perceived by their urban counterparts. But the subgroups of the Riah ultimately integrated and became the tribes of the *makhzan*, meaning that they put themselves in the service of the new state. Only one, the Ouled Said, remained dissident. Until the seventeenth century, chroniclers accorded them the most pejorative attributes and Ibn abi Dinar judged them very harshly.

The new Turkish power struggled to subjugate the countryside. Othman Dey led many armies against the interior regions to suppress them. But he also attempted negotiations to put an end to the abuses committed by the Bedouins in the rural regions and to regulate the royalties they owed. Ramadan Bey continued the policy of repression against the dissident groups. Mourad was brought in to organize long expeditions against the southern regions, all while placing Islamized former captives, the Mamluks, at the very heart of certain tribes. He named his own Mamluk, Hassan, Caid of the great tribe of the Drids: Hassan settled among the Bedouins, married several of their daughters and ensured that there would be many "Bedouinized" Mamluk descendants.[6] It was through this policy of alliances that the Turks constructed a social link to the countryside. Caid Hassan's descendants assimilated into Bedouin lifestyles, while also bringing with them their city ways. In the Tunisian memory, the Caid of the Drids is a very colorful character.

The Founding Alliances

The high officers of the army and the holders of certain political offices chose their spouses from among the influential families. The most important case, for it would give rise to a strong lineage, was that of Othman, who allied himself with the Zhani, an old family said to be from Tunis.[7] At least one daughter was born from this marriage, and her father, in turn, gave her in marriage to Youssef Dey. Seventeenth century documents mention the free woman 'Aisha bint Mass'oud al-Zhani, who established *habous* goods for al-Ksar mosque in Tunis. Othman Ddey's first wife must have belonged to this same family of notables, founders of the *waqf*. As for his second wife, Ltifa, who was involved in the slave trade on behalf of Abu al-Gaith al-Quachach, she was the daughter of Sheikh Muhammad Kshour. He was a scholar, close to the saint, who participated in the saint's economic affairs.[8] Othman had other unions, which lasted for unknown lengths of time. When he died, he left behind two daughters and four sons.

Through his two known marriages, Othman Dey searched for notability as well as the acquisition of property. Did he nurture the ambition to pass on his power? During his lifetime he offered his daughter in marriage to Youssef, his assumed successor. Youssef did succeed Othman, but on the advice of his counselor 'Ali Thabit, refused to marry Othman's daughter. 'Ali Thabit did not want the Zhani family, the fiancée's maternal grandfather, to gain power, probably so that he would remain the only person of influence.[9] The dey's counselor played an important role in the political life of the regency right up to his death in 1631. He was even the most powerful local figure. To this end, he had not only to distance himself from anyone who could overshadow him, but also to position himself at the center of power by marrying his daughters to influential men. Following 'Ali Thabit's advice, Youssef Dey took concubines. The sources allow us to identify one by the first name of Kmar, a Corsican and the sister of the renegade Youssef Coursou Turki, who gave birth to the dey's son Muhammad.[10] We do not know the identity of the mothers of Youssef Dey's three other known children, Ahmad, Mustafa, and Fatma.

The first great dey, Othman, had envisaged passing on power to his descendants through his daughters. Was this a practice from distant Anatolia—different from the Mediterranean and Arab heritage in force in local society—giving a daughter preeminence over a son and the *khal*, the role that other cultures accorded to the paternal uncle? Othman's wish was granted, for his daughter married Mourad Bey and, thanks to a complex game of alliances, his descendants remained in power until 1902.[11]

18

Deys, Beys, Alliances, and Successions, 1611–40

Between the death of Othman Dey in 1611 and that of Osta Mourad in 1640, the deylical and beylical families built many alliances among themselves. The succession of power was no longer the business of institutions or the militia, but rather the strategy of dynasties, which shared political and economic power. The focal point of this familial system was Othman, founder of a line that grew through marriages among Turks, renegades, and locals. Sensing his impending death after a bad fall from a horse, he gave his opinion on who should succeed him: he cast aside the presumptive dey, 'Ajam, in favor of Youssef, who was promised to his daughter.

Youssef Dey, Othman's Successor: 1611–37

Youssef was a Janissary in Tripoli. Exiled after committing a grave offense, he headed to Tunis to register with the *diwan*. Al-Wazir al-Sarraj reports that Youssef began his career modestly, in the shadow of Othman.

The soldier had protected his leader by discreetly following him during his nighttime security checks across the city.[1] He climbed the ranks and became *chaouch* in the *diwan*. Othman Dey saw in Youssef a potential successor and engaged him to his daughter. The strategy failed in the short term due to Othman's death. Youssef, advised by his right-hand man, 'Ali Thabit, broke off his engagement with Othman's daughter and married a captive instead. Nevertheless, Othman's two daughters were married, one to Mourad Bey and the other to his son Hamouda, creating one of the most powerful Turkish houses in Tunis.

As for Youssef, he occupied the position of dey for twenty-six years, until his death. He became rich and powerful, amassing a fortune thanks to the immense profits generated by piracy and transactions with renegades

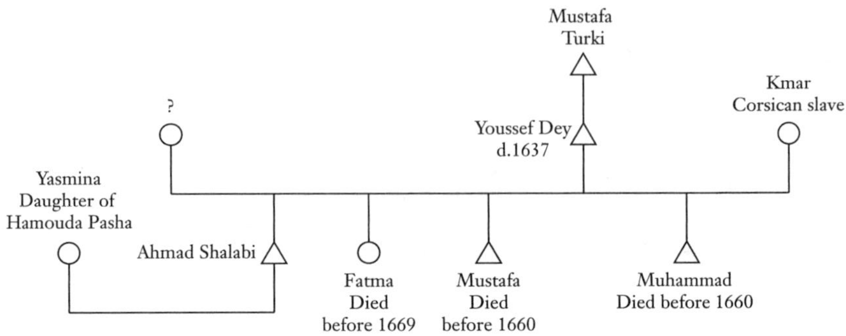

6. The house of Youssef Dey

and important Andalusian merchants, especially Mustafa de Cardenas, head of the Andalusian community. Youssef Dey established his own house and surrounded himself with several renegades: Moratto Maltaise; Hendrich de Giovanni, his "scrivanno maggiore" or first secretary; Regep, the *guardian-bashi* (captain of the guard) of his prison; Veneziano, who belonged to the important Riadino family; Henry de Jehan Flaman: a slave, letter carrier, and writer; and Carali, *guardian-bashi*.[2] Behind these men and the jobs they performed, one gets a glimpse of the importance of overseas networks and commercial transactions, especially human trafficking.

Youssef Dey was also supported by locals. 'Ali Thabit, especially, became a central figure: he was wealthy, owned palaces and slaves, and actively participated in human trafficking. Ibn abi Dinar praises him, while the hagiographic account *Nour al-armash* depicts him as a greedy, bad man. Under Youssef, he became the most powerful local figure. His family benefited from his position of privilege, and his son-in-law confiscated proceeds from the Zawiya al Quachachia.[3]

'Ali Thabit is a key figure in the period of Youssef Dey. According to al-Wazir al-Sarraj, who tends to report tall tales, 'Ali Thabit was a Bedouin and a fortune-teller who predicted a glorious future for Youssef, whom he had met on the way to Tunis. Several years later, Youssef became *chaouch* of the *diwan* and found 'Ali Thabit once again. This was the start of an important collaboration between the two men. Present at the death of Othman, it was 'Ali Thabit who hastened to grant the *bay'a* to Youssef, who occupied the position of dey for almost twenty-six years.

Osta Mourad Genovese, General of the Deys' Galleys

Othman Dey's right-hand man, general of the galleys of Bizerte and advisor to Youssef Dey (1611–37), Osta Mourad Genovese, held the position of dey from 1637 to 1640.

He was born in the region of Genoa, at Levanto or Albisola, to a sailor, the "boss" Francesco di Rio di Levante detto il marmararo. It is unclear how he arrived in Tunis, and if he even came as a captive. We find him close to Othman Dey, in a position resembling that of a secretary and right-hand man. He was already involved in maritime affairs and associated with the Genoese Osta Hassan, who became one of the greats of Tunis and later Osta Mourad's son-in-law. Between 1605 and 1611, they sold ships and many captives. Business flourished, and Mourad became a moneylender and mediated between the Christians and the authorities of Tunis. His career took a new turn with Youssef Dey's rise to power, and he became one of the richest men in Tunis. His first high position was as captain general of the galleys of Bizerte. The consular archives document him in this position from 1615 to 1637. The galleys of Bizerte constituted the state's fleet, made up of six galleys of twenty-six benches each, mounted by the Janissaries. They were renowned for being well armed and well equipped. They went out to sea twice a year, in the fall and in the spring, on the orders of Osta Mourad.

It is impossible to understand this renegade's career without understanding the familial network that supported him. His numerous family members were associated with navigation and commercial activities between Marseille, Genoa, Livorno, and Tunis. Osta Mourad's father, Francesco Rio, was prominent in the ransoming of slaves on behalf of Genoa. He died in 1600. Giovanni Rio, one of Osta Mourad's cousins, pursued the same activity from 1608 to 1609. Bortoloméo Rio, Mourad's brother, was an established trader in Tunis who did business in Marseille, Genoa, and Livorno. His nephews had strong ties to Tunis: Jacomo Rio was based there until 1641, and Gian-Battista Lavagna Rosso was a merchant who lived in Tunis and had an extensive business career there between 1626 and 1661.

Agostino Rio was present in Tunis when Mourad's inheritance was being distributed. On the opposite shore of the Mediterranean, a certain man called Francesco Rio, who lived in Livorno, was working with his cousins in Tunis to sell goods. Livorno was a base for the reselling of goods obtained through piracy. This family group supported commercial and charitable activities, such as the ransom of slaves. They were present and active in the principal commercial markets of the Mediterranean, through which both licit and illicit goods flowed.

Osta Mourad Genovese also leaned on the support of a core group of renegades, his captives whom he had encouraged to repudiate Christianity: Giafer Veneziano, Morato Rais, and a French renegade by the name of Loys Cravier, originally from Toulon. Osseino Genovese, son of Geronimo Bianco, the companion of Osta Mourad became his *kahia* when his affairs prospered and later, his son-in-law.[4]

There is no question of Osta Mourad Genovese's success. He became an important figure in Tunis, possessing enough slaves to require a *bagno*, or area for grouping captives, a house in Tunis, another in La Goulette, a residence in the countryside, and a property in Slimân. His family, strengthened by his support, abused its power. Two merchants testified:

> But during the lifetime of Morat Dey, king of this realm, Jacques Rio, Jean Baptiste, and Augustin Lavage Rosso, Genoese merchants and his nephews, detained Pierre Compian, a merchant from Marseille, in their uncle's prison for sixteen months, weighed him down with irons and chains, usually four or five at a time, treating him worse than a thief under the pretext that Compian owed them money. The consul had him released and declared to the dey that the merchant had been poorly treated by Jacques Rio, who had put him on the chain of his absolute power.[5]

As long as he was general of the galleys, Osta Mourad was loyal to French interests. Starting in 1616, multiple consular letters document that "there is nobody who feels more affection for our country than Lord Osta Morat," or that he "never hesitates to advise the French galleys," or that "he feels a great veneration for the king of France and considers him the most generous ruler of the land." Between 1616 and 1621, Osta Mourad tried to obtain the pashalik of Algiers. He played a role in the French-Algerian accord of 1620, which was broken when Radjeb rais attacked a French ship, massacred its occupants, and sank it. Two sailors managed to escape the massacre and make it back to the port, where they sounded the alarm about what had just occurred. The Turkish ambassador was in Marseille at the time for an official visit. When they heard the news of the massacre, the local populations attacked the ship where the ambassador was staying, killing him and the forty-five people who were with him. The Algerian corsairs resumed their efforts against the French even more forcefully, but Tunis did not follow the example of Algiers. France sincerely hoped for Osta Mourad's appointment, which would have led to the establishment of a durable peace and respect for the peace treaties. He would have made another attempt in 1626.[6] Mourad the Genovese's authority grew and he was recognized by the French king. He played the role of negotiator and established a climate of trust between the corsairs and their French patrons.

His fortune grew in parallel to his power and his captives numbered in the thousands. When Youssef died in 1637, Osta Mourad was appointed dey. It is difficult to ascertain quite how he was appointed. Had he carried out a coup with the support of three hundred well-armed renegades? Or had he received help from Mami of Ferrara, Youssef Dey's lieutenant, who used Mourad to test the reaction of Turkish soldiers when faced with a renegade's rebellion? Was Mami of Ferrara working for himself or for the son of Youssef Dey? Mami of Ferrara would have been a sort of regent while Youssef Dey's son was a minor and too young to succeed his father in 1637.[7] We must not forget that Mourad was the only convert to reach the position of dey. His descendants were among the notables of Tunis and were aligned with the family of Othman Dey.

19
The Mouradite House

The Mouradite house was founded by Mourad, a renegade originally from Levie in Corsica. Taken captive during a corsair attack, he fell into the hands of Ramadan Bey, who took on the responsibility of educating him.

Ramadan Bey, Master of Mourad

Ramadan Bey is as celebrated as he is unknown. He is famous for his palace and for the renegades who belonged to his house, yet we must still speculate about his identity. The most extensive bibliography comes from al-Wazir al-Sarraj. It draws on information written on Ramadan Bey's tombstone that identifies him as the son of Hussein, a Turk from Algiers, and an Italian captive. Al-Wazir also tells the story of Ramadan's mother, captured on the day of her wedding and sold in Algiers to a Turk who then married her. She gave him one son, Ramadan. After being widowed, the former captive returned to her homeland and found her first fiancé and married him. When she lost her second husband, she asked Ramadan, who had by this time become a prominent figure, to allow her to settle in Tunis with her son from her second marriage.

Ramadan accepted this proposition on the condition that the child be converted. This is how the former captive, still Christian, came to end up in Tunis with her young son, baptized Rajeb.[1] Ibn abi Dinar considers Ramadan Bey to be a renegade from Algiers. Whatever his origins, it is important not to confuse him with the other Ramadan, his namesake, who participated in the conquest of Tunis in 1569 and was killed in Tripoli in 1584. Our Ramadan Bey was commander of the land army and died in 1613. He focused on pacifying the interior regions. Like all the most powerful men, he drew on the support of a group of renegades who made up his house. Among them was Mourad.

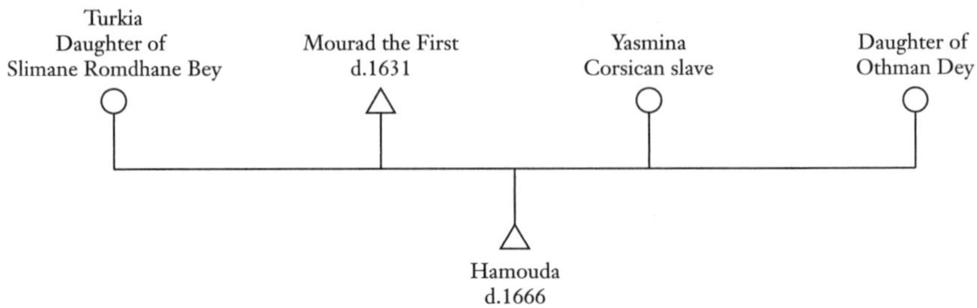

7. The unions of Mourad the First

It is difficult to follow his trajectory step by step, but several indications lead us to believe that Mourad began working with the coral companies in 1591, along with other Turks, including Othman. Shortly thereafter, he is recorded in the archive under the title of caid. In March 1605, the caid Mourad joined Caid 'Ali Napolitano and Caid Rajeb in the business of exporting leather and cartons of sugar. They were referred to as customs officers because they arranged for the export of certain products over which they had a monopoly. In 1607, he continued to work commercially, providing goods to be sold in Marseille, which in turn allowed him to purchase silk fabric. He carried out these economic activities alongside his military responsibilities, and he prided himself on his riches, which would be a decisive factor in his rise to power.[2]

The Unions of Mourad the First

We know of three women who had unions with Mourad: Yasmina, a Corsican captive; Turkiya bint Slimane Bey (Slimane Bey was the son of Ramadan, Mourad's master); and lastly the daughter of Othman Bey. Mourad's marriage with Turkiya is well documented by al-Wazir al-Sarraj and a seventeenth-century French chronicle, which was long considered anonymous but is now attributed to Guilleragues, ambassador of France to Istanbul between 1680 and 1685. The diplomat collected the family history directly from Muhammad al-Hafsi, son of Hamouda Pasha Bey, whom he had met in Istanbul.[3] Although his version of the story was romanticized, the characters and the events are real. According to this first version, Slimane Bey would have married Mourad to Yasmina, who died after giving birth to her son Muhammad, known as Hamouda. Shortly after this loss, Slimane Bey found Mourad kissing the hand of his daughter Turkiya. He threatened to kill his slave, but then changed his mind and decided to marry them instead. According to the second version of the story, as told by al-Wazir, Turkiya was Mourad's first wife. He secretly took a concubine, Yasmina, who gave birth to Hamouda in the house of the Dabbabs, close friends of Mourad's.[4] But the young woman did not survive the birth. Upon learning of her husband's secret concubine and the woman's death, Turkiya decided to raise the child herself. While these two accounts differ on other matters, they agree that Mourad had two wives, at the same time or successively, and that both died young. The rest of the story, told by Guilleragues, describes Mourad's deep grief after the loss of Turkiya. He mourned for one year, abandoning his responsibilities, even those of the king, leaving them to the dey, Youssef. He suggested that Youssef marry Othman Dey's eldest daughter and that he ask for the hand of the youngest for his son Hamouda. This double union would have taken place around the year 1630.

Succession: Institutions or Dynasties?

The alliances that Turkish leaders (or those who had been assimilated) sought with local families, and which were reinforced through repeated early marriages among their own children, allow us to reconsider relations between the deys and the beys by looking at the connection between power and kinship. These Turkish families put in place strategies for the transfer of political power, material goods, and intangible prestige that was at the foundation of these great houses and passed on through carefully considered rules for marriage. A Turkish aristocracy, largely mixed-race, was in the process of being established and gaining political power.

With the death of Mourad's master Ramadan in 1613, the question of succession in the role of *bey al-amhal*, or Bey of the Camp, arose. The position was sought not just by Mourad, but also by Rajeb, Ramadan's brother. Mourad asked Youssef Dey to arbitrate, and Youssef Dey advised him to approach Sghaier bin Sandal, whose true identity remains somewhat ambiguous. He chose Mourad over Rajeb. Rajeb sought support for his candidacy from the Ouled Khmakhim. For some time, there were several beys of the camp in Tunis who led their campaigns sometimes together, sometimes separately. In 1613, Mourad was distinguished for his bravery in the war against the Turkish army of Algiers. His military expeditions were led in conjunction with his commercial activities.

In November 1615, along with Rajeb Bey, the brother of his master, he sold eight hundred hides to Livorno for a sum of 9,000 pieces of eight, which they received on August 20, 1617 through an intermediary, the Corsican Antonio Petro. In August 1617, he freed captives for ransom, and the act designating him as the "very illustrious Morato bei corso" was signed not in the consulate of France, but in the bey's own home. Mourad gained importance, established his house, and surrounded himself with his own renegades, including caid Ja'far Genovese and 'Ali Coursou: the number of renegades grew alongside the bey's riches. In May 1620, he acted as the intermediary in the sale of sugar to Florence.

In January 1623, he was named supreme commander of the camps of Tunis, which proved that he had supplanted the other beys who occupied the position at the same time as him. During this period, he was accused of wanting to pardon two young sailor captives. Several years later, he wanted to pardon two children—a boy of nine and a girl of eleven—probably to increase the number of his renegades. His business prospered and he remained in negotiation with Mustafa de Cardenas, head of the Andalusian community.[5] His principal activity remained investing in piracy and the sale of goods and captured ships. In 1624, he sold a boat filled with its cargo of wheat at 3,500 pieces of eight for the boat, and six reals for each *qafiz* of wheat. During his rise to power, Mourad Bey did not cut ties with his native Corsica and maintained strong family relations. On May 20, 1627, he gave money to his nephew in Tunis, Alexandro de Santo, from Levie. The men who worked for him, recruited from among the renegades, continued to multiply: 'Ali Rais of Marseille; Giuseppe Forte de Trapani, described as Mourad's slave and "spaliere" or right-hand man; Osta Regeppe, his *guardian-bashi*; his prison guard (a post reserved for captives); Morat, his renegade, whose Christian name was Vincenzo, and who was the nephew of Luca Bele Barba, from the island of Meso de Raguse.[6] In 1628, he participated in the second war against the Turks of Algiers alongside other generals—notably Rajeb, who was not up to the task.

In 1631, he led an army in the south of the region against the *wirghimma*. At this time, Bekir, the acting pasha, died. 'Ali Thabit, friend and counselor of Youssef Dey, died in the same year. Mourad benefited from these events and asked the Sublime Porte to grant him the title of pasha. In April 1631, the notary archives designated him "Mouratto Pasha." Then he ceded his position of bey to his son Hamouda.[7] Not long after, in June 1631, Mourad died. His premature death prevents us from understanding his intentions.

The political configuration changed in 1631. With the death of Mourad and 'Ali Thabit, a generation was vanishing. 'Ali Thabit's death deprived

Youssef Dey, who by then was advanced in age, of a powerful supporter. He followed his friend not long after, dying in 1637. The period of the triumvirate—pasha, dey, and bey—was coming to an end.

Hamouda Pasha Bey and the Centralization of Power

The first decade of the sixteenth century corresponded with the establishment of the great houses and the appearance of the first families of Turkish notables, products of the unions among the Janissaries, renegades, and local families. The policy of alliance-making expanded so much that under Hamouda Pasha Bey there came to be a true social network that depended more and more on the acquisition of large estates. It was thanks to this double policy of matrimonial politics and the inscription of Hamouda's power in physical space through the ownership of land and property that he was able to challenge his rivals. Succeeding his father proved to be a long and difficult struggle from which Hamouda emerged a winner.

Hamouda, Bey and Pasha: 1613–66

Hamouda was the son of Mourad Coursou and a Corsican captive, Yasmina, who died shortly after giving birth. No source gives the exact date of his birth, but it probably occurred in 1613. His father's wife, Turkiya bint Slimane, took care of him as a child. As an adolescent, he was entrusted to three renegades who belonged to the house of his father and took charge of his education. Among them was Ja'far, a corsican of Souboulla, who was his closest adviser. Hamouda would later marry Ja'far's daughter.

When his father died in 1631, Hamouda was eighteen years old and was considered an accomplished man. Ibn abi Dinar described him as such:

> He was of medium height, a handsome face, with a pale complexion, with an attractive appearance, well-proportioned. Nobody expressed themselves with such hardness and softness, such beauty and reason . . . a man of morality and of great intelligence, he knows how to make the right decisions. He never expresses his animosity and distinguishes himself by a great generosity, that of men who do not fear poverty. His friends and enemies alike testify to this.[8]

But human qualities alone were not enough to secure power, and the rise of Hamouda was not a simple formality, as the chronicle of Ibn abi Dinar suggests. His father appointed him bey after having sought and obtained the post of pasha from Istanbul. But Mourad died two months later, depriving Hamouda of his support. As for the rank of bey and the military responsibility associated with it, it was shared between two other powerful men: Rajeb and Slimane, brother and son, respectively, of Ramadan Bey, Mourad's master. Hamouda Pasha Bey had two formidable rivals, even though, until then, no position had been inherited and the meritocracy appeared to still be governed by a separation of responsibilities. However, Hamouda avoided conflict with them, and for good reason: he had inherited from his father the status of an unfree man, a product of captivity. As such, he was the Mamluk of Slimane Bey, who inherited him. Conscious of the precariousness of his position, Hamouda Pasha Bey let things play out naturally over time. His ambition came into the open with the deaths of two important figures, Rajeb Bey, and later, Osta Mourad Dey. His career developed progressively and he was able to benefit from many opportunities.

The Beylical Phase

Hamouda did not show excessive ambition during the first ten years. He carried out the task begun by his father: repression of the recalcitrant tribes, especially the Ouled Said, whom he fought in the region of the Hamma and against whom he led a terrible war until he subdued them in 1635. He also attacked the Ouled Shanouf, who controlled the region of El Kef, and secured their surrender. He continued the pacification of Jbal Matmata, subjugated the great Arab leaders, bargained with them, and recruited horsemen among the men of these tribes whom he entrusted to the command of his Mamluks. He also cut a deal with the sheikh of a group in the borderland, by which he assured the security of the west. Word of these victories, which took place over nearly seven years, spread throughout the countryside and assured Hamouda Pasha Bey's fame. The security of all the territories within the regency remained the bedrock of political legitimacy. This beylical period demonstrated Hamouda's physical and military capabilities: he was a truly distinguished general, whose campaigns were crowned with success. In other words, he earned his post through merit and not because of his origins, as had Rajeb and Slimane, who according to Ibn abi Dinar were lousy military leaders. Hamouda was careful not to claim the title of pasha that his father had held between April and June 1631.

Throughout these years, Hamouda made sure to increase his property and land assets. He bought property, or confiscated it under the guise of the public interest, and then quickly designated it as *habous* so that it would be protected for his children. He continued the policy of patrimonialization begun by his father. Mourad Bey had in effect acquired the "Great House," *al-dar al-kubra* (which currently belongs to the prime minister), and several annexes that he had designated as *habous* for his son Muhammad (Hamouda) in March 1628. Creating a *habous*, at least in theory, offered a way to secure a property and prevent not only its partitioning but its confiscation by the state. Hamouda continued his father's strategy, which consisted of rebuying, expanding, and embellishing the great palaces in Tunis and its outskirts, and investing in farmlands and orchards. The notary acts do not always demonstrate how property was acquired, but all indications lead us to believe that some of these transactions were cover-ups for confiscations. In 1633, several houses in the Turkish quarter, at the foot of the Kasbah, were constituted as *habous* for the benefit of his daughter 'Aisha. The Sénia of al-Ibdilliya and its outbuildings, important Hafsid properties in La Marsa, were acquired by Hamouda Pasha Bey before 1636 and designated as *habous* for the benefit of his young children, Mourad and Yasmina.

The Great Estate of the Bardo

Hamouda Pasha Bey acquired the great domain of the Bardo. The seller was none other than the council of the Janissaries. The deed of sale was properly signed by the leaders of the *diwan*: *agha*, *kahia*, the high oudhabashi officers, several veterans, the *Agha* of the Kasbah and his *kahia*. The deed was also signed in the name of the institution responsible for those properties left without an heir, *dar al-ashghal wa-l-mawarith*, as well as by Osta Mourad, who had recently become the dey of the *'askar*.[9] Hamouda wanted this beautiful acquisition to be unlike anything else. Who did this ensemble of properties, destined to become a palatial city, belong to? The deed does not specify how the council of Janissaries came to own it. Let us note, however, that this purchase occurred just as Osta Mourad was appointed dey, the highest authority at the time. A bargain had been made! Slowly, Hamouda Pasha Bey continued his climb.

The Great Muhassaba

With the death of the dey Osta Mourad in 1640, Hamouda Pasha Bey set the record straight with Slimane Bey, known as the great *muhassaba*. This settling of scores occurred at the beginning of the reign of Ahmad Khouja Dey. Hamouda Pasha Bey submitted two documents: freedom papers for Mourad granted by his master Ramadan Bey, as well as the latter's will, which accorded Hamouda Pasha Bey one-third of Ramadan's properties. Al-Wazir al-Sarraj reports that these documents were forgeries executed under duress by Sheikh al-Ghariani.[10]

Given these new circumstances, Slimane Bey fled, likely weakened and without support, and accorded Hamouda Pasha Bey a galliot, a drinking establishment, and a large tract of land in Ras Tabia. The bey was quick to offer all of these to the new dey, Ahmad Khouja. The scope of these two deeds was large. The act of freedom made Mourad the First and his descendants free men. Thus, Hamouda Pasha Bey was no longer a Mamluk. The inheritance allowed him to recover properties of great value, to impoverish Slimane, and to buy the goodwill of a newly appointed dey, who he then went to for favors. These decisions show a Hamouda Pasha Bey determined to consolidate more and more power and to claim symbolic spaces: both the famous palace of Ramadan Bey and the elaborate living space on the second floor that had belonged to Slimane Bey, a symbol of success for this beylical family, passed to Hamouda at an unknown date and in an unknown way. On December 15, 1659, he gave it to his son, Mourad, who immediately designated it as a *habous* for his descendants.[11]

Hamouda Pasha Bey's Rise is Challenged

Several influential people opposed Hamouda, notably the powerful commander of the caids, 'Abdallah bin Khouran. When he showed his reservations about Hamouda, all his belongings were confiscated, and he ultimately aligned himself with the bey. Mustafa de Cardenas, the sheikh of the Andalusians, a rich and enterprising man connected to Youssef Dey and Mourad Dey through important commercial interests, was ruined and driven out of the area. Hamouda punished and ruined his secretaries and his close advisers, Abi al-Qasim al-Gafsi, 'Ali Hoaua, and the family of the Banu Sandal. The latter, secretaries of his father, had contributed to his rise. By depriving these men of their fortunes and positions, he eliminated embarrassing witnesses from his past, most of whom were locals, and depended more and more on the Mamluks. It seems that these men may have challenged the concentration of powers in the bey's hands; this opposition deserves to be interrogated.

The way power had been distributed among the pasha, dey, and bey since 1591 is not in itself proof that power had been institutionalized. The prerogatives of each position were not well defined, nor were the rules of appointment. Each time that one of the three positions fell vacant, the configuration was once again called into question, and a redistribution was organized by all the powers in Tunis—the military council; the corsair and commercial milieu, in which all the renegades were involved; and the Andalusians and locals—while at the same time pressure was exerted by European diplomats in Istanbul, who were protecting their own interests.

As he discredited all those who showed a hint of opposition, Hamouda reinforced his social alliances.

The Unions of Hamouda Pasha Bey

The first wife of Hamouda Pasha Bey was the daughter of Othman Dey. We do not know much more about this union. One of his concubines was called Fatma. She was the daughter of Turkiya, now set free from Hmida Sharfi, although it is unclear whether Fatma was Hmida Sharfi's daughter.[12] Fatma bore Hamouda a daughter, Aisha, and a son, Ahmad, who died around 1645.[13] His second wife was Hiziya, daughter of 'Ali Thabit, the mother of Mourad and Yasmina (who were named after the bey's parents). Her two children, who benefited from the *habous* of al-Ibdilliya, were described as small in 1635. His third wife was Khdija bint al-Caid Ja'far, mother of Muhammad al-Hafsi. The last wife was Mira bint Muhammad al-'Askri, whom Hamouda married late in life and who bore him Hassan and Mna, who were still young when their father died in 1666.

Hamouda Pasha Bey's four or five wives, not counting his legal concubines, came from two influential families, those of Othman Dey and of 'Ali Thabit. He remained loyal to the renegades of his father, marrying the daughter of Ja'far, whose family had begun to rise to the ranks of the nobility. His last known wife, Mira, came from a tribal milieu, that of the Hnansha in the region of El Kef.

With these different wives, he had several children, only some of which survived him. In 1643, a *habous* document listed all his children: Mourad, Ahmad, Muhammad al-Hafsi, Yasmina, Aisha, and Khadija. These three daughters and Ahmad died during their father's lifetime, and so when Hamouda died, his heirs were Mourad, Muhammad al-Hafsi, and two young first cousins, Mira's children, Hassan and Mna. It was with Hamouda that the matrimonial alliances between the Mouradite beys and the local tribes began, and these alliances developed with his descendants.[14]

The Alliances of Hamouda Pasha Bey's Children

Hamouda Pasha Bey attached vital importance to marriages, and organized banquets for the occasion that were famous for their splendor. In 1648, he

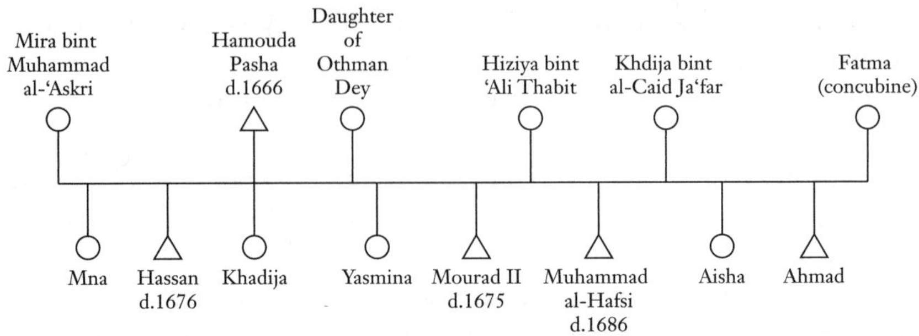

8. The house of Hamouda Pasha Bey

married Mourad to the daughter of Youssef Dey. This marriage united two powerful houses, that of the Mouradites of Youssef Dey and that of 'Ali Thabit, Mourad being the son of Hiziya bint 'Ali Thabit. Mourad also had another wife, the daughter of Ibrahim Shalbi, secretary of the *diwan*.[15] In 1655, Hamouda married Muhammad al-Hafsi to the daughter of 'Abd al-Rahman, Pasha of Tripoli. In 1658, he married Hassan to the daughter of Othman Pasha of Tripoli. It is likely that Hassan was still very young at this point and that this was an arranged child marriage. In 1659, he organized the marriage of his grandson Muhammad, son of Mourad, to the daughter of Ahmad Shalbi, son of Youssef Dey.[16] As for the girls, they were both married to sons of Youssef Dey.

The Establishment of the Janissaries' Council

Hamouda Pasha Bey had to put in place the Janissary council in a way that would allow him to control the appointment of the deys, who could be serious contenders for power.

Ahmad Khouja, dey from 1640 to 1647, was a Turk from Sinope, a city on the Black Sea, who arrived in Tunis around 1625. He held a variety of positions in the *diwan*, notably that of *khouja*, or secretary. He was married to Turkiya, daughter of al-Hajj Muhammad Aranout. At the death of Osta Mourad, the *diwan* of the Janissaries appointed Ahmad Khouja to replace him, as he had always shown affection for the orphans of the Janissaries. Whether it's true or not, this line of reasoning shows that the council of the Janissaries had once again taken up the role that it had been assigned after the mutiny of October 1591, that of appointing the dey. In fact, the *diwan* had barely exercised this responsibility since the period of Othman.

From this point of view, the death of the great renegade, the powerful corsair Osta Mourad, was certainly a turning point in political life. Ahmad Khoudja resisted the power of Hamouda Pasha Bey: he refused to permit him to establish a cavalry. Hamouda Pasha Bey must have offered a huge quantity of jewels to the wife of the dey to obtain this right.[17]

After him, the office of the dey was held by men from the council of Janissaries, who had negotiated their power grabs with Hamouda Pasha Bey: Muhammad Laz (1647–53); Mustafa Laz (1653–65); and Mustafa Karakouz (1665–66). The bey had distanced a serious contender, Muhammad Grig, who threatened to diminish his power. The latter, as his name indicates, was a Greek renegade who could perhaps have ushered in the return of corsairs to the deylical position.

The Phase of the Pashalik: 1658–62

In a grandiose ceremony in April 1658, Hamouda was given the firman according him the position of pasha. The title was bestowed on him after several delays. The dey Mustafa Laz informed him that some had opposed Hamouda's appointment by sending secret messages to Istanbul, out of fear that if the bey became pasha, he would escape the control of the Janissaries. The institutional rivalries resumed once again, and the deys, protectors of the militias, wanted to keep the bey under their control.

Hamouda Pasha Bey's final act remains an enigma. In 1662 or 1663, he sent a delegation to Istanbul to announce that he was stepping down from the position of pasha. Then he divided power among his three sons. Mourad became Bey of the Camp, which was a way of implicitly identifying him as first in the line of succession. The second, Muhammad al-Hafsi, was appointed Governor of the provinces of Kairouan, Monastir, Sousse, and Sfax. The last, Hassan, still a child, was given the provinces of Frigua.

It was the end of an era. Hamouda Pasha Bey died on April 14, 1666, following a frightening and surprising experience: from his window, he saw the body of "Ali al-Fillari hanging from the door of the Kasbah. A week later, he died. Immediately, the dey Mustafa Karakouz was dismissed. This was a dangerous precedent that threw the region into the downward spiral of civil war.

Conclusion

The Regency of Tunis emerged from a long period of struggles and rivalries between the Spanish and the Ottomans in which the crucial issue had been control of the Mediterranean. The Battle of Lépante, which unfolded in October 1571, was a stunning military victory for Spain and its allies. Paradoxically, this date also signaled the beginning of the end of the Spanish in the Mediterranean and paved the way for the Ottoman Turks' arrival in Tunis three years later. The fate of Ifriqiya had been sealed: it would be in the fold of the empire for the next three centuries.

Between 1535 and 1574, events accelerated. The Hafsid state was disintegrating and its territory shrinking. Small regional powers were beginning to appear. A religious leader claimed to have carved out a kingdom from the rubble and took Kairouan as its capital. Several coastal cities were the subject of rivalries among the Spanish, corsairs serving the Ottoman Empire, and traders ready to defend their autonomy. These multiple sovereignties, based as much on legitimacy (more or less contested) as on violence, allowed for the reorganization of the former Hafsid space. Numerous configurations were possible because of the complexity and fragility of alliances, as well as an inconsistent balance of power. It was not yet certain that from this muddle, the Ottomans would emerge victorious.

Everything began with the new Spanish crusades against the Maghrebi coastline and the raising of a string of forts that hosted garrisons intended to protect Spanish galleys en route to their Italian possessions. The Mediterranean became a place of confrontation between Christians and Muslims, religious orders of Knights and the Barbarossa brothers, each waging their own holy war. When 'Arrouj Barbarossa won control of Algiers, the situation in the region changed for the intrepid corsair and his brother,

Khayriddine, who nurtured the ambition to build a string of cities on the shore, facing the sea and engaged in piracy.

With 'Arrouj's death, Khayriddine gave shape to this plan. He put himself under the protection of the Ottoman Empire, stood up to Spanish expansionism, and actively helped the Moriscos establish themselves in the coastal cities of the Maghreb. In the view of contemporary observers, by the seventeenth century Algiers had become an Andalusian city governed by the Turks. The consolidation of the *oujak* of Algiers was a first step toward control of the entire Maghrebi coast. Khayriddine's ambitious project would have resulted in the detachment of the coasts from their distant backcountries, but it did not see the light of day. Neither did the Spanish pretensions to maintain the forts along the Tunisian coast, which would have made La Goulette, Mahdia, Kélibia, Tripoli, and other cities into Spanish enclaves for an indeterminate period. (Melilla and Ceuta retain the status of Spanish enclaves until this day). There were two colonial projects: one military and defense-oriented, the other of settlement, in which the Andalusians would constitute the linchpin. But the vision of a Maghreb open to the sea and cut off from its continental territories would never materialize: from the heart of the steppes, a voice rose up, crying of the Christian danger and rallying the Bedouins to defend Islam.

'Arafa Shabbi, founder of a brotherhood that was widespread in the central steppes, purported to establish a religious state that would stand up to Hafsid power, in a compromise with the Christians. The Spanish occupation of Tunis in 1535 and the suffering to which the Tunisians were subjected gave 'Arafa Shabbi the opportunity to present himself as a savior, prepared to help the populations defend their honor and property (Ibn abi Dinar speaks of sixty thousand deaths, which is probably an exaggeration, but even so gives an indication of the burning memory of the event one century later). Supported by the great tribe of the Hnansha, his most loyal followers, 'Arafa Shabbi set off on a political adventure and transformed Kairouan into the capital of this embryonic state. But exercising power proved to be a true test. To retain it, 'Arafa and his followers were compelled to ally themselves time and again with their former enemies—the Hafsids, and even the Spanish—blurring the divide between Muslims and Christians that had been the basis of their propaganda and the spread of their *da'wa*. The Shabbi were not easily accepted by the people of Kairouan, who saw in 'Arafa an obscure and unremarkable scholar, one whose shallow knowledge of religion was "only good for sheep herders" and was not convincing to the *ulama* of a city known for its tradition of legal debate. Several Kairouan families allied themselves with the Turks from Tripoli: the state founded by 'Arafa and transferred to his grandson was swept away by Dargouth in 1557. His followers disappeared into the Sahara, their attempt to maintain a maraboutic dynasty doomed to failure.

The Hafsids—exhausted by fratricidal rivalries, held hostage by the Bedouins, and abandoned by the Spanish, who held them in low esteem—were left completely powerless, and dispersed, ending their lives in exile and austerity. After a century of crusades against the Muslims, the Spanish abandoned the Mediterranean for a great adventure across the Atlantic. The triumphant Turks became the masters of Tunis.

The former Hafsid territory was, by this time, completely shattered. The Ottoman Turks controlled some cities, especially the coasts, but vast stretches escaped their reach. The regencies of Tripoli and of Tunis were constructed from territorial "debris" and regional reshapings that the different governors were scrambling to reconstitute amid confusion and, oftentimes, geographic ignorance. One of the pashas of Tripoli tried to detach the cities of Sousse, Monastir, and Kairouan from Tunis by claiming that they were closer to his province!

This chaotic situation lasted a dozen years, and the imperial correspondence with successive governors reveals the total absence of territorial control. Orders, counter-orders, false information, accusations, and complaints circulated around the cities of the Maghreb and Istanbul, giving rise to successive appointments and dismissals. The Ottoman machine, so well-oiled in other provinces, here seemed to be dysfunctional. What was going on in these peripheral regions?

The conditions of the occupation of the Maghreb were unprecedented in Ottoman history. Since the founding of Algiers, the corsairs had solicited the help of the sultan and had been placed under the protection of the empire, asking for the support of the Ottoman military and its symbolic protection. Its first pasha, Khayriddine, governed Algiers by relying on the support of his men, all former Christian captives who had converted, the majority from Mediterranean regions, and whom he had raised and initiated into the trades of the sea. Despite their Islamization, these men were considered slaves of the master and maintained relations of *wala*, or vassality, which implied both submission and solidarity. This relation of master to slaves led to the establishment of houses, in the sense of groups of persons linked through relations of interdependence, often reinforced by matrimonial alliances. This notion of a house is fundamental for understanding how power functioned in the *oujak*s of the Maghreb: we have always believed that the pasha governors were chosen and appointed from Istanbul, when in fact, the imperial capital often merely endorsed suggestions from the provinces themselves. Sometimes an Ottoman Turkish dignitary would seek the position of pasha in one of the *oujak*s, but would fail in his mission and ask to be relieved of the position. The success of the pashas depended, in large part, on ties and networks that they maintained in the region. This partially explains the "waltz of the pashas," who circulated from one capital to the next and refused to be appointed somewhere else, as Haydar Pasha did when he was removed from Tripoli. It was difficult to govern one or the other province if one did not know the rules by which it operated—or rather, by which it did not operate. In the beginning, most pashas exercised the menial duties of *kahia* or caid that gave them military, administrative, and fiscal powers. Strengthened by their experiences, these men could then claim the role of pasha, and alternately govern Tunis, Algiers, or Tripoli. The first house of the corsairs was Khayriddine's, and most of the pashas were part of it: in addition to Khayriddine's own son, three-time pasha of Algiers, Dargouth and 'Ilj 'Ali also belonged to this house. The status and wealth of Khayriddine's dynasty sparked jealousy in Istanbul and became a subject of suspicion, for they feared the eventual risks of succession. Khayriddine's dominance, obtained through the dynamism of piracy and the fabulous riches it brought in, was dealt with in two ways. First, the Ottomans tried to weaken Khayriddine's house by depriving it of its leaders. They appointed them to such high positions as captain pasha, or grand admiral of the fleet, an honor that was given to two men of great value, Khayriddine and his lieutenant, 'Ilj 'Ali. Their respective talents were thus put in the service of the central state, reducing the risk that their region would break off. The second method they used to try to weaken Khayriddine's house, after his death, was by preventing all forms of "créolization" of power (the mixing of Turkish men and local women) and hereditary succession, using a weapon that hurt some candidates more than others: the disgrace of illegitimacy. The best example is Hassan, Khayriddine's son. He became Pasha of Algiers during his father's lifetime. He allied himself with the Kabyles and married a Kabyle woman, establishing a form of power that included the indigenous population. Hassan was distanced from Algiers several times through intrigues fomented at the highest echelons of power. Even though he held the position of pasha three times, he nevertheless ultimately abandoned Algiers and his family, ending his life in Istanbul and cutting himself off definitively from the Maghreb. Certain great houses of Istanbul understood that they had no interest in promoting the integration of the Turks into the indigenous milieu, nor in protecting the unity of the three *oujak*s. In 1587, with the death of Kilidj 'Ali Pasha, the sultan decided to give up on the unification of the *oujak*s. From that time on, each province embarked on its own individual path, all while retaining much in common with the others, insofar as they were all imperial possessions.

Each with its own tone, the three provinces remained connected to the empire through ties of vassalage that were strongly expressed both politically and symbolically. The pashas represented the sultan himself. The Friday *khutba* was pronounced in his name and the currency minted with his effigy. The three provinces were oriented toward the sea, due to piracy, all while remaining attached to their hinterlands (even if they did not completely control them). Tied to Mediterranean commerce and especially piracy, a similar social elite, made up of Janissaries, Anatolian Turks, and converted Christians (the renegades) established themselves as the dominant group. This group distinguished itself from the indigenous population through a set of cultural codes: language, customs, clothing, Hanafi rites, octagonal minarets, and *souq al-Atrak* (Turkish souq), expressing the Ottomanization of the great cities of the Maghreb.

Building on the foundation of these shared traits, the three provinces evolved individually. The time had not yet come for the establishment of three distinct territorial states, still imperfectly constituted around their respective capitals. But it was necessary to bury the notion of unifying the Maghreb, which the Hafsid dynasty had pursued with varying degrees of success ever since the distant Almohad expansion. More than its neighboring provinces, the Regency of Tunis seemed to have initiated a territorial centralization based on the former Hafsid territory and the capital's historic past. On top of this there was undoubtedly a social alchemy between the group that took power and certain local houses, *al-buyutat*, or great families, whether old or recently formed.

Understanding the history of the Regency of Tunis and of the entire Maghreb in the sixteenth century comes back, in part, to grasping the process by which an outside group, formed in part by Christian captives and in part by commoners, transforms into a social and political elite. This question addresses a more general problem, that of the legitimacy of rulers.

On what premise would a dominant group base its power? Social legitimacy, religion, or charisma? In the face of the Christian advance during the sixteenth century, could the defense of religion be invoked as the only discourse legitimizing the exercise of power? Did another form of legitimacy exist—a social form, for example?

The Ottoman Turks presented themselves under the cover of Islam to protect the Maghrebi coasts from the Spanish invasion. But this marker of legitimacy, the sultan being the Commander of the Faithful, was not enough to open doors for them, and they were fought and hunted for decades. In Tunis at this time, the Hafsid house—which was deteriorating in interminable internecine fights between brothers and fathers and sons and had called for help from the Spanish, who defiled even the holy sites—lost its legitimacy. The Shabbia would also go down this path, but quickly, the inanity of their discourse, coupled with their political incapacity reduced them to meandering and dispersion. From this moment on, the Turks triumphed over local resistance, whether in the territories joined to Tunis or to Tripoli, where they also encountered opposition from a preacher who claimed to be a prophet, whom they would have to fight to impose their power. This effervescent "popular" Islam, claiming to realign societies in the right direction by combatting depraved regimes, was based upon simplistic preaching and did not bear the weight of a political project. 'Arafa Shabbi was criticized for his religious knowledge, which was "only good for the herdsmen," according to the scholars of Tunis. However, this is no reason to downplay religion as a powerful source of social cohesion. Indeed, religious discourse becomes most effective when articulated as part of the social: it could, therefore, give rise to a durable state. This is what happened in Morocco, which escaped Turkish rule despite several attempts at occupation. There, the Ottomans found themselves faced with another force: the *shurafa*, families claiming descent from the Prophet Muhammad, who managed to block the Janissaries' way. The role of the *shurafa* in the sixteenth century was essential in social representation and political legitimacy. Their numbers proliferated alongside the arrival of the Moriscos, for several Andalusian families claimed this heritage.

Algiers, Tripoli, and Tunis did not have the opportunity to oppose the Ottoman Turks by playing the card of the Arab nobility. Only the new masters of the land were aware of the rivalry with the *shurafa*, who had also contested Ottoman power in the Arab peninsula. The Turks, who presented themselves as the defenders of Sunni orthodoxy, accorded them special treatment. In Tunis, the *shurafa*, organized under the authority of a *naqib*, were represented in the council of the pasha. They were allowed to wear identifying marks—a green turban—and were even exempted from certain taxes. Did they have more access to power? The question deserves to be posed to better understand the speed with which the Turks integrated into local society and the relative passivity of the local populations in the face of the brutality and violence of the military regime.

The hypothesis that we suggest privileges the path of matrimonial alliances between Turks and *shurafa*, or alternatively, between Turks and maraboutic families or brotherhoods. The reconstitution of the marriages of the first generation of Janissaries of Tunis, which was possible thanks to an intensive study of *habous* documents from the period, helps us to understand the appeasement of relations between the communities, the gradual recognition of the Turks' social legitimacy, and the failure of all attempts at Hafsid restoration. These alliances, which derived their significance more from symbolism than from numbers, overshadow the fact that the Turks of Tunis were not all Muslims by origin, and that many had recently converted. They also show the social power of women, for Sharifism as well as maraboutic charisma were transmitted through the mother. Thus, the sons of Turks born of these unions, and from among whom the members of the dominant group recruited, benefitted from a double legitimacy: they belonged to the occupying body through their fathers and to the nobility through their mothers. This double legitimacy was reinforced through strong inbreeding in these families, whose descendants also united through ties of marriage.

However, despite their recognition and integration, this new Ottoman Turkish political formation, mostly mixed-race, was still not able to establish a modern state according to the model that was in place in Europe at the time. Despite the autonomy that it seemed to enjoy, the government of Tunis was firmly attached to the empire and to the sultan caliph, who remained its principal source of legitimacy. The intensity of movement and the strength of the ties between Tunis and Istanbul were expressed in correspondence from the council of the sultan, the complaints lodged by the indigenous population, and appointments and removals of Maliki judges (there are several examples of this in the *ajwiba* of 'Addoum), some of whom went to the imperial capital to assert their rights. These and other clues show the strength of the ties between the regency and Istanbul, which was never questioned, even if the powers of Tunis, just like Algiers and

Tripoli, exhibited indiscipline, arrogance, and disrespect for orders. There was a simple mismatch between their reciprocal economic interests with regard to corsair activity that did not go so far as to drive a desire for secession. The idea of the autonomy of the province of Tunis was developed by diplomats, mostly French, charged with liberating captives, who appeared in Tunis brandishing imperial orders that the council of the Janissaries refused to enforce. Even though the foreign policy of the Ottomans undermined the interests of the houses of the corsairs of Tunis, the conflict did not involve a rupture with the "nourishing mother" and regulated itself through backdoor means.

The node of relations among Istanbul, Europe, and the Maghreb remained the question of piracy. The practice had been assimilated into a holy war and remained accepted by the Muslim states, on the condition of respect for certain rules. When piracy developed in Tunis under Othman Dey, it immediately took on a fierce, lawless character that was unknown in previous eras. Othman Dey associated with sailors of multiple nationalities—English, Dutch, and Mediterraneans of all kinds—who carried out extortion at sea with the complicity of many European partners who were involved in the operations at different stages, from the sale of ship rigging to the flow of merchandise. This was a vast traffic in which the high officials in charge of European ports and even certain Ottoman ministers participated. In the face of the influx of riches and the growth of traffic, the words of diplomats fell on deaf ears, and a veritable comedy played out for identifying those responsible. At this moment, the pashas (who were, don't forget, the official representatives of the sultan) claimed to lose power and be under the menace of the rais and the council of the Janissaries. A simple game, for in the seventeenth century, almost all the pashas of Tunis were renegades who had personally commanded pirate ships!

In the seventeenth century, the question of autonomy seemed to be an exaggerated interpretation of relations between Tunis and Istanbul. The group in power was not motivated by any sentiment of local belonging, which would have pushed it to create an independent state. On the contrary, all its interests remained under the roof of the empire, all while working toward the consolidation of local authority. What form could this authority take without creating major conflicts? From the beginning, the enormous possibilities for enrichment and the strong rivalries that they generated excluded individual strategies and transmissions in direct lines in favor of the establishment of houses, which neutralized all possibility of competition that could lead to violence. For this reason, the powerful families of the deys, the beys, the *agha*, the pasha, and the caids wove among themselves solid ties of kinship and alliances. Together, they took hold of various sources of wealth and monopolized their exports to Europe: oil, wax, and wool collected in the interior helped fuel industries north of the Mediterranean. Add to this all the products taken from the captured boats and resold with the help of European traders. As such, the role of caid of customs took on a vital importance, and it was exclusively proffered to those close to the men in power.

Through the game of marriages and alliances, houses were built, and they concentrated economic power in their own hands. The money earned through corsair activity was invested in the land and the palaces, but also in charity work, the founding of mosques, madrasas, and public water fountains. The renegades and former soldiers managed to enhance their standing and make their mark on the city. Tunis saw a relative social peace, despite plagues in 1605 and 1622 that decimated the population.

The government of the regency was shared among three authorities: the pasha, representing the sultan and exercising by delegation the role of the first magistrate; the dey, powerful protector of the militia; and the bey, the general of the armies. This tripartite organization was shaken up by Mourad Bey when he demanded, and obtained, the title of pasha and ceded the role of bey to his son. Did the former captive, now rich and powerful, nurture dynastic ambitions? Probably, if he wanted his dynasty to maintain power: only Mourad did not have daughters, and his house would be built by his son and his renegades. It seems that such a pretension was not accepted.

Muhammad (known as Hamouda), the son of Mourad and Yasmina, a Corsican captive, painstakingly built up the house of his father beginning in 1631. But in 1662 or 1663, the aging Hamouda decided to renounce the title of pasha, which he had sought four years earlier, and to divide the land over which he had reigned for thirty years among his three daughters. He offered to the eldest the role of *bey al-ambal* and the two others, territory and the title of bey. The act was surprising coming from a great prince who sacrificed the grandeur of his state for the peace of his family. How should we interpret this decision, which broke apart the territorial centrality that had been painstakingly assembled since the Ottoman Turks occupied Tunis?

Hamouda Pasha Bey, who died in 1666, had reigned for more than thirty years, consolidated his frontiers, and reinforced strong institutions.

And then, on the eve of his death, he destroyed his own project. Sharing the territory among his heirs revealed a patrimonial conception of power in which the sovereign, equating the territory he governed to his private property, transmitted an inheritance to each of his descendants. Was it to avoid wars between brothers that he brought back into question the foundations of the fragile centralization begun under Turkish rule? What he ultimately left as a legacy was the cities and lands just emerging from a checkered Middle Ages, which his sons would fight over in a civil war from 1675 to 1686, and whose knot we have still not untangled. The territory had exploded again. The men who had arrived in the sixteenth century were integrated into the cities, while the disparities between the cities and countryside widened. The countryside was populated by tribal groups—some settled, some transhumant. Successive political powers continued to try to exert control over it with the goal of containing the tribes: civil war in the Mouradite house gave them the opportunity to return to the political scene.

For the moment, it was the tent of the empire that united this world.

Notes

Chapter 1

1 *La Revue Tunisienne*, published by the Institute of Carthage since 1894.
2 Braudel, *La Méditerranée.*

Chapter 2

1 Berque, *L'intérieur du Maghreb, XV-XIXè siècle,* Gallimard, 1978.
2 Berque, *L'intérieur du Maghreb, XV-XIXè siècle,* Gallimard, 1978.
3 Gauthier, *L'islamisation de l'Afrique du nord, les siècles obscurs du Maghreb,* Payot, 1927.
4 Berque, *L'intérieur du Maghreb, XV-XIXè siècle,* Gallimard, 1978, 56–59.
5 Al Wancharissi, *Al Mi'yar*, vol. 10, 413, 418, 462.
6 Braudel, *La Méditerranée*, 44.
7 Brunschwig, *La Berbérie orientale*, vol. 1, 118, 136.
8 Marmol y Carvajal (Luis), a Spanish historian of the sixteenth century, taken prisoner following the expedition of Charles V against Tunis in 1535. He returned to Spain after eight years in captivity and published his *Description Générale de l'Afrique* (General Description of Africa), translated into French by Perrot d'Ablancourt (Paris, 1967, 2 vol.).
9 Brunschwig, *La Bérbérie orientale*, 134.
10 Laroui, *L'Histoire du Maghreb*, 236.
11 Sinan Chaouch, *Fondation de la Régence d'Alger*, 279.

Chapter 3

1 Sinan Chaouch, *Fondation de la Régence d'Alger*, 307.
2 Haedo, *Histoire des rois d'Alger*, 42.
3 Sinan Chaouch, *Fondation de la Régence d'Alger*, Editor's note no. 6, 307.

Chapter 4

1 Hammer, *Histoire de l'Empire ottomane*, 119.
2 Temimi, "Lettre de la population algéroise."
3 Plantet, *Correspondance des deys d'Alger*, vol. 1, xvi.
4 Haedo, *Histoire des rois d'Alger*, 68.
5 Sinan Chaouch, *Fondation de la Régence d'Alger*, 307, 325.

6 Ben Hamoucha, Mustapha, "De Grenade à Alger, ou la politique urbaine ottomane face au problème andalou," in *Revue des Etudes Ottomanes*, Oct. 1995, 47. The author remarks that from the analyses of the *waqfs* and from the study of the establishment of Andalusian properties it is possible to conclude that Algiers was practically an Andalusian city run by the Ottomans.
7 Sinan Chaouch, *Fondation de la Régence d'Alger*, vol. 5, 119.
8 Hammer, Histoire . . . op.cit. vol. 5, p. 119.

Chapter 5

1 This chapter is written using the testimonies of Sandoval, a historian of Charles V, cited by Venture de Paradis in Sinan Chaouch, *Fondation de la Régence d'Alger*, annex, 337–40.
2 Hammer, *Histoire de l'Empire ottomane*, 120.
3 Sinan Chaouch, *Fondation de la Régence d'Alger*, 179.
4 Sinan Chaouch, *Fondation de la Régence d'Alger*, 337–40.
5 De La Primaudaie, "Documents inédits," 212.
6 Ibn abi Dinar, *Al Mu'nis*, 163–64.
7 De La Primaudaie, "Documents inédits," 212.
8 Hammer, *Histoire de l'Empire ottomane*, 122, note 5.
9 Hammer, *Histoire de l'Empire ottomane*, 122, note 5.
10 Hammer, *Histoire de l'Empire ottomane*, 122, note 5.
11 Hammer, *Histoire de l'Empire ottomane*, 122, note 5.
12 Rousseau, *Les Annales Tunisiennes*, 408–414, citing M. CH. Weiss, Extract from the state papers of Cardinal Granvelle, unedited collection of documents on the history of France, vol. 2, 368 and onward.
13 Rousseau, *Les Annales Tunisiennes*, 408–14.

Chapter 6

1 Feraud, "Kitab al Adouani."
2 Monchicourt, *Etudes kairouanaises*, 106–107.
3 Shabbi, *'Arafa*, 94.
4 Ibn abi Dinar, *Al Mu'nis*, 164.
5 Shabbi, *'Arafa*, 46.
6 Monchicourt, *Etudes kairouanaises*, 57.
7 Monchicourt, *Etudes kairouanaises*, 52.
8 Ibn abi Dinar, *Al Mu'nis*, 167; He cites him as sihr (relative by marriage and in this specific case, son-in-law). Shabbi, *'Arafa*, 46.
9 Monchicourt, *Etudes kairouanaises*, 58, note 27.
10 Monchicourt, *Etudes kairouanaises*, 121.
11 Ibn abi Dinar, *Al Mu'nis*, 167.
12 Moncvicour études Kairounaises, 109.
13 Ibn abi Dinar, *Al Mu'nis*, 111–112, document discovered by the muphti of Kairouan, Muhammad al-Joudi, and translated by Monchicourt.
14 Shabbi, *'Arafa*, 109.

Chapter 7

1 Pignon, "Un document inédit sur la Tunisie," 71, note 48. Pignon denies the giving of a grant from Tabarka to Lomellini in exchange for the liberation of Dargouth.
2 Karli-elli: Ottoman province.
3 Sinan Chaouch, *Fondation de la Régence d'Alger*, 131.
4 Monchicourt, *Etudes kairouanaises*, 139.
5 Monchicourt, Charles, "Episodes de la carrier tunisienne de Dragut," in *Revue tunisienne*, 1918.
6 Monchicourt, *Etudes kairouanaises*, 140.
7 Monchicourt, *Etudes kairouanaises*, 145.

Chapter 8

1 The list of governors is reconstituted according to Haedo, *Histoire des rois d'Alger*, and De Grammont, *Histoire d'Alger*.
2 A number calculated with much precision in Sinan Chaouch, *Fondation de la Régence d'Alger*, 256.
3 Haedo, *Histoire des rois d'Alger*, 71.
4 Haedo, *Histoire des rois d'Alger*, 78.
5 Haedo, *Histoire des rois d'Alger*, 83.
6 Rostom Pasha was known for corruption, according to Bayat Fadhil, *Studies in Arab History in the Ottoman Period*, Beirut, 2002, 107.
7 Haedo, *Histoire des rois d'Alger*, 118.
8 Haedo, *Histoire des rois d'Alger*, 118.
9 Haedo, *Histoire des rois d'Alger*, 118.
10 Haedo, *Histoire des rois d'Alger*, 128.
11 Haedo, *Histoire des rois d'Alger*, 132.
12 Roxelane died in 1558.
13 Temimi, *Etudes sur l'histoire du Maghreb*, d. 21, 154.
14 de Cervantes, Miguel, *Don quichotte de la Manche*, Seuil, 1967, vol. 1, 44; also Haedo, *Histoire des rois d'Alger*, 140.

Chapter 9

1 Haedo, *Histoire des rois d'Alger*, 148.
2 Temimi, *Etudes sur l'histoire du Maghreb*, d.10, 149.
3 Haedo, *Histoire des rois d'Alger*, 151.
4 Ibn abi Dinar, *Al Mu'nis*, 172.
5 De Grammont, *Histoire d'Alger*, 104.
6 Haedo, *Histoire des rois d'Alger*, 152.
7 Haedo, *Histoire des rois d'Alger*, 167.
8 Temimi, "Les Régences d'Alger,"d. 89, 118.
9 Temimi, Abdeljelil, "Les Régences . . ." article cited, d. 50, 53, 55, pp. 99-101.
10 There is an abundant history of the bastion of Tunis, *la Nova Arx*. For illustrative purposes, see Djelloul, Néji, *Les fortifications en Tunisie*, l'Agence de Mise en Valeur du Patrimoine et de la Promotion Culturelle, 1999, 79.

11 Monchicourt, *Etudes kairouanaises*, 192.
12 Monchicourt, *Etudes kairouanaises*, 192.
13 Monchicourt, *Etudes kairouanaises*, 193.
14 Monchicourt, *Etudes kairouanaises*, 195.
15 Monchicourt, *Etudes kairouanaises*, 202.
16 Letter of Philip II, King of France, to the viceroy of Naples, archives of Simancas, Mapas, planos y dibujos, 7–131; estado, legago 487 (we consulted a copy in the archives in Barcelona). On 'Ilj 'Ali, see de Cervantes, *Don Quichotte*, 449–50.

Chapter 10

1 Ibn abi Dinar, *Al Mu'nis*, 292.
2 Monchicourt, *Etudes kairouanaises*, 176.
3 Temimi, Abdeljelil, "La propriété fonciere et le régime des za'amat et des timar dans la Régence de Tunis 1574–1588" in *Revue d'histoire arabe et d'études ottomanes*, no. 11–12, October 1995, supporting documents 1 and 2, 198–200.
4 Sameh, *Les Turcs ottomanes*, 261.
5 Temimi, "Les Régences d'Alger," d. 125, 127; 138–39.
6 Temimi, "Les Régences d'Alger," d. 53, March 5, 1572, 100.
7 Temimi, "Les Régences d'Alger," d. 2; 274.
8 Temimi, Abdeljelil, "Les Régences . . ." article cited, d. 125, 127, pp. 138-139.
9 'Addoum, Qasim, *Kitab al-ajwiba*, edited by al Hila Med Habib, published by Bayt Hikma 2006, 11 [s
10 Idem, vol. 1, pp. 138-139.
11 'Addoum, *Kitab*, vol. 1; 318-320.
12 Sameh, *Les Turcs ottomanes*, 88.
13 Sameh, *Les Turcs ottomanes*, 93.
14 Sameh, *Les Turcs ottomanes*, 270.
15 Temimi, "Les Régences d'Alger," article cited, d. 167; 156–57.
16 Sameh, *Les Turcs ottomanes*, 267.
17 Saadaoui, Ahmad, *Tunis ville ottomane*, Tunis: Center for university publications, 1990, 13.
18 Sameh, *Les Turcs ottomanes*, 278.
19 Sameh, *Les Turcs ottomanes*, 179.
20 Savary de Brèves, *Négociations de la France dans le levant*, vol. IV, 315.
21 Haedo, *Histoire des rois d'Alger*, 176.
22 Savary de Brèves, *Négociations*, vol. 4, 313, 315, 327.
23 Haedo, *Histoire des rois d'Alger*, 178.
24 Haedo, *Histoire des rois d'Alger*, 204.

Chapter 11

1 Moalla, Asma, "Le jund de la Régence de Tunis, 1574–1650," in *Arab Historical Review of Ottoman Studies*, August 2004, 189-196.
2 Bayat, *Etudes*, 118.

3 Temimi, “Les Régences d’Alger,” d. 188; 165.
4 Bacrouch, *Formation sociales barbaresque*.
5 Temimi, “Les Régences d’Alger,”, d. 31, October 24, 1568, 89.
6 Ibn abi Dinar, *Al Mu’nis*, 174.
7 Moalla, “Le jund,” 189–96.
8 Pignon, Jean, “La milice des janissaires de Tunis au temps des *deys* (1590–1650)” in *Cahiers de Tunisie*, vol. 4, 178.
9 Temimi, “Les Régences d’Alger,”d. 24, August 14, 1567, 86.
10 Temimi, “Les Régences d’Alger,” d. 131, May 31, 1577, 141.
11 Temimi, “Les Régences d’Alger,” d. 50, September 13, 1571, 99.
12 Temimi, “Les Régences d’Alger,” d. 132, October 24, 1568, 89 [L1].
13 Temimi, “Les Régences d’Alger,” d. 121, October 18, 1576, 136.
14 Temimi, “Les Régences d’Alger,” d. 121, October 18, 1576, 136.
15 Grandchamp, *La France en Tunisie*, vol. 1, 108–110.
16 Raymond, *Les Grandes villes arabes*, 71.
17 Temimi, “Les Régences d’Alger,” d. 210, September 1588, 174.
18 Temimi, “Les Régences d’Alger,” d. 7 and 150; 149.
19 Temimi, “Les Régences d’Alger,” d. 218, September 13, 1588, 179.
20 Temimi, *Etudes sur l’histoire du Maghreb*, d. 194, 167.
21 Temimi, *Etudes sur l’histoire du Maghreb*, 190.

Chapter 12

1 Sabbagh, Leila, *La société arabe syrienne au début de l’époque ottomane*, University of Damascus, 1975.
2 Temimi, “Les Régences d’Alger,” d. 94, 121.
3 Temimi, Temimi, “La propriété foncière,” d. 19, undated, 208.
4 Temimi, *Etudes sur l’histoire du Maghreb*, d. 172, February 11, 1582, 229.
5 Sameh, *Les Turcs ottomanes*, 89.
6 Haedo, *Histoire des rois d’Alger*, 67.

Chapter 13

1 De Grammont, *Histoire d’Alger*, 129.
2 Haedo, *Histoire des rois d’Alger*, 211, supports the view that he is Turkish.
3 Saadaoui, *Tunis au XVIIe siècle*, 151.
4 Haedo, *Histoire des rois d’Alger*, 130.
5 De Grammont, *Histoire d’Alger*, 130.
6 Ibn abi Dinar, *Al Mu’nis*, 201.
7 Temimi, “Les Régences d’Alger,” d. 194, June 1585, 167.
8 Temimi, “Les Régences d’Alger,” d. 147, May 1579.
9 Temimi, “Les Régences d’Alger,” d. 211, September 1588, 175.
10 Temimi, “Les Régences d’Alger,” d. 148.
11 Temimi, “Les Régences d’Alger,” d. 148.
12 Temimi, “Les Régences d’Alger,” d. 210, 211; 174–75.
13 Ibn abi Dinar, *Al Mu’nis*, 200.
14 Ibn abi Dinar, *Al Mu’nis*, 200.

15 Bacrouch, *Formation sociale barbaresque*, 34.
16 Ibn abi Dinar, *Al Mu'nis*, 201–202.

Chapter 14

1 Ibn abi Louhayya, *Nour al Armâch*.
2 Ibn abi Louhayya, *Nour al Armâch*, 23–24.
3 'Addoum, *Kitab*, vol. 2, 8.
4 Ibn abi Louhayya, *Nour al Armâch*, 364–65.
5 Ibn abi Louhayya, *Nour al Armâch*, 322.
6 Ibn abi Louhayya, *Nour al Armâch*, 44.
7 Ibn abi Louhayya, *Nour al Armâch*, 340.
8 Dossier no. 1 of the Mouradite period, in the national archives, indicates a *yoldach*, the brother of the dey Othman, see Blili, Leïla, "Parenté et pouvoir dans la Tunisie houssaynite," doctoral thesis, University of Tunis, 2005.
9 Ibn abi Louhayya, *Nour al Armâch*, 450.
10 *Khouja, Dhayl*, 184.
11 Ibn abi Louhayya, *Nour al Armâch*, 141.
12 Ibn abi Louhayya, *Nour al armâch*, 459.
13 Ibn abi Louhayya, *Nour al armâch*, 459.
14 Grandchamp. *La* France *en Tunisie*, vol 3, p. 308.

Chapter 15

1 Grandchamp, *La France en Tunisie*, vol. 2, Act of June 15, 1609.
2 Grandchamp, *La France en Tunisie*, vol. 3, 389 et seq., full text as related by Foucques.
3 Grandchamp, *La France en Tunisie*, vol. 2, Act of June 15, 1609.
4 Savary de Brèves, *Relation des voyages de Monsieur de Brèves faits aux royames de Tunis et d'Alger*, Paris, 1628 (followed by three theses, one of which is titled *Discours sur l'Alliance qu'a le roi avec le Grand Seigneur, et de l'utilité qu'elle apporte à la Chrétienté*).
5 Masson, Paul, *Les Compagnies du corail: Etudes historique sue le commerce de Marseille au XVIème siècle et les origines de la colonization française en Algérie, Tunisie*, Paris, Marseille, 1908.
6 Grandchamp, *La France en Tunisie*, vol.1, November 1578.

Chapter 16

1 'Addoum, *Kitab*, vol. 6, 126.
2 Saadaoui, *Tunis au XVIIe siècle*, 167.
3 'Addoum, *Kitab*, vol. 6; 18, 24.
4 'Addoum, *Kitab*, vol. 6, 126.
5 Grandchamp, *La France en Tunisie*, 3. Foucques' testimony, 389 onward.
6 Haedo, who speaks of him as the twenty-seventh "king" of Algiers (211), could not have known that it was the same person who governed Tunis. Several references in 'Addoum, *Kitab*, vol. 1, 19; vol. 2, 43; vol. 5, 130, 279; vol. 10, 26, 299, 300.

7 Grandchamp, *La France en Tunisie,* vol. 2, témoignage de Foucques, p. 389 et suivantes.
8 Al-Wazir al-Sarraj, *Al Hulal,* 2, 348–49.
9 Grandchamp, *La France en Tunisie*, vol. 3. These claims appear in several places: 18, 21, 27, 43, 46, 81, 93, 102.
10 Grandchamp, *La France en Tunisie*, vol. 3, 60.
11 Sameh, *Les Turcs ottomanes*, d. 9 joumada II 1017, October 30, 1607, 296.
12 Grandchamp, *La France en Tunisie*, vol. 3, 140, 208: there are several mentions of "Fassali" and "Fagali."
13 Grandchamp, *La France en Tunisie*, vol.3. According to the chancellery acts, Muhammad Bey lived until Apil 2, 1609. One act dating to June 22, 1609, refers to the heirs of Muhammad Bey.
14 Grandchamp, "Une mission delicate."
15 On this conflict, see Bernard Roy, "Deux documents inédits sur l'expédition algérienne de 1628," in *Revue tunisienne*, no. 122, 1917.

Chapter 17

1 On the population of Tunis, see Paul Sebagh, *Tunis au XVIIe siècle, une Cité barbaresque au temps de la course*, Paris, 1989.
2 'Addoum, *Kitab,* vol. 6, 127–28. Chérif, Mouhamad al Hédi, "Témoignage du mufti Qasim 'Addoum" in *Cahiers de Tunisie*, no. 77–78, 1972, 39–50.
3 Saadaoui, Ahmad. *Tunis au XVIIè siècle. Des actes wazfd l'époque des deys et des beys mouradites,* Université de la Manouba, 2011. The first indication of a café seems to appear during the time of Youssef Dey, according to Ahmad Saadaoui, on the basis of his study of the *habous* act of 'Ali Thabit.
4 Sebagh, *Tunis*, 123–24.
5 Monchicourt, *La Région du Haut Tell.*
6 Chérif, Mouhamad al Hédi, *Pouvoir et société dans la Tunisie de Hussayn bin 'Ali*, vol. 2, University of Tunis, 1986, 79.
7 Saadaoui, *Tunis au XVIIè siècle*. Op. cit. 108.
8 'Addoum, *Kitab,* vol. 6, 56–57. There are several examples of the mufti 'Addoum accusing Kshour of corruption.
9 Al-Wazir al-Sarraj, *Al Hulal,* vol. 2, 351.
10 Saadaoui, Ahmad, *Tunis . . . op.cit.*, 73–75.
11 Blili-Temime, Leïla, "Parenté et Pouvoir dans la Tunisie Houssaynite," doctoral thesis defended in May 2005, accepted for publication.

Chapter 18

1 Al-Wazir al-Sarraj, *Al Hulal,* vol. 2, 351.
2 Grandchamp, *La France en Tunisie*, vol. 3, 307–308, 318, 322.
3 Ibn abi Louhayya, *Nour al Armâch*, 140.
4 Complete biography of Moratto Genovese in Jean Pignon, "Osta Moratto Turcho Génovésé, dey de Tunis (1637–1640)" in *Cahiers de Tunisie*, no. 11, 331–62.

Grandchamp, Pierre, *La France . . . op. cit.* vol. 3. This indication does not mean that Mourad did not occupy this function before 1615.

5 Grandchamp, *La France en Tunisie*, vol. 4, act of June 20, 1631, "Ossaino Génovésé, gendre de Osta Morat."
6 Pignon, "Osta Moratto."
7 Pignon, "Osta Moratto."

Chapter 19

1 Al-Wazir al-Sarraj, *Al Hulal*, 355–56.
2 Grandchamp, *La France en Tunisie*, vol. 3; Ibn abi Dinar, *Al Mu'nis*, 228.
3 Sebagh, ed., *Une Histoire des revolutions*, 61.
4 Al-Wazir al-Sarraj, *Al Hulal*, 371–72.
5 Grandchamp, *La France en Tunisie*, July 1623.
6 Grandchamp, *La France en Tunisie*, vol. 3, 342, May 1630.
7 Grandchamp, *La France en Tunisie*, vol. 4, April 1631.
8 Ibn abi Dinar, *Al Mu'nis*, 229.
9 Saadaoui, *Tunis aux XVII è siècle*, 484.
10 Al-Wazir al-Sarraj, *Al Hulal*, 407.
11 Saadaoui, *Tunis aux XVII è siecle*, 502.
12 Saadaoui, *Tunis aux XVII è siècle*, 237–39.
13 Saadaoui, *Tunis aux XVII è siècle*, 239.
14 Blili-Temime, "Parenté."
15 Al-Wazir al-Sarraj, *Al Hulal*, vol. 2, 147.
16 Ibn abi Dinar, *Al Mu'nis*, 212.
17 Al-Wazir al-Sarraj, *Al Hulal*, vol. 2, 407–08.

Bibliography

Many specialized academic works relating to the period indirectly informed this book, but are not all included in the bibliography. References have not been expressly cited where information is already well known, so as not to weigh down passages that provide a synthesis. Directly relevant sources are listed alphabetically, and include published sources in Arabic and French, as well as historical material.

'Addoum, Qasim. *Kitab al-ajwiba*. Edited by Hila Habib. 10 vols. Tunis: l'Académie tunisienne des Sciences, des lettres et des Arts, Bayt al-Hikma, 2004.

Ahmed, Kacim. *al-Iyala al-tunisiya 'ala daw' fatawa Qasim 'Addoum, 1574–1600.* Tunis: Fondation Temimi, 2004.

Bachrouch, Taoufic. *Formation sociale barbaresque et pouvoir à Tunis au XVIIe siècle.* Tunis: l'Université de Tunis, 1977.

Bayat, Fadhil. *Dirasat fi tarikh al-'arab fi-l 'ahd al-'uthmani : u'ya jadida fi daw' al-watha'iq wa-l-masadir al-'uthmaniya*, Benghazi, 2003.

Bergna, Constanzio. *Tarâblus min 1510 ila 1850.* Translated by Tillissi Khalifa. Tunis: Maison arabe du livre, 2009.

Berque, Jacques. *L'intérieur du Maghreb, XV–XIXe siècle.* Paris: Gallimard, 1978.

Blili, Leïla. "Parenté et pouvoir dans la Tunisie Houssaynite." Doctoral thesis, University of Tunis, May 2005, published in parts as *Sous le toit de l'Empire*, with volumes 2, and 3 scheduled for release November 2020.

Boubaker, Sadok. *La Régence de Tunis au XVIIe siècle, ses relations commerciales avec les ports de l'Europe*. Tunis: CEROMA, 1987.

Braudel, Fernand. *La Méditerrané et le monde méditerranéen à l'époque de Philippe II.* 3rd ed., 2 vols. Paris: Armand Colin, 1976.

de Brèves, Savary. *Relation des voyages de Monsieur de Brèves faits aux royames de Tunis et d'Alger*, Paris, 1628.

———. *Négociations de la France dans le levant,* 1628, vol. IV, 315.

Brunschwig, Robert. *La Bérbérie orientale sous les Hafsides des origines à la fin du XVe siècle*. 2 vols. Paris: Maisonneueve, 1947.

Chaouch, Sinan. *Fondation de la Régence d'Alger, histoire des frères Barberousse 'Arrouj et Khaïr-ed Dîn*. Algiers: Grand Alger Livres, 2006.

Cherif, Mouhamad al-Hédi. "Témoignage du mufti Kacim 'Addoum sur les rapports entre les Turcs et les autochtones dans la Tunisie de la fin du XVIe siècle." *Les Cahiers de Tunisie* (1972): 77–78.

De Grammont, Henri-Delmas. *Histoire d'Alger sous la domination turque, 1550–1830*. 2nd ed. Algiers: Bouchene, 2002.
De La Primaudaie, Elie. "Documents inédits sur l'occupation espagnole en Afrique, 1506–1574," Archives de Simancas, *Revue africaine* 21 (1877).
De la Véronne, Chantal. *Oran et Tlemcen dans la première moitié du XVIe siècle*. Paris: Geuthner, 1983.
Farrugia de Candia, Jean. "Monnaies frappées à Tripoli et à Gafsa par Dragut." *Revue tunisienne* (1936): 200–201.
Feraud, Louis-Charles. "Les Harar, seigneurs des Hanenchas." *Revue Africaine* 18 (1874): 167–69.
———, trans., "Kittab al Adouani ou le Sahara de Constantine et de Tunis." *Recueil des notices et des mémoires de la société archéologique de la province de Constantine*. Algiers : Constantine: L. Arnolet, 1868.
Gauthier, Emilie-Felix. *L'islamisation de l'Afrique du nord, les siècles obscurs du Maghreb*. Paris: Payot, 1927.
Grandchamp, Pierre. *La France en Tunisie au XVIIe siècle*, inventaire des archives du Consulat de France à Tunis de 1582 à 1705. 9 vols. Tunis, 1920–33.
———. "Une mission délicate en Barbarie au XVIIe siècle: Jean-Baptiste Salvago, Drogman vénitien à Alger et à Tunis." *Revue tunisienne* no. 30, second trimester, 1937: 299–322.
Haedo, Diego. *Histoire des rois d'Alger*. Translated by H-D de Grammont. Algiers: Éditions Bouchène, 2004.
Ibn abi Dinar, Muhammad. *al-Mu'nis fi ahbar Ifriqiya wa Tunis*. Edited by Chamam Muhammad. 2nd ed. Tunis: Libraire El-Atika, 1967.
Ibn abi Louhayya, al-Montacir. *Nur al-armash fi manaqib al-qushash*. Edited by Boujarra Houcine and A'issa Lotfi Tunis: Librairie Alatika, 1998.
Kouja, Houssayn. *Dhayl basha'ir ahl al-iman fi futuhat al-'uthman*. Edited by Tahar Mamouri, Tunis: Dar al-'Arabiya li-l-Kitab, 1975.
L'Africain, Leon. *Description de l'Afrique*. Paris: Maisonneuve, 2 vol., 1956.
Laroui, Abdallah. *L'Histoire du Maghreb: un essai de synthèse*. 2nd ed. Casablanca: Centre culturel arabe, 1993.
Marmol y Carvajal, Luis. *Déscription génerale de l'Afrique*. French translation by Perrot d'Ablancourt, Paris. 1667, Paris Chez Louis Billaine, en la grand' Salle du Palais, a la Palme.
Moalla, Asma, "Le jund de la Régence de Tunis 1574–1650." *Arab Historical Review of Ottoman Studies*, August 2004, 189–96.
Monchicourt, Charles. *Etudes kairouanaises: Kairouan et les chabbias, 1450–1592*. Tunis: J. Aloccio, 1939.
———. "Les Hafsides en exil de 1574 à 1581." *Revue tunisienne*, first trimester (1936): 98–103.
———. *L'expédition espagnole de 1560 contre l'île de Djerba*. Paris.
———. *La Région du Haut Tell en Tunisie: Essai de monographie historique*. Paris : A. Colin, 1913.
Pignon, Jean. "Un document inédit sur la Tunisie." *Les Cahiers de Tunisie* (1961): 119–219.

———. "La malice des janissaires de Tunis au temps des *deys* (1590–1650)." *Les Cahiers de Tunisie*, vol. 4, 178.

———. "Osta Moratto Turcho Genovese, dey de Tunis (1637–1640)." *Les Cahiers de Tunisie*. No. 11, third trimester, 1955, 331–62.

Plantet, Eugène. *Correspondance des deys d'Alger avec la cour de France 1579–1833*. 2 vols. Paris, 1889; repr. Tunis: Bouslama, 1981.

———. *Correspondance des beys de Tunis et des consuls de France avec la cour, 1577–1830*. Paris, 1889; repr. Tunis: Bouslama, 1981.

Raymond, André. *Les Grandes villes arabes à l'époque Ottoman*. Paris: Sindbad, 1985.

Roy, Bernard. "Deux documents inédits sur l'éxpédition algérienne de 1628." *Revue tunisienne*, no. 122, 1917.

Rousseau, A. *Les Annales Tunisiennes*. 2nd ed. Tunis: Bouslama, 1985.

Saadaoui, Ahmad. *Tunis au XVIIe siècle: Des actes de Waqf de l'époque des deys et des beys mouradites*. Tunis: Faculté des Lettres, des Arts et des Humanités de la Manouba, 2011.

———. *Architecture et arts funéraires*. Tunis: Centre de Publications universitaires, 2010.

———. *Tunis ville ottoman*, Tunis: Centre de publications universitaires, 1990.

Sabbagh, Leila, *La société arabe syrienne au début de l'époque ottoman*. Damascus, University of Damascus, 1975.

Sameh, Aziz. *al-Atrak al-'Uthmaniyyun fi Ifriqya al-shamaliya*. Translated by Adham Abdesselem. Cairo, Tripoli, London: Dar al-Firjani, 1991.

Sebagh, Paul, ed., *Une Histoire des révolutions du royaume de Tunis au XVIIe siècle, une oeuvre de Guilleragues?* Paris: L'Harmattan, 2003.

———. *Tunis aux XVIIe siècle, une Cité barbaresque au temps de la course*. Paris : L'Harmattan, 1989.

———. *Tunis, histoire d'une ville*. Paris: L'Harmattan, 1998.

Shabbi, 'Ali.*'Arafa Shabbi, ra'id al-haraka al-wataniya fi al-'ahd al-hafsi*. Tunis, Tripoli: Dar al-'Arabiya li-l-Kitab, 1982.

Temimi, Abdejlil. *Etudes sur l'histoire du Maghreb ottomane au XVIe siècle*. Tunis: Fondation Temimi pour la recherche scientifique et l'information, May 2009. *Dirasat fi tarikh al-Maghrib al-'uthmani fi al-qarn al-sadis 'ashar.*

———. "La propriété fonciere et le régime des za'amat et des timar dans la Régence de Tunis 1574–1588." *Revue d'histoire arabe et d'études ottomanes*, no. 11–12, October 1995, supporting documents 1 and 2, 198–200.

———. "Iyalât al Jazâ'ir wa Tûnis wa Tarâblus min khilâli al muhimmé defteri 1559–1595." *Revue d'histoire arabe pour les Etudes ottomans* 34 (October 2006): 76–143.

———. "Rissâla min sukkân al Jazâ'ir ilâ al sultan salîm al awaal 1519." *Revue d'histoire maghrebine* (1976): 95–97.

Von Hammer-Purgstall, Joseph. *Histoire de l'Empire ottomane depuis son origine jusqu'à nos jours*. 2nd ed. Vol. 5. Istanbul: Hachette Livre BNF, 2017.

Al Wancharissi, Ahmad. *al-Mi'yar*. 10 vols. Beirut: Dar al-Gharb al-Islami, 1990.

al-Wazir al-Sarraj. *al-Hulal al-sundusiya fi al-akhbar al-tunisiya*. Edited by Hila Habib. 2 vols. Beirut: Dar al-Gharb al-Islami, 1984.

Index

Page numbers in *italics* indicate Figures.